DYNAMIC CONTEMPLATION
Inner Life for Modern Man

DYNAMIC CONTEMPLATION

Inner Life for *Modern Man*

by PAUL HINNEBUSCH, O.P.

SHEED AND WARD   NEW YORK

Imprimi Potest:
  Clemens E. Collins, O.P.
  Prior Provincialis
  Province of St. Albert the **Great**
  November 4, 1969

Nihil Obstat:
  Paul E. Couture, S.S.E.
  Censor Deputatus

Imprimatur:
  † Robert F. Joyce
  Bishop of Burlington
  January 20, 1970

The Nihil obstat *and* Imprimatur *are a declaration that a book or pamphlet is considered to be free from doctrinal or moral error. It is not implied that those who have granted the* Nihil obstat *and* Imprimatur *agree with the contents, opinions or statements expressed.*

Acknowledgements

We are most grateful to Sister Mary Henry Soniat, O.P., of St. Mary's Dominican High School, New Orleans, for typing the manuscript and for many valuable insights and suggestions which we have incorporated into this book.

Part IV, St. John's Course in Contemplation, originally appeared in *The Bible Today*, February, 1968, and is reprinted here with the permission of the editors.

Chapters ten and eleven originally appeared, in a slightly different form, in *Sisters Today*, January, 1969, under the title, "Dynamic Contemplation." They are used here with the permission of the editor.

Symbols Used in This Book

When the documents of Vatican II are quoted, the citation is followed immediately by the initials of the first two Latin words of the document and the number of the paragraph quoted, e.g., (*AG* 8). Symbols of the documents quoted in this work:

AG—Ad Gentes, Decree on the Church's Missionary Activity

GS—Gaudium et Spes, Pastoral Constitution on the Church in the Modern World

LG—Lumen Gentium, Dogmatic Constitution on the Church

NA—Nostra Aetate, Declaration on the Relationship of the Church to Non-Christian Religions

PO—Presbyterorum Ordinis, Decree on the Ministry and Life of Priests

SC—Sacrosanctum Concilium, Constitution on the Sacred Liturgy

Biblical References and Symbols

Throughout this book, except where otherwise indicated, the Scripture quotations are from *The Holy Bible, Revised Standard Version,* copyrighted 1946 and 1952 by the Division of Christian Education of the National Council of the Churches of Christ in the U.S.A.

Quotations from other versions are indicated by these symbols after the reference:

a—*Anchor Bible,* copyright 1966 by Doubleday & Company, Inc.

c—*Holy Bible,* copyright 1962 by the Confraternity of Christian Doctrine

j—*The Jerusalem Bible,* copyright 1966 by Doubleday & Company, Inc.

s—*The New Testament,* translated by Francis Aloysius Spencer, O.P., copyright 1937 by the Macmillan Company

v—The Latin Vulgate

A Note Concerning Chapter One

The first chapter deals with some fairly difficult theological points, and the reader who is untrained in theology is urged to persevere in reading it. The rest of the book will be easier reading. Theology has traditionally attributed three kinds of knowledge to the human mind of Christ: beatific, infused and acquired. The difficult portions of chapter one deal with this knowledge.

Introduction

The Title

"If you use the word 'contemplation' in your title, no one will read even the opening sentence. 'Contemplation' is a word which 'turns people off.' They will label your book 'irrelevant' and will never even open it."

That was the warning issued by my friends when I chose the title for this book.

But I replied, "One way of being relevant to the times is by standing up to the cry 'Irrelevant!' when the cry is false and is due to widespread misunderstanding."

The very reproaches urged against contemplation—for example, that it is static, individualistic, uncommitted—are the clue to its relevancy, for they show what the reproachers need and are seeking. The title, *Dynamic Contemplation,* brings out our point that Christian contemplation is not guilty of the accusations leveled against it but that it provides abundantly the very things its opponents accuse it of not giving.

Contemplation is accused of being static, concerned only with looking at the past, gazing at changeless truth and beauty. It seems to have nothing to offer to contemporary man, who has a very dynamic view of the world. All things are in evolutionary process, moving forward in a marvelous progression, and it is man's responsibility to be actively, creatively involved in forwarding this process. The future is all important!

Again, the contemplative is accused of being too individualistic, of being wrapped up in a selfish "me and Jesus spirituality," of having no concern for his fellowmen, of trying to escape reality. He is not human enough. He is uncommitted to the responsibility of active involvement in building a more human world. He is impractical, lost in idle speculation, a dreamer who contributes nothing to human progress.

These accusations were never really true of authentic Christian contemplation. Perhaps the various oriental non-Christian contemplatives were trying to escape from reality by losing their identity in the divinity. Perhaps the philosophers and the Greek Platonic contemplatives were static, concerned only with gazing at the changeless eternal ideas and essences, in complete detachment from everything.

But the Christian who contemplates the living God, Father, Son and Holy Spirit, and this God as actively revealing and communicating himself to man in the paschal mystery of Christ, becomes intensely involved in the dynamic forward thrust of the kingdom of God because he becomes totally committed to Christ and his work. Indeed, his infused contemplation is a baptismal participation in Christ's own contemplation, a sharing in Christ's own light and love which led him to do what he did in his paschal mystery.

Existential Contemplation

Therefore we thought at first of calling our book "Existential Contemplation," to show that Christian contemplation is not a dry, intellectual process in which one stands back and admires mere abstractions or ideas. Christian contemplation is a living movement of love and leads to an ever deeper commitment, an ever more total involvement in the life of God's people and in God's project for the universe. Indeed, we shall see that "the situation in which the

Christian contemplative finds himself enters into the very texture of his contemplation."[1]

The word "contemplation" unfortunately has too many connotations of apartness, of separation. This is because most people wrongly associate contemplation only with the cloister or with withdrawal into the desert when in fact, because it is a baptismal fullness, contemplation is for all Christians. Because it is wrongly identified with separation, the reality of contemplation is rejected as though it were the opposite of commitment and presence with our fellowmen, as though the contemplative were selfish and unconcerned about others.

The authentic Christian contemplative, however, is not one who stands apart from his fellowmen doing nothing. Any contemplative who is uninvolved in the paschal mystery of Christ and in the full mission of Christ and his Church is not a Christian contemplative. The authentic contemplative is a presence among men; and indeed, says Vatican II, the Church is not fully present in any region where the contemplative life has not been established (*AG* 18).

Therefore, we thought of calling this book "Incarnational Contemplation," to show that true Christian contemplation does very much involve one in the life of the Church, the continuation of Christ's own incarnation. That title would express the Christian paradox that contemplation of God and action among men are not at all contradictory. Contemplation and Christian action are one: contemplation penetrates the totality of Christian life, and Christian life opens one ever more fully to contemplation. The contemplation of God and the service of fellowmen are elements of one and the same movement of Christian love.

Eschatological Contemplation

Again, we thought of the title "Eschatological Contemplation," to show that true contemplation is no enemy of the creative action

1. Père Chenu, quoted by P. R. Regamey, *Un Ordre Ancien dans Le Monde Actuel* (Paris: Cahiers Saint Jacques, 1958), p. 51.

advocated by the contemporary theology of hope. On the contrary, because it involves one ever more deeply in the Lord's paschal mystery, it sweeps one along into the dynamic thrust towards the full Christian hope.

The Bible is the story of mankind's call back, through the call of Abraham, into the divine presence from which all of us had departed through sin. The journey back is accomplished in the person of Jesus, the first man to see God, Jesus, the contemplative par excellence. Only in him can the rest of us see God and live in communion with him.

The whole life of Jesus, his total paschal mystery, is his going back to the Father from whom he came: "I came from the Father and have come into the world; again, I am leaving the world and going to the Father" (Jn. 16:28). This is the eschatological journey in which all of us must join. In Christ, we go to the Father. Him we shall see with Jesus. Shoulder to shoulder with our fellowmen, we are ever facing toward the Father with Jesus; we are moving to him in a dynamic progression. The Father will receive us into his presence; with him we shall speak face to face in a communion of love.

"Face-to-Face"

No doubt "contemplation" is a word which "turns off" many of our contemporaries so perhaps we should find a new word for the same marvelous reality. Of course, if we do use a new word, we risk losing sight of many of the marvelous riches connoted by the old word in nearly two thousand years of living Christian tradition. Our problem is to induce our contemporaries to search for these riches by convincing them that contemplation is really the sort of reality they long for.

In the Scriptures, some of the key words in speaking of contemplation are "face" and "presence," "communion" and "knowing."

Our contemporaries speak much of openness, of listening and response, of dialogue, of sensitivity to others. The Scriptures are the story of sensitivity between God and mankind, of dialogue, of presence, of personal communion between them, of the obstacles to that sensitivity and openness and of the remedies for the obstacles.

The man who seeks communion with God is said to seek the face of the Lord. "My heart has said of you, 'Seek his face.' Yahweh, I do seek your face; do not hide your face from me" (Ps. 27:8,j).

To hide one's face is to refuse to communicate; it is to expel another from one's presence and love. "How much longer will you hide your face from me? Look and answer me, Yahweh my God!" (Ps. 13:1, 3,j). Man cries to the Lord to turn to him: "Let your face smile on us and we shall be safe" (Ps. 80:3,j).

In reality, it is always the Lord who is the first to turn his face to man. The living God looked upon the man he had formed from the dust of the earth and breathed into his face the breath of life; and man became a living being, alert to the Lord who had made him (Gen. 2:7).

It is always man who is the first to turn his face away from God: "The man and his wife hid themselves from the presence of the Lord God among the trees of the garden" (Gen. 3:8). . . . . "Cain went away from the presence of the Lord," though the Lord had turned to him after his sin (Gen. 4:16).

The Lord repeatedly turns his face to the man who has turned from him. "The Lord God called to the man and said to him: 'Where are you?' " (Gen. 3:9). He called Abraham from the midst of a race of men who had fallen into idolatry and said, "Walk in my presence and be perfect" (Gen. 17:1,c). The whole Bible is the story of the return of mankind to the divine presence, to the face-to-face encounter of love, to the dialogue of friendship, the communion. "Abraham was called the friend of God" (Jas. 2:23). "Face to face I speak to Moses (as one man speaks to another—Ex. 33:11), the presence of the Lord he beholds!" (Num. 12:7–8,c). "The skin of his face shone because he had been talking with God!" (Ex. 34:29). Man has been called back, to become again "the image and glory of God" (1 Cor. 11:7).

In short, contemplation is being face-to-face with God in a dia-

xiv   *Dynamic Contemplation*

logue of love, in a communion of life and friendship. For when
the Lord turns his face to man, he breathes into the face of man his
Holy Spirit of love and life, and man comes alive, "alive to God in
Christ Jesus" (Rom. 6:11).

> You hide your face, they are dismayed:
>   you take back your spirit, they die,
>   returning to the dust from which they came.
> You send forth your Spirit, they are created;
>   and you renew the face of the earth (Ps. 103:29–30,gr).

Man breathes in the divine Spirit and breathes it out again in the
cry of love and desire, "Father!"

Authentic contemplation, then, is ever existential, incarnational,
eschatological. It is dynamic, involving us in Christ's paschal mystery, his journey to the Father at the head of the People of God.
With him, we shall see God "face-to-face."

A Better Word Than Contemplation?

Shall we speak then of contemplation as "presence with God"?
That, too, would "turn off" those of our contemporaries who are so
concerned about presence with men. Christians, however, and
Christ are present with men precisely for the purpose of making
God present to them and bringing them into communion with God.
"Love does not consist in gazing at each other, but in looking out-
ward together in the same direction," in the direction of God.[2]

Shall we speak of contemplation as "communion with God"?

The biblical term, "communion with God" (*koinonia*), includes
a great deal more than infused contemplation. In fact, it embraces
the total Christian reality.

Each of the essential elements of the Christian communion, however, includes some measure of Christian contemplation. The truly
Christian presence to our fellowmen, for example, is possible only

2. A. de Saint-Exupery, *Wind, Sand and Stars* (New York: Harcourt,
Brace and World, 1939), p. 229.

in some sort of contemplative light—in Christ's own light—and all Christian apostolate is rooted in a presence with God in Christ. Jesus appointed men of his own choosing "to be *with him* and to be sent out to preach" (Mk. 3:14).

Concerning the necessary integration of contemplation with apostolic activity, Père Plé writes:

An authentic act of theological charity for neighbor is not possible without a "contemplative" love of neighbor, or rather, without that understanding of neighbor given by faith. Only the penetrating insight of faith permits us to love neighbor as God loves him and to encounter the other in the secret depths where God calls him to himself. If our service of neighbor is not thus enlightened by our faith, if neighbor is not a "mystery of God" for us, it is because we are not loving him with charity. Thought of in this way, apostolic activity is not possible without this contemplation of God in the object of the activity and at the time of the activity. Contemplation and action are thus really one. To the degree that charity and its divine object become the predominant end of life, a choice between contemplation and action is no longer necessary; in the act of charity for neighbor the two are integrated in a higher unity. *In actione contemplativus.*[3]

We shall not speak explicitly in this book concerning the heights of infused contemplation. By showing that contemplation is not irrelevant to contemporary life, we shall, perhaps, inspire some of our readers to search out again the masterpieces which have been written on that subject. Our concern, rather, is to place contemplation in the total context of the Christian life, showing how ordinary daily Christian living must be shot through with it. Without some measure of contemplation, life cannot be Christian and the apostolate cannot be authentic.

We wish to say no more than this: contemplation is a normal and necessary element of ordinary Christian life. The Church's troubles today are not because Christians have been too contemplative but because they have not been contemplative enough. They

3. A. Plé, "Apostolic Action as a School of Perfection," *Apostolic Life* (*Religious Life* X) (Westminster: Newman, 1958), pp. 151–152.

have not seen themselves, their fellowmen, their world clearly enough in the light and love of Christ.

It is true that the word "contemplation" is pagan in origin and is not found in the Gospels. However, the *reality* signified by the term "Christian contemplation" is very much in evidence in the Scriptures. It is manifest in Mary pondering in her heart the things spoken concerning Jesus (Lk. 2:19,51). It is praised by Jesus when he says, "Blessed rather are those who hear the word of God and keep it" (Lk. 11:28), "holding it fast in an honest and good heart, bringing forth fruit with patience" (Lk. 8:15).

Contemplation is love's delight in the presence of the God who is love and who reveals himself to the pure of heart (Matt. 5:8). It is the joy of the heart in turning to God, its true treasure (Matt. 7:21), and in doing all it can to bring others to share in this treasure. It is the response of one's whole personality to the living and personal God who reveals himself in the very gift of himself to the heart.

We propose to show how Christian contemplation is an essential element in the full response to baptismal grace and how it is a dynamic functioning of this grace. But since contemplation is a participation in Christ's own light and love, we shall consider in the earlier chapters Christ himself as the contemplative par excellence. Then, after considering the relationship of Baptism and contemplation, we shall endeavor to show the role of the Lord's Prayer and the eucharistic sacrifice in bringing us ever more fully into the Lord's own contemplation. Since the Christian contemplates above all God as he has revealed himself in Christ his Son, we shall study, in the midst of our considerations on the Lord's Prayer, St. John's lessons in contemplation in which he teaches us to behold the Lamb of God.

Not only is Christian life necessarily contemplative, but all apostolic activity springs from contemplation and brings others into this contemplation. The Church is ever saying, like the first disciples: "We have seen the Lord!" (Jn. 20:18,25). "Come and see with us!" (Jn. 1:46; 4:29).

Contents

INTRODUCTION:

TITLE AND PURPOSE OF THE BOOK   ix

I Jesus the Contemplative   1
1   Jesus, the Contemplative   3
2   The First Man to See God   16
3   The Contemplative Process in Jesus   28
4   More on Our Lord's Contemplative Process   40
5   What Jesus Saw in the World and in Men   46
6   "Lord, Show Us the Father!"   53
7   "Beholding the Glory of the Lord"   62
8   The Cross and the Transfiguration   69
9   They Were Not Listening   76

II Christian Contemplation: A Fullness of Baptism   85
10   Contemplation: A Fullness of Charity and Hope   90
11   Faith is Necessarily Contemplative   97
12   Coming to Self-Awareness Through Prayer   104
13   The Nature of the Spirit's Witness   110
14   Experiencing a Divine Person   119
15   Various Manners of the Spirit's Witness   123
16   The Witness of the Spirit in the Eucharist
     and in Penance   136

III   The Apostolate of Contemplation   149
    17   Coming in Community to Contemplation   152
    18   Contemplation and Our Daily Work   162
    19   The Apostolate of Contemplation   174
    20   Building a World Open to God's Self-Revelation   185
    21   Imaging God to Others—in Family Life and in
         Celibacy   192
    22   "Love is From God"   206

IV   St. John's Course in Contemplation   213
    23   "Behold the Lamb of God!"   219
    24   The Lamb's Self-Revelation   227

V   The Our Father and the Eucharistic Sacrifice   239
    25   The Lord's Sacrifice is the Lord's Prayer   242
    26   Dynamic Involvement in the Lord's Prayer   250
    27   "Thy Will Be Done"   262
    28   "Lead Us Not Into Temptation"   274
    29   Why Jesus Prayed Alone   285
    30   To a Loveless World . . .   292

DYNAMIC CONTEMPLATION
Inner Life for Modern Man

I
Jesus, the Contemplative

1
Jesus, the Contemplative

Since Jesus was like the rest of us in all things except sin (Heb. 4:15), so, too, he went through the process of contemplation—even its darknesses! This process was a basic and essential element in his personal paschal mystery.

The Contemplative Process: The Search for Meaning

The contemplative process—at least in its roots and initial stages— is a coming to self-awareness as much as it is a becoming aware of God. It is the search for meaning; it is a process of interpretation of self and of the world of men and things in which we live, a process which ultimately finds all true meaning in God.

Man grows in self-understanding through reflection upon his experience of life. Prior to reflection upon himself, he already possesses a consciousness of himself; he has an immediate experience of his existence in the world of men and things. But this lived experience necessarily gives rise to images and ideas by which he interprets his life and the reality in which he lives.

It is necessary for man thus to think about himself and his world. Otherwise, he cannot live humanly. For, unlike the animals, he is not endowed with a natural instinct to guide his life. His life program is not innate in him. Therefore, he must try to find and develop it by reflection upon his immediate experience of life.

Thus consciousness, the immediate experience of self, is not the same as express knowledge, the concepts in which man clearly interprets and articulates his prereflective experience. Consciousness can be an intuitive awareness distinct from one's interpretation and articulation of this awareness in concepts and words. One can be vividly conscious of himself long before he finds a reasonably adequate way of expressing that consciousness. Such intuitive self-awareness is, indeed, the necessary basis of all self-interpretation in ideas and words.

In coming to self-understanding, a man reflects not only upon his experience of his existence in the world of men and things but also upon his experience of himself in relationship with God. For sooner or later every man is granted some sort of experience of God; sooner or later "the true light enlightens every man" (Jn. 1:9). To every man is offered at some time or other the grace of communion with God; and the very offer is a grace in which there is at least a minimal experience of God. They who accept the offer and are faithful to further graces will have varying experiences of God and of themselves in relationship with God.

All this is material for man's reflection in coming to self-understanding. This search for meaning, for the meaning of self and of one's world, is the contemplative process which should find its normal fullness in the immediate experience of God himself in infused contemplation.

The Contemplative Process in Jesus

Did Jesus go through this process of coming to self-understanding?

The very first time that Jesus speaks in the Gospels, it is clear that he already knows who he is: "Did you not know that I must be busy with my Father's affairs?" (Lk. 2:49,j). Yet in this same place in the Scriptures we are told that Jesus went through a process of growth in knowledge.

The scene of the finding, in which Jesus affirms with absolute clarity his consciousness that he depends directly and personally upon the

Father, is framed in the Gospel between two sentences, or more exactly, by the same sentence twice repeated in almost identical words: 'And the child grew and became strong, filled with wisdom; and the favor of God was upon him'; 'And Jesus increased in wisdom and in stature and in favor with God and man' (Lk. 2:40,52).

The intention of the Evangelist is evident: he wants to give full value, by their very contrast, to two simultaneous facts, each as important as the other: this child who grows like all children, and is not different from them except in a more perfect way of growing, is also he who, without having learned it from any creature, knows he is the Son of God and knows the existence God has determined for him.[1]

For Christ to grow in self-understanding, then, does not mean that there was ever a time in his human consciousness when he was unaware that he was Son of God. Certainly everything in the Gospels indicates that during the time of his public mission he knew who he was and why he came. The Church firmly believes that his first-person statements clearly indicate a consciousness of his divine Sonship. Moreover, he was fully conscious of the fact that he could forgive sins and was Lord of the Sabbath. In the contemporary Jewish context this could only mean that he was conscious of possessing the fullness of divine power: "Who can forgive sins but God alone?" (Mk. 2:7). Seen in this light, his claim to divine sonship is to be interpreted in fullest validity.

Moreover, in order to fulfill his mission of revelation, Jesus had to have some sort of direct vision of God in which he clearly knew the Father, and himself as Son of the Father: "No one has ever seen God; the only Son, who is in the bosom of the Father, he has made him known" (Jn. 1:18). "Truly, truly, I say to you, we speak of what we know, and bear witness to what we have seen" (Jn. 3:11). "Not that anyone has seen the Father, except him who is from God; he has seen the Father" (6:46). "I know him, for I come

1. Jacques Guillet, "Croissance de Jesus Christ," *Christus*, 55 (1967), p. 383–84.

from him, and he sent me" (7:29). "I speak of what I have seen with my Father" (8:38).

These assertions, made precisely to guarantee the truth of his teaching, leave the inevitable impression that the Father, in telling what Jesus as man was to say and speak, gave him as man the most perfect spiritual insight possible, even a direct perception of God. . . . The vision of God is invoked by Jesus as the guarantee of the truth of his message; and as that message was understood by the human intellect of Christ, only the vision itself can have been the source of that understanding.[2]

Did Jesus Grow in Self-understanding?

But if Jesus had this vision of God and this full knowledge of his mission as he went about his public preaching, did he reach this fullness of knowledge in a process of growth? At the age of twelve, for example, was his awareness of God as his Father but one stage in his growth in self-understanding? Did he possess the beatific vision from the very beginning of his human life?

As ordinarily understood by theologians, Christ's beatific knowledge included not only the face-to-face vision of God but also the objective knowledge of all things, past, present and to come. But if Jesus from his earliest infancy and throughout his life on earth had enjoyed this all-inclusive vision, it would seem that he could not possibly have grown in self-understanding. In the fullness of beatific knowledge he would always have known himself perfectly.

Therefore, a number of recent theologians such as Karl Rahner and Jean Galot,[3] without denying that Jesus always knew he was God, have endeavored to explain his knowledge of his divinity, not as beatific vision, but as an intuitive experience of his divine Person,

2. Bernard Leeming, "The Human Knowledge of Christ," *Irish Theological Quarterly*, 19 (1952), pp. 251–52.

3. K. Rahner, "Current Problems in Christology," *Theological Investigations* (Baltimore: Helicon, 1961), 1:168–70; "The Human Knowledge and Consciousness of Christ," *Theology Digest*, 12 (1964), 53–55; Jean Galot, "The Knowledge and Consciousness of Christ," *Ibid.*, 48–52.

a consciousness of who he was which did not necessarily include a knowledge of all things, nor even the details of his own mission. By growing in the understanding of his mission and the manner in which it was to be carried out, he would be growing also in self-understanding; for a man is fully himself and comes to full self-knowledge only in carrying out his true mission in life.

To maintain that Jesus always had the beatific vision involves many difficulties which are hard to reconcile with the scriptural evidence. For example, how could the beatific vision, the state of final beatitude, be reconciled with Christ's genuine inner suffering, or with the reality of his full human freedom in executing his mission in obedience? To know in beatific vision, from the first moment of his existence, the minutest details of his earthly career, says Rahner, seems to deny to the human nature of Jesus any active role in salvation and to reduce his humanity to a kind of inert facade behind which the divinity alone accomplishes our redemption.[4]

Knowing everything present and future in the last detail would paralyze his true personal growth through free decision. A free decision, says Rahner, presupposes a certain area of the unknown into which the deed can plunge forward.[5]

Jesus did make human decisions in carrying out his mission. He did come to his perfection as true man by making free choices in the light of the situations in which he found himself. "He called to him men of his own choosing, and they came to him" (Mk. 3:13,c). When these men of his choosing explicitly professed their faith in his messiahship (Mk. 8:29), he saw that the time was ripe to take them apart from the crowds to instruct them more fully on the nature of that messiahship as characterized by suffering and death (Mk. 9:29–31).

Moreover, before each decisive step in his career he prayed, St. Luke tells us. For example, before choosing the twelve, before evoking from his disciples their profession of faith, before setting

4. *Ibid.*
5. *Ibid.*

out for Jerusalem to face death Jesus prayed (Lk. 6:12; 9:19; 9:28,31). This praying may indicate his asking for light concerning the details of his Father's will. He made his decisions in view of the situation at hand and in the light which came to him from his Father.

Thus, Jesus "knew that his hour had come to depart out of this world to the Father" (Jn. 13:1). He knew it, says Yves Congar, "by 'infused knowledge' and by the experience of the events in which the drama was developing and gradually reaching its resolution."[6]

The infused knowledge could have been granted to him from the Father only when the situation required it, for the details of his mission were not necessarily known to him in his immediate consciousness of his divine sonship.[7]

Thus, Jesus carried out his mission not like a computer fully programmed to the last detail as to what he was to do (and if he saw all things in the beatific vision he would seem to be so programmed) but as a true man living according to decisions which he made as the situation required.

Perhaps all this seems to indicate that on earth Jesus did not have the beatific vision with a detailed knowledge of everything past, present and future. But it cannot mean that he had no vision of God and of himself as Son of God. The problems concerning the human knowledge of Christ are as old as Christology itself, and no doubt they will never be satisfactorily solved by theologians. For Christ is a divine mystery, and we cannot know for sure just what he knew or did not know. The living tradition of the Church, in spite of its awareness of these problems, has nevertheless unwaveringly maintained that Jesus did have the beatific vision throughout his life on earth.[8]

6. Yves Congar, *Jesus Christ.* (New York: Herder & Herder, 1966), p. 54.
7. Cf., Galot, *op. cit.,* p. 51.
8. Leeming, *op. cit.,* pp. 234–35.

Christ Always Knew He Was God

In suggesting that Jesus did not have the beatific vision, Karl Rahner does not deny that Jesus always knew that he was God, and thus, no doubt, Rahner remains within the tradition. But he explains this knowledge as Christ's subjective consciousness of himself as the divine Person of the Son rather than as objective knowledge of the divine essence and of all things known in that essence. At the root of his human consciousness, according to Rahner, Christ experienced the person of the eternal Word as the personal support of his human nature.[9] In a knowing being, being and consciousness are simultaneous factors of one same reality, so that a thing may be said to exist to the degree that it is present to itself in knowledge. At the highest level of being, the spiritual level, being and self-awareness coincide, so that here being *is* consciousness; being is being-with-oneself in self-awareness.[10]

Now the hypostatic union is the communication of the divine being of the Word to the human nature of Christ. If then it is true that self-awareness is a function of one's mode of being, then the participation of Christ's human nature in the infinitely perfect being of the Word must have a necessary corollary in the human consciousness of Christ. A hypostatic union without this consciousness of the union is impossible. Christ's immediate awareness of himself as Son of God during his earthly life, then, according to Rahner, was not the beatific vision. It was simply his basic awareness of himself in the hypostatic union. Such a self-awareness is his human consciousness of himself as Son of God.[11]

This basic experiential fact of his sonship at the subjective pole of his consciousness, according to Rahner, is something which is

9. Cf., Gutwenger, "The Problem of Christ's Knowledge," *Concilium,* vol. 11. (New York: The Paulist Press, 1966), p. 99.

10. Gutwenger, *ibid.;* Rahner, *Theology Digest* 12 (1964), p. 54.

11. *Theology Digest, ibid.*

not reflective and not thematic (that is, not expressed in clear intellectual concepts). "But it becomes the subject of reflection without, for that, exhausting it. The immediate consciousness of the divine becomes thematic and reflective in Christ's encounter with the world. To interpret himself, he uses the material which the opinions, the language, the customs and the ideas of his environment and his age provide him with. One can understand that in this way this thematic self-interpretation of Christ becomes a progressive historical process."[12]

Since consciousness of his divine sonship is inseparable from the hypostatic union, Jesus would always have been aware of himself as Son of God from the very first instant of his human consciousness and, through reflection, he would have come to an ever deeper human self-understanding. Any child's dawning experience of himself is born with him, for he is a living being endowed with a variety of powers of living awareness. The face of the tiniest infant already begins to manifest the light of the intelligence which is the very root of his life, the source of the consciousness which is identical with his living being. He soon begins to reflect upon this conscious experience of self which begins with life itself; and he develops through reflection to an express knowledge in clear concepts in which he interprets and articulates his prereflective experience.

From his very birth Jesus, too, must have had this sort of prereflective consciousness of who he was. But the profundity of the infant Jesus is that of God.

The self of whom he was conscious was not a mere human self, but a divine self, the Second Person of the Blessed Trinity. Christ's human self-consciousness, then, touched God, so to speak, immediately. His awareness of himself was awareness of God. This must have been by direct vision, by intuition. For it is inconceivable that God, even though man, should not be aware that he was God.[13]

12. Gutwenger, *op. cit.,* pp. 103–04.
13. Leeming, *op. cit.,* p. 138.

Yet it is conceivable, according to the thesis of Rahner, that Christ's initial self-awareness could develop in a human way through reflection. He was God, not a mere created intelligence, and what he was must have had resonances in his human consciousness from the very beginning as a direct intuition of his divine sonship. As he developed humanly and, as any child does, began to reflect on this direct experience of himself, he grew in human self-understanding.

Obscurity and Growth in Christ

However, whether we explain his knowledge of who he was in terms of beatific vision throughout his life or in Rahner's terms of an intuitive self-awareness which develops thematically through reflection, we have to admit, with the Scriptures, that there was growth and crisis in the life of Jesus. Truly, from the beginnings of his human consciousness his human mind was enlightened by the Word which he was, "the true light which enlightens every man" (Jn. 1:9). But along with this fundamental knowledge of his divine sonship, and in no way derogating from it, there was in Jesus real growth, "leaving him *in fieri* (in becoming), in some sense unequal to himself, subject to the very real trial of obscurity, of effort, as long as he was in the state of subjection and of suffering."[14] The obscurity and effort seemed to be most intense of all in the garden and on the cross: "My Father, if it be possible, let this cup pass from me" (Matt. 26:39); "My God, my God, why hast thou forsaken me?" (Matt. 27:46).

And yet in the measure necessary for each situation, in his obscurity and effort, Jesus was enlightened by the Word-he-was with some kind of infused knowledge. With the help of this interior light, along with the data presented by each situation in which he found himself, he was able to make decisions and carry out his mission in full human freedom. It was truly as *man* that the Word

14. Maurice Blondel, "Au coeur de la crise moderniste," *Lettres présentées* par R. Marlé (Paris, 1960), p. 245. Quoted by Guillet, *op. cit.*

of God worked out the salvation of man. He truly went through the contemplative process, even its obscurities: "My God, my God, why hast thou forsaken me?" (Matt. 27:46).

Our Lord's Contemplative Process and Ours

We have gone into these difficult theological questions in order to throw some light on our own contemplative process. In coming chapters we shall consider more fully the contemplation of Jesus— his awareness of his heavenly Father and his own divine sonship, his contemplative search to do always the things pleasing to the Father, the attentiveness of his human mind and heart to the light and love which came to him from the Father in the Word and Holy Spirit.

No matter how poorly or clearly Jesus may have understood himself in human concepts, no matter by what process he may have come to the fullness of his self-understanding, the apostles have accurately interpreted for us, in the light of the Holy Spirit given to them as the fruit of Jesus' glorification, what Jesus in his intuitive contemplation of God always knew he was.

Thus, in no uncertain terms, St. John presents Jesus in his maturity as knowing with fullest clarity who he was and what his mission was. He calls himself "the one whom the Father consecrated and sent into the world" (Jn. 10:36). John tells us authoritatively that Jesus had the interior experience of his divine origin: "Father, glorify thy Son . . . with the glory which I had with thee before the world was made" (Jn. 17:1–5). He had also the awareness of the unique mission which this entailed, namely, the revelation of the Father whose only Son he was, and the bringing of men into a participation in his own relationship with the Father: "Father, I have manifested thy name to the men whom thou gavest me out of the world. . . . The glory which thou hast given me I have given to them" (Jn. 17:6,22).

Moreover, St. John and St. Paul seem to indicate that Jesus while on earth knew and loved each one of us as distinct persons:

From the time of St. Peter until today those who love Christ have believed he knew them and loved them personally. During his appearance at the lakeside, our Saviour asked St. Peter for the third time if he loved him and "Peter was grieved that he said to him the third time: Lovest thou me? And he said to him: Lord, thou knowest all things, thou knowest that I love thee" (Jn. 21:17). St. Peter in those words voiced the conviction of all Christians: Christ our Lord knows us each individually, our weaknesses and our sins, our sorrows, aspirations and resolves. Still more, he suffered and died for each of us individually: "He loved me and delivered himself for me" (Gal. 2:20). That love of Christ was a personal love, involving, therefore, personal knowledge.[15]

St. John persistently presents Jesus as knowing what was in the hearts of men. This would seem to entail a very real difficulty for the thesis that Jesus did not have the beatific vision during his life on earth. How could he have known each one of us individually if not in beatific vision? Possibly, of course, his knowledge of the hearts of men such as St. Peter, Nathaniel and the Samaritan woman was an infused knowledge that came to him when he was in the situation involving him with these people. His words to Nathaniel indicate that his knowledge of this man's heart derived from his divine knowledge: "Before Philip called you, when you were under the fig tree, I saw you" (Jn. 1:48). Since the divine plan of salvation called for it and the situation required it, the knowledge flowed from the divine Word to the human mind of Jesus when he began to deal with Nathaniel.

As for Christ's personal knowledge of each one of us, certainly he has such knowledge here and now in his beatific vision in glory, and each one of us as an individual can be certain that we are embraced in his love and knowledge. It is certain that he died for every single one of us, whether or not each of us was distinctly and individually before his human mind as he hung on the cross. Now, in the glory of his resurrection, he knows each one of us personally; he calls each one of us by name as he called "Mary!" on the morning of his resurrection (Jn. 20:16).

15. Leeming, *op. cit.*, p. 135.

No matter what the manner in which he had all this knowledge, it remains true that during his life on earth, and especially in his passion, Jesus was subject to real obscurity and effort, and this on behalf of us whom he loved personally. Jesus, we must say again, is a divine mystery whom we shall never adequately explain.

His contemplative process may, indeed, have had all the normal darkness of man's contemplation of God in this life. But because of the contemplative attentiveness of his human mind and heart to the interior light of the Word, and through his human openness to the experience of the Father's love for him in the Holy Spirit, he ever lived true to what the Son of God ought to be in human nature, a true man in filial obedience to the will of the Father, a man who in full freedom steadfastly chooses to accomplish the mission the Father has given him.

Likewise, our contemplation has to be above all an attentiveness to the same Word working in our hearts by his Holy Spirit, an attentiveness to Jesus who is this Word and who gives us a participation in the same light and love which illumined his own mind and enflamed his own heart; for now in his glory and beatific vision he certainly has this light and love in its infinite fullness.

Possibly, then, even Jesus may have come to an ever deeper understanding in human concepts of what from the beginning he grasped in a prereflective awareness. Certainly, our Christian life of prayer and contemplation is a coming to ever clearer consciousness of what we already are by the grace of Baptism, sons of God in Christ. It is an ever fuller acceptance of this, an increasingly perfect expression of it in our living, an ever deeper participation in the Lord's paschal mystery, "who, though he was in the form of God, did not count equality with God a thing to be grasped, but emptied himself, taking the form of a servant, being born in the likeness of men. And being found in human form, he humbled himself and became obedient unto death, even death on a cross" (Phil. 2:6–8).

To say that in his human form he experienced in some way the limitations of human knowledge does not at all dishonor him. It glorifies God all the more, who thus manifested the infinite depths of his love in becoming like us in all things except sin, redeeming us by living our very life. And he gives us courage in our dark nights, for he himself experienced them with us.

2
The First Man To See God

Jesus was the first man to see God.

St. John declares, "No one has ever seen God; the only Son, who is in the bosom of the Father, he has made him known" (Jn. 1:18).

Not even the great Moses had seen God. When Moses said to Yahweh, "Do let me see your glory," the Lord refused him and gave him only an imperfect, obscure revelation of himself, saying, "My face you cannot see, for no man sees me and still lives. You may see my back; but my face is not to be seen" (Exod. 33:18,20,23,c).

This incident between Moses and God was no doubt in St. John's mind when he said, "No one has ever seen God"—not even the great ones of Israel! But Jesus can make him known, for *he* sees him. As only Son, he is in the Father's bosom; as Son he abides in the Father's love. "We saw his glory, the glory that is his as the only Son of the Father" (Jn. 1:14,j).

Jesus can show God to us only because he himself first has seen him. "No one knows the Father but the Son, and anyone to whom the Son chooses to reveal him" (Matt. 11:27). In these words, Jesus claims for himself a knowledge of God which no one else has, and a power to show him to others. "To know," in biblical language, means "to experience in love." Jesus claims a love and knowledge of the Father which is on a par with the Father's love and knowledge of him: "No one knows the Son except the Father, and no one knows the Father except the Son."

Even if Jesus did not speak these words exactly in the way the Evangelist has expressed them, even if in his earthly career he did not find adequate human concepts and words to express his direct intuition, his experiential consciousness, of who he was, the Evangelist is telling us clearly that Jesus did have this consciousness. We shall try to show that this intuition was an awareness of the Father's unique love for him as eternal Son. But like any man's contemplative experiences, it was too great to be expressed in mere human concepts and words.

Jesus sees the God whom no man before him had ever seen, and only he can show this God to others: "Everyone who has heard and learned from the Father comes to me. Not that anyone has seen the Father, except him who is from God; he has seen the Father" (Jn. 6:45–46). That is, before the coming of Jesus there were ways of hearing God and learning from him—Moses "saw God's back." He had some sort of mystical experience of God "in a mirror dimly" (1 Cor. 13:12), but this was not yet seeing God. One who hears God and learns from him comes to Jesus, for only Jesus has seen the Father, and only he can show us the Father. "No one comes to the Father but by me" (Jn. 14:16).

Jesus ever serenely contemplates this Father, and, therefore, he can make him known. Whenever he speaks, he speaks about the Father. "Out of the abundance of the heart the mouth speaks" (Matt. 12:34). The Father is ever on his lips because he is ever in his heart; he abides in the Father's love which he is ever experiencing. His whole mission is to manifest the Father: "Father, I have glorified thee on earth, having accomplished the work which thou gavest me to do. I have manifested thy name to the men whom thou gavest me out of the world" (Jn. 17:4,6).

To manifest his Name is to manifest his Person, for in biblical thinking, there is an identity between name and person. The name *is* the person whose name it is.

How He Is in the Father's Bosom

The Son is ever in the bosom of the Father, that is, in the deepest intimacy of the Father's love, ever experiencing that love in its fullness. That is why he is able to reveal the secrets of divine love which no one else has seen. "We speak of what we know, and we bear witness to what we have seen," Jesus insists to Nicodemus, who doubts his revelation of divine love, the love which wills to beget us as his children in the rebirth of water and the Spirit (Jn. 3:11).

"We speak of what we know," that is, what we have experienced in love. Only because Jesus has personally experienced the Father's love, only because he ever dwells in the bosom of that love, can he reveal it as a Father's love for us, too. Jesus—a man—aware of himself as God's own Son, understands how all men can be called to participate in divine sonship, and he proclaims this truth.

In their divinely guaranteed post-resurrectional explanation of Jesus and his life and sayings, there is one thing which the Gospels certainly make clear. Throughout his life on earth, Jesus was always somehow aware of himself as Son of God and was ever experiencing the Father's love. "You are my beloved Son; in you I am well pleased" (Mk. 1:11). These words, addressed to him by the Father at his baptism, express what Jesus had always experienced. Even as a child, he was conscious of his heavenly Father and of his own divine sonship. When Mary spoke of one father—"Your father and I have been looking for you anxiously"—the child Jesus spoke of another Father: "Did you not know that I must be in my Father's house?" (Lk. 2:48–49). And out of his experience of his Father's love for him, Jesus says to his disciples, "As the Father has loved me, I also have loved you" (Jn. 15:9).

"God so loved the world that he gave his only Son" (Jn. 3:16). "Loved" and "gave" are practically synonyms; divine love is ever a giving. It is a love which reveals itself and proves itself by giving with infinite generosity. "The Father *loves* the Son," says Jesus, "and has *given* all things into his hands" (Jn. 3:35). The Father's

boundless love for Jesus was ever manifest in the boundless gifts
he had given him. But all the other gifts of the Father to Jesus—
such as the power to give eternal life to whomever he wills (Jn.
17:2)—are only the consequences of the first, the infinite gift, the
gift of divine sonship, the gift of divinity bestowed upon his lowly
humanity.

Even if on earth Jesus did not have the beatific vision, he did
have a direct intuition of his divine sonship. He knew he was Son
of God; he was ever humanly aware of the boundless generosity of
the Father's love for him. With his human mind and heart, he was
conscious that the Father was loving him with the same infinite
divine love he had had for him from eternity. He expresses this
realization that his sonship is the fruit of eternal love when he says,
"Father, I desire that they also, whom thou hast given me, may be
with me where I am to behold my glory which thou hast given me
in thy love for me before the foundation of the world" (Jn. 17:24).

Thus, truly, Jesus experienced in his human heart the Father's
eternal love for him as Son. All that infinite love of the Father is
showered upon him, and he knows it!

Thus he experiences his Father's love for him shortly before he
faces the terror of his passion: "The hour is coming, indeed it has
come, when you will be scattered, every man to his home, and will
leave me alone; yet I am not alone, for the Father is with me" (Jn.
16:32). How often Christians have been able to testify that they,
too, have had a remarkable experience of the love and presence of
God shortly before God would ask a great sacrifice of them!

"We speak of what we know"—what we have experienced in
love—"and bear witness to what we have seen" (Jn. 3:11). On
earth, Jesus certainly saw the Father in the sense of his intuition of
his divine sonship and his experience of the Father's love for him
as eternal Son. Now that he has been glorified in the Father's full
presence with the glory which he had with him before the world
was made (Jn. 17:5), he sees the Father face to face, the first man
ever to see him thus.

He who is thus in the bosom of the Father manifests the Father to us by sending the Holy Spirit into our hearts to bear witness that we, too, are sons in the Son. In this witness of the Spirit, we, too, can experience the Father's love.

The Joy of Jesus in Revealing the Father

In his intuition of his divine sonship, in his experience of his Father's love for him, we said, the Man Jesus could understand how all men are called to divine sonship. If he, a man, had received the gift of divinity, it was so that he might share it with all his fellow-men. He is conscious that the Father's love for him includes a love for all of us; he is aware that the Father's love in bestowing the glory of divinity upon his personal humanity willed thereby to embrace the whole world of men in that same fatherly love. hast given him power over all flesh, to give eternal life to all whom thou hast given him" (Jn. 17:2). St. Luke records that one day Jesus became "enraptured with joy in the Holy Spirit and said, 'I give praise to thee, O Father, Lord of heaven and earth, because, having hidden these things from the wise and clever, thou hast revealed them to little ones. Yes, Father, for such was thy gracious will!'" (Lk. 10:21,s).[1]

Continuing this praise and thanksgiving, Jesus mentions still more explicitly the motive for his joy, namely, the Father has entrusted *him* with the privilege of revealing the Father. "All things have been delivered to me by my Father; and no one knows . . . who the Father is except the Son, and he to whom it is the pleasure of the Son to reveal him" (Lk. 10:22,s).

Thrilling with joy in his Father's love for him, his human heart can thrill in the thought of extending that love to all his fellow-men: "As the Father has loved me, so have I loved you" (Jn. 15:9). That is why he is ever speaking about the Father; that is why he reveals the Father's love: "Father, I have made known to

1. Last phrase, RSV.

them thy name, and I will make it known, that the love with which thou hast loved me may be in them, and I in them" (Jn. 17:26).

His joy in the Father is just too much to keep to himself. It floods from his heart and fills the hearts of all to whom he reveals the Father: "These things I have spoken to you that my joy may be in you and that your joy may be full" (Jn. 15:11).

In revealing the Father, Jesus communicates divine sonship to those to whom he reveals him. For the grace of adoption as sons and the revelation of the Father are one and the same grace. In the very grace by which we are adopted as son, the Father is made known to us; for only when the Spirit of the Son is sent into our hearts can we experience God as Father and cry, "Abba!" (Gal. 4:6).

With joy, Jesus can report to the Father that he has accomplished his mission of love. "I glorified thee on earth by accomplishing the work thou gavest me to do. . . . The glory thou hast given me"— divine sonship!—"I have given them. . . . I revealed thy name to them, and will reveal it, in order that the love with which thou lovest me may be in them, and I in them" (Jn. 17:4,22,26,s).

This is the love Jesus has experienced, this is the love he desires to reveal and share. Only he who has personally experienced the Father's love can reveal it, only he who is in the bosom of the Father's love can share it. Christian contemplation is thus a participation in Christ's own experience of the Father's love for him and, consequently, a sharing in his own joy in the Father.

Christ's Joy and Serenity in Sacrifice

The Father rejoices eternally in the Son, and he continues to rejoice in that Son when he becomes Man. He expresses this joy, saying, "Thou art my beloved Son; with thee I am well pleased" (Mk. 1:11).

Jesus also rejoices in the Father, finding delight in always "doing what is pleasing to him" (Jn. 8:29). He finds joy even in sacrificing his life, for such is the will of the Father.

The Father in turn rejoices in him, because Jesus has so loved him: "For this reason the Father loves me, because I lay down my life, that I may take it up again. . . . This charge I have received from my Father" (Jn. 10:17-18).

At the Last Supper, when the disciples are saddened by his imminent departure, Jesus says, "If you loved me, you would have rejoiced, because I go to the Father; for the Father is greater than I" (Jn. 14:28). In saying, "I go to the Father," Jesus is referring to his sacrificial death. He rejoices in his sacrifice, for it is his way to the Father. And it is his way of bringing us to the Father. His disciples, too, should rejoice that he goes to the Father, for when he is with the Father he will have his fullness of joy. And they should rejoice that he thus shows us the way to that joy.

Our Lord's joy in the thought of returning to the Father, then, is the anticipation of his full personal joy in the Father's presence—"Father, glorify thou me in thy own presence with the glory which I had with thee before the world was made" (Jn. 17:5),—but it is far more than that. Jesus means also, and primarily: "If you loved me, you would rejoice that in my sacrifice I act as a true son of the Father, that I prove myself his true Son—for my obedient love for him in obedience even unto death reveals how lovable he really is, and shows you how to love him."

How wonderfully, indeed, Jesus must have experienced the Father's love for him, when, to reveal that love to the world, he willingly gives his very life on the cross. "God so loved the world that he gave his only Son" (Jn. 3:16). The Father's love for the Son is most clearly manifest in the Son's response in love for the Father even to the point of laying down his life in obedience. "I do as the Father has commanded me, so that the world may know that I love the Father" (Jn. 14:31).

"For this reason the Father loves me, because I lay down my life that I may take it up again (Jn. 10:17-18). That is, the Father is delighted with the Son's wholehearted cooperation with his plan of love, and responds to the Son's self-sacrifice by the glory his love pours out upon him in the resurrection, thus acknowledging him as his beloved Son, manifesting him to the world, fully empowering him to give the Holy Spirit of sonship to all his fellowmen, so that the Son can say with joy: "Go to my brothers and say to them, I am ascending to my Father and your Father"—your Father now, as well as mine (Jn. 20:17).

So lovable is the Father, then, so much joy does Jesus personally find in him, that he must spread this joy far and wide. He must offer himself in sacrifice so that all can love the Father and find joy in him, even as Jesus does. "These things I have spoken to you that my joy may be in you and that your joy may be full" (Jn. 15:11).

Christ's Prayer in the Holy Spirit

Jesus is *ever* Son of the Father. In eternity and in time, he exists in the same basic relationship with the Father, a relationship of mutual love. Father and Son love one another in the Holy Spirit; they find their joy in one another in the Holy Spirit. The Holy Spirit *is* their love; he is their joy. In thanking the Father for revealing himself, Jesus "thrilled with joy in the Holy Spirit" (Lk. 10:21,bj).

This thrill of joy gives us a deep insight into our Lord's contemplative life. The Holy Spirit was his incessant bond of love with the Father, the Holy Spirit was his bond with the Father in prayer. For prayer is a relationship in love. Infused contemplation is an experience of God in the union of love.

If on this occasion Christ's prayer to the Father in the Holy Spirit was a thrill of joy, on other occasions his prayer was humble submission and confidence and courage in that same Holy Spirit. In St. Mark's account of the agony in the Garden, Jesus cries out, "Abba, Father, all things are possible to thee; remove this cup from me; yet not what I will, but what thou wilt" (Mk. 14:36).

When we pray the Son's own prayer, "Abba, Father," we pray it in the Spirit of Jesus (Ga. 4:6). So, too, our Lord's cry in his agony,

"Father," was in that same Holy Spirit, who was ever our Lord's bond of love with the Father, the love in whom his heart rose in prayer to him. His human mind and heart, his human prayer and action, were ever "led by the Spirit" (Lk. 4:1,14,18; 10:21). Whether in his thrill of joy or in his cry of humble submission and loving confidence, Jesus ever prayed in the Holy Spirit. This same Holy Spirit inspires our prayers, too, and in them takes us to the Father.

The Holy Spirit dwelling in us is the source of all prayer and communion with God. He is the Giver of the ever fuller enlightenment and love—a participation in Christ's own light and love—which brings baptismal grace to its dynamic fullness. Whoever wishes to pray, then, must be convinced that the source of all prayer, the Holy Spirit, dwells in him. He must learn to be responsive to him, attentive to his inspirations; for it is he who inspires and perfects our prayer. "The Spirit helps us in our weakness; for we do not know how to pray as we ought, but the Spirit himself intercedes for us with sighs too deep for words. And he who searches the hearts of men knows what is the mind of the Spirit, because the Spirit intercedes for the saints according to the will of God" (Rom. 8:26–27).

The Serenity of Jesus

In great peace of conscience, Jesus was ever serenely certain that the Father was with him and that he was pleasing the Father because he was doing the Father's will. "He who sent me is with me; he has not left me alone, for I do always what is pleasing to him" (Jn. 8:29).

This serene assurance of conscience came from his steady contemplation of the Father: "Truly, truly, I say to you, the Son can do nothing of his own accord, but only what he sees the Father doing" (Jn. 5:19). That is, Jesus contemplates the Father's work of salvation, the mystery of the Father's salvific will, and ever sees himself as one entrusted with this work of salvation: "My Father is working still, and I am working. . . . The Son can do nothing of his own accord, but only what he sees the Father doing" (Jn. 5:17, 19).

In each situation, before he acts, Jesus always looks to see what the Father wills. The Evangelists, especially St. Luke, show us Jesus at prayer before each significant step in his mission.[2]

Fruit of His Contemplation

The fruit of this contemplation is our Lord's repeatedly renewed acceptance of his mission and his total dedication in carrying it out: "This is the will of him who sent me, that I should lose nothing of all that he has given me, but raise it up at the last day" (Jn. 6:39).

Christian contemplation is always like that. Like Christ, the Christian contemplates not just abstract attributes of God as the philosopher does, nor a God in whom one tries to annihilate self in escape from life's misery, as so many oriental contemplatives seem to try to do. No, the Christian contemplates God as a Father of men, God in his mystery of salvation, God in his saving action, God in his desire to give himself to men in Christ.

Such contemplation springs first into the gift of self to God in filial love, and then into an apostolate. The fruit of true Christian contemplation is always salvation action, above all the action of offering self with Christ for the salvation of the world. Whoever contemplates the mystery of saving love—the God who so loves that world that he gives his only Son—consecrates self with that Son for the continuation of that work.

For in contemplating the saving God, one discovers God's will to use his people in continuing his saving work. With Isaiah one hears God say, "Whom shall I send?" and with Isaiah one generously responds, "Here I am, send me!" (Isa. 6:8–9). The will of God which we contemplate is not an arbitrary will, but is the mystery of salvation, the salvific plan to bring all of us into the hands of the Father, into the bosom of his love. In contemplating this mystery,

2. Luke 3:21; 6:12; 9:18; 9:28–31; 18:1; 22:32; Mk. 1:38; Jn. 17.

we experience the God who is love, and consecrate ourselves to his work of love. Contemplating self in the light of God's saving will to discover how one can be at the services of this divine love, one discovers one's vocation, one's true mission in that saving work.

Christ's Serenity and Ours in the Depths of Trial

Throughout his mission, Jesus continues to contemplate his Father and to respond to him; he is always conscious of his Father's presence and love for him: "He who sent me is *with me;* He has not left me alone, for I always do what is pleasing to him" (Jn. 8:29).

This ever-continuing prayer of Jesus, this experience of the Father's presence with him, of his Father's love for him as Son, is his steadying support in all his trials. It is the cause of his majestic serenity which shines forth from him throughout the Last Supper and his Passion: "The hour is coming, indeed it has come, when you will be scattered, every man to his home, and will leave me alone. Yet I am not alone for the Father is with me.

"I have said this to you, that in me you may have peace. In the world you have tribulation, but be of good cheer, I have overcome the world" (Jn. 16:32–33). The peace and courage of Christ's heart—the fruits of his contemplation of the Father and his salvific will—are offered to us, and will be ours when, with Jesus, we contemplate the Father and his saving mystery, and respond with Jesus: "Thy will be done. Father, into thy hands I commit my spirit" (Matt. 26:42; Lk. 23:46).

They who would deny to Christ a knowledge of his divine sonship during his life on earth claim that lack of this knowledge makes him all the more like us in our trials; it gives us courage and comfort in our agony and death to know that even Jesus was in the dark! On the contrary, it was the courage and serenity of Jesus in his agony which gives us hope and courage in facing sufferings and death; and his serenity came precisely from his consciousness of his Father's love and presence. Even if in the midst of his agony and in the deepest darkness of his crucifixion his experience of his

Father's love did fade away, still it was the memory of what he had vividly experienced previously that enabled him to say with serene surrender, "Father, thy will be done! Father, into thy hands I commit my spirit!"

Any number of Christians can testify that this is how it happens. It is the memory of Christ's love for them in the past which fortifies them in the severe trials to which he puts them. Those past experiences of God in prayer left their permanent effect on them, preparing them for the trial which was ahead. And the very faith and hope by which they persevere in trial, along with the darkness itself during which they hope, are an experience of God who is near, but veiled in the darkness.

It was because Jesus was Son of God and experienced his Father's love, and therefore was able to drink courageously and willingly the chalice of our human misery to the full, that we have hope and courage. To be told about Jesus who suffered and died and rose again is not enough. If we are to have faith and hope in suffering and death and other trials, we must somehow experience in faith and prayer our sonship in the Son.

3

The Contemplative Process
in Jesus

Before he acted in each situation, Jesus always looked to see what his Father willed: "The Son can do nothing of his own accord, but only what he sees the Father doing" (Jn. 5:19). "I do always what is pleasing to him" (Jn. 8:29).

But did Jesus really *need* to look to the Father to learn? Did he really have to consult the Father before he acted? Was he not God, and, therefore, did he not already clearly know all things? Those who heard him speak were certainly impressed by the confidence and firmness with which he spoke; he was completely sure of himself in whatever he said. "They were astonished at his teaching, for he taught them as one who had authority, and not as the scribes" (Mk. 1:22).

But was it merely because he was God that he knew so clearly what to say and do? Was there also a human factor in the certitude of his knowledge? Did his human mind grow in the understanding of his mission? And, if so, in this growth did not his human mind function in the way that human minds usually do, or should?

For he was like us in all things except sin. The Scriptures say that he grew to perfection and that he learned. "Although he was a Son, he *learned* obedience through what he suffered, and *being made perfect* he became the source of eternal salvation to all who obey him" (Heb. 5:8–9).

To learn obedience, to grow through obedience to his perfection as man, to be genuinely obedient in a human way, surely this Man, though Son of God, had to learn what the Father willed; he had to look to the Father to see what was pleasing to him. Contained in his consciousness of who he was, Son of God made man, was the consciousness of his mission to make all men adoptive sons of God. But in a human way he searched to discover the details of how this mission was to be accomplished.

And how did he discover these details of the Father's will? Did he find them only in knowledge directly infused into his human mind by the Father? Or did he not seek and find them also in the normal human ways? Did he not discover the Father's will in the usual signs given to men: in the Word of God in the Scriptures, in the situations in which he found himself, in the needs of his fellowmen to which he responded, in his own experience of human life, his experience of what it really means to live as man? Certainly the Scriptures show Jesus reacting to human situations, questioning men to discover what was in their hearts, making his decisions accordingly, and thus fulfilling the Father's will that he meet the needs of men where he found them.

But always he interpreted these ordinary human signs of God's will with the aid of an interior light, the light of the Holy Spirit who dwelt in him, the light of the Word which he was. For this, too, is normal human procedure. No man is authentic man unless he receives knowledge both from the world of men and things about him, and from the Word and Spirit of God. And neither knowledge is complete without the other; they complement one another. In fact, the external signs of God's will do not make full sense without the inner light from the Holy Spirit, in which alone they can be interpreted with full accuracy and ultimate meaning. "By the gift of the Holy Spirit man comes in faith to the contemplation and full appreciation of the mystery of the divine plan" (*GS* 15).

It is quite obvious in the Scriptures that Jesus saw all things more clearly than did his fellowmen. He penetrated more profoundly than they the meaning of everything to which he directed his attention. His teaching, for example, which caused such astonishment in his hearers, was not learned merely from the Scriptures. It was so striking in contrast to the teaching of the scribes, the experts on the meaning of the Scriptures, that it must have come from another source in addition to the Scriptures.

If he interpreted the Scriptures so clearly, spoke of them with such authority, announced the scriptural Kingdom with such assurance, it could only be because his human mind read the Scriptures with a fuller participation in the divine light than did the experts of his times; and he had this fuller light because he was the Word. Similarly, he read the message of God in nature, in his fellowmen and their needs, in every situation, with this fuller light. No less than the great prophets before him, he was possessed by the Spirit of God by whom his human mind was endowed with a divine light. Like the prophets, he was aware of being moved by the Spirit. "The Spirit of the Lord is upon me," he proclaimed in the synagogue at Nazareth, "because he has anointed me to preach good news to the poor" (Lk. 4:18). St. Luke points out repeatedly that Jesus was ever led by the Holy Spirit in the accomplishment of his mission.

But it was more than a case of being led by the Holy Spirit. Jesus was the Word, and within the unity of his person which existed with the existence of the Word, he was ever deeply conscious of himself as true Son of God and profoundly experienced the Father's love for him as his divine Son. But in this consciousness, if what we said in our first chapter is correct, he did not necessarily know all the details of how he was to live as man, nor the ultimate details of his mission on earth. This was something he had to seek to find; he had to look to see what his Father willed. His very awareness of his divine sonship, his experience of his Father's love for him, his love in response to the Father's love, urged him on in this contemplative process of coming to a deeper human understanding of himself and of his mission.

How Does the Son of God Live as a Man?

Jesus needed a deeper understanding of himself in the sense that he had to learn in a human way how a Son of God lives as a man, how a man lives as Son of God.

For Jesus "thought it not robbery to be equal to God" (Phil 2:6, Douay). In the full consciousness that he was Son of God, he could not but *live* as Son of God. He "emptied himself" (2:7), not by abandoning his divinity or denying it, but by living his Sonship in the way *a man* must live divine Sonship—"in human form," in "the form of a servant" (2:7–8), in obedience unto death. God "cannot deny himself" (2 Tim. 2:13). Of one thing, therefore, Jesus could not possibly empty himself: his divinity, his divine sonship and "all that is implied in this divine sonship: the complete dedication to God, his unique mission and love, his sinlessness."[1]

As man, then, Jesus had to live as Son of God, Son of God in human form. He had to be true to his divine sonship by living it in an authentic human way. This he had to learn to do, as any child has to learn to live a human life. The implicit question of his childhood days, as he learned from his parents and from his daily experience of human life, was this: "What does it mean for a man to be Son of God; how does one live divine Sonship in human nature?" For deeply aware of his divine sonship and of his Father's love for him as Son, in love's response he eagerly desires to be a *worthy Son,* fully responding to that love by doing always the things pleasing to the Father in total consecration to his holy will.

"How does the Son of God live as a man?" Such was the basic question in our Lord's human, contemplative search for meaning. And the answer could be found only in the experience of living a human life, learning from living, growing in self-understanding in the normal processes of human growth. He learned the human condition from men by experiencing it with them. He accepted the

1. Piet Schoonenberg, "He Emptied Himself"—Philippians 2:7 *Concilium,* vol. 11. (New York: The Paulist Press, 1966), p. 58.

human condition, Son though he was, precisely because he was Son, and had to live as Son in whatever situation he found himself.

In his living of human life, he saw the true meaning of human life as no other man could ever have seen it; for only he who was God, ever enlightened by the Word he was, could learn in this human experience the full reality of what it means for man to live as God; and this meaning he has revealed to us. He learned from his human experience what he had to teach to us: how all men are to live as Sons of God in their grace of divine adoption.

Our Lord's Personal Need for the Life at Nazareth

Since only in the actual living of human life could the Son of God learn to live as a man, he truly needed his thirty years at Nazareth.

If the example of the life of Jesus at Nazareth is so forceful, it is precisely because God did not will it first of all as an example for us, but primarily as a necessity for his Son. . . . Jesus himself had need of those thirty years, for the work that he had to accomplish, for the man he had to be. . . . He needed those thirty years to become what he had to be, a man of his people, of his era, of our humanity.[2]

He needed the life at Nazareth to become fully himself; that is, Son of God living an authentically human life (and in this very living of it, working out our redemption), a life which grows to perfection through seeking to know how God wills that he should live and freely choosing to act accordingly.

In his experience of human life at Nazareth, then, Jesus learned from Mary and Joseph and from the local community how human beings live, how *he* must live to be truly man and truly Jewish. For in willing that his Son live as man, God willed that he live in a specific time and locality; by his very nature, man is circumscribed by time and place. The child Jesus, therefore, had to learn to be a Son of God in his Palestinian environment and in his Jewish religion and culture; he had to grow to self-understanding in terms of this particular human situation in which he found himself.

2. Guillet, *op. cit.,* pp. 385–386.

Jesus Learning from the Scriptures

In a special way he learned from his people's Scriptures how a man of this people must live. In his spontaneous eagerness to respond to his heavenly Father's love for him, he found in the Scriptures man's way of responding to God's love. He learned these Scriptures in the synagogue at Nazareth where they were read aloud each Sabbath. Even before that, he learned them from his mother, who was so given to pondering the Word of God that she must have known most of the key passages by heart and with profound insight.

Jesus needed his years at Nazareth to become what he had to be for us. Aware from his early childhood that he was in this world for a specific purpose, in filial love for the Father he sought to discover that purpose in explicit detail that he might faithfully carry it out. For, we said, the details of his mission were not necessarily clearly revealed to him in his consciousness of his divine sonship.

Is not this why he sought knowledge from the teachers in the temple when he was twelve years old, "listening to them and asking them questions"? (Lk. 2: 46). He was about his Father's business, seeking to know in what precise manner he was to carry it out. No doubt he was asking the teachers questions concerning the Scriptures, for did not the Scriptures reveal the plan of God? If it is true that he sought the Father's will in the Scriptures, then why not with the aid of the experts in the Scriptures? To say that he sought understanding is not to say that he was confused, or in doubt, or in error, but simply that he was growing, seeking fuller understanding.

One might object that as God he would have immediate insight into the profound depths of the Scriptures as soon as he read them, or even without reading them; though this would be to forget that his human mind was not his eternal divine mind. We are speaking of this *Man's* mind and his human understanding. Even we, when we read the Scriptures, often receive from the Holy Spirit insights into their meaning which no human beings have taught us. This is true enough, but usually these insights come only in the course of a pondering search. Why should it not have been so with Jesus in his human growth? And why should not the divine light have come to him sometimes with the aid of a human interpreter?

Father Yves Congar explains the twofold source of Christ's understanding of divine things:

At the same time that the soul of Jesus was being enlightened by the knowledge which the Father directly communicated to him of his design of salvation and of the way to accomplish all that had been foretold, his soul was acquiring, through meditation, a deeper understanding of the texts which had spoken of him.[3]

Insight was directly infused into his human mind from the Father and from the Word which he was. But these graces of insight no doubt often came to him from God in the way they normally come to other men: in the midst of a situation in which he was seeking his Father's will or the details of his vocation, or while meditating on the Scriptures. The full light can never come from human experience alone, nor from the Scriptures alone, nor from human teachers alone, but only from the interior light received from the Father. And yet both sources of insight—divine enlightenment and human experience—are necessary for any man, including Christ. Interior divine grace can be interpreted for human living only in human experience. "His consciousness," says Congar, "coordinated the lights that it received within the different 'registers' to which we have referred, and attained the absolute fullness of meaning of the Scriptures and of the design of God."[4]

If the twelve-year-old Jesus was asking questions of the teachers in order to learn from them rather than to teach them, no doubt he quickly surpassed the teachers in understanding the very Scriptures they explained. For he had a better light than they for penetrating their meaning. His very questions amazed the teachers, no doubt because what he asked revealed an insight into the Word of

3. Congar, *op. cit.*, pp. 61–62.
4. *Ibid.*, p. 62.

God surpassing their own. The Child's questions were probably pursuing directions which had not even occurred to the teachers. Jesus had an insight into clues which he was following up, and which he would pursue until he had reached full understanding of his mission.

Did his return to Nazareth in subjection to Mary and Joseph, for example, result from some clarification in his mind concerning the master-role of obedience in his life and in the Father's plan of salvation? Had he been quizzing the teachers, perhaps, on the Suffering Servant poems of Isaiah?

> Morning by morning he wakens, he wakens my ear
> to hear as those who are taught.
> The Lord has opened my ear,
> and I was not rebellious,
> I turned not backward.
> I gave my back to the smiters,
> and my cheeks to those who pulled out the beard (Isa. 50:4–6).

Jesus Learning from the Servant Poems

For there is no doubt that Jesus was especially struck by the Servant poems in Second Isaiah.[5] In later years when his sacred passion was near at hand, he described himself and his mission in terms of this Servant: "For the Son of Man also came not to be served but to serve, and to give his life as a ransom for many" (Mk. 10:45).

Surely these poems showed him in a special way how a man of his people should live. Second Isaiah emphasizes that the people of Israel is God's servant for the accomplishment of his purposes (Isa. 43:10; 44:1,21). The people as such has failed miserably in this mission (Isa. 42:19–25); but some mysterious individual member of that people, as the true Israel (49.3), succeeds admirably in accomplishing the will of God, in the midst of great sufferings (53:10–11).

All that Jesus will explain to his disciples after his Resurrection,

5. Isaiah 42:1–9; 49:1–7; 50:4–11; 52:13–53:12.

opening their minds to understand the Scriptures (Lk. 24:45), "he himself had first learned, beginning with his human knowledge of the Scriptures, as much by meditation as by enlightenment received from his Father. . . . Jesus had been the first to read and to understand the Scriptures in reference to himself and his mission. He had understood himself . . . as the holy Servant foretold by Isaiah, in the measure that he meditated on the sacred texts, and then in the measure that everything was being fulfilled."[6]

Father Schoonenberg, too, suggests that our Lord's deepest enlightenment concerning his mission as revealed in the Servant poems came to him in the course of the events in which they were being fulfilled:

At his Baptism, Jesus may not have seen yet that the painful end of the Servant of Yahweh would be his. . . . What happened immediately after his baptism (the voice coming from heaven, 'Thou art my beloved Son; with thee I am well pleased'—Mk. 1:11) must be understood . . . as a divine experience for Jesus himself; as such, it implies that, from that moment, he recognized in himself the figure of the Servant of Yahweh.[7]

The words from the Father at his Baptism were a clear echo of Isaiah 42:1, the first Servant poem. How often men and women have had this experience of hearing scriptural words as though they were addressed directly and personally to themselves, giving an effective thrust and new direction in the working out of their vocation. Should not Jesus be like us in this, as in all else? Is not this God's way of working with men; is it not normal for men to receive such communications from God?

The Servant of Yahweh as described in the first poem is a preacher of the Word of God. In this experience at his Baptism, Jesus was confirmed in his mission as preacher of the good news; as it were, he received from the Father the "go-ahead; now is the time!"

6. Congar, *op. cit.*, p. 62.
7. Schoonenberg, *op. cit.*, p. 63.

At the start of his preaching, suggests Schoonenberg, Jesus thought of himself chiefly as this preacher. But did he clearly see that his word would be rejected, and that "his death would have the significance of that vicarious sacrifice of atonement described in the fourth Servant poem (Isa. 53)?"

Only when the opposition grows and these opponents develop a truly deadly hatred of him, there dawns upon him the significance of the violent death which awaits him. Now he recognizes from the circumstances that his Father's will for him is to fulfill the function of the Servant of Yahweh to the end, to die in order to bring the many to righteousness.[8]

The events, then, revealed to Jesus the way his mission was to be worked out, but the events as understood in the light of those scriptural passages, and through an interior enlightenment enabling Jesus to see clearly the meaning of the events and of the Scriptures. Such is the way God speaks to all of us, if, like Jesus, we are ever intent to do always the things that please him.

That Jesus received successive infused lights from the Father only as necessary for carrying out his mission, or when he looked to the Father to see what he would have him do, is perhaps indicated in our Lord's words: "Truly, truly, I say to you, the Son can do nothing of his own accord, but only what he sees the Father doing; for whatever he does, that the Son does likewise. For the Father loves the Son, and *shows* him all that he himself is doing" (Jn. 5:19–20).

Jesus does not say "has shown" as if revealing absolutely everything all at once in beatific vision, but "shows," as if indicating a continuing process which was still in progress when Jesus spoke these words. Of course, perhaps Jesus is merely emphasizing the identity of his own work with God's life-giving work, without intending to say how or when his personal light is received from the Father.

8. *Ibid.*

Jesus the Servant, the True Israel

The people of Israel, servant of Yahweh, had failed in their mission. But Jesus shows himself the true Israel, succeeding where his people had failed. He succeeds because he is Son of God in fullest reality! In the consciousness of this reality and in the power of this Sonship, he can only act as a Son of God "in the form of a servant," becoming "obedient unto death, even death on a cross" (Phil. 2:7–8).

His success in being truly Son and Servant, coming to his human perfection as Son of God in filial obedience, makes him the cause of divine sonship in all those who are obedient in his obedience. "Although he was a Son, he learned obedience through what he suffered; and being made perfect he became the source of eternal salvation to all who obey him" (Heb. 5:8–9).

The reality of Jesus coming to his true personal fulfillment through a genuine process of human growth and free choice in obedience is explained very well indeed by Schoonenberg's suggestion that Jesus grew in the understanding of his mission in the very process of carrying it out faithfully. He matured in a truly human way, freely accepting the situations in which he found himself. "All human life grows out of situations which are not chosen by ourselves but which we accept and make our own as we become more mature."[9]

The Contemplative Process in the Living of Life

Truly, the contemplative process is admirably illustrated in Jesus. In perpetual attention to the Father whose love he experiences, in seeking the Father's will in reflecting upon the Scriptures, in experiencing their fulfillment in the events of his life, he comes to the fullness of his self-awareness in relationship to his heavenly Father; he *knows* the Father in the very living of his life, in the scriptural sense of *knows*. To *know*, in biblical language, is no mere intel-

9. *Ibid.*, p. 62.

lectual knowledge; it is the experiencing of a reality in the very living of it in love. The man, Jesus, comes to know his Father in all human fullness only by lovingly living the totality of his life entirely for the Father, in authentic sonship.

Thus his process of coming to self-understanding can come to completion only in the understanding and fulfilling of his mission. For a man is fully himself, and fully experiences and understands himself, only in actually living his God-given mission. Jesus was totally himself by being totally given over to God and to the many for whom he gave his life as Servant of Yahweh (Mk. 10:45).

Thus, the contemplative process in which we come to full awareness of ourselves as sons of God in grace requires not only a persevering attention to God in prayer, but a dedicated endeavor to live as his sons, thus becoming fully aware of God our Father in the very living of our sonship. Contemplation requires involvement in life. Light comes not just directly from God. It also comes in the very events of life which we understand in God's light.

4

More on Our Lord's Contemplative Process

Jesus Learning from the Jewish Liturgy

If Jesus learned in the very experiencing of human life how as Son of God he must live as a man, and if he learned from this life as enlightened by the Scriptures, he learned it also by participating in the liturgy of his people.

As a child, he learned the religious attitudes of his people, experiencing them as he worshipped the Father with his people in the synagogue and in the temple, and listening to the Scriptures which gave meaning to that worship.

For if the Jewish scriptures and liturgy were God's will for the people into which he was born, then they were God's will for the Son of God made man.

But here again, his awareness of his divine sonship, his experience of his Father's love for him, enabled him to put inexpressibly deeper meaning into this worship than any other man had ever been able to do. As he participated in the liturgy, his contemplative reflection helped to bring to ever more explicit understanding his intuitive experience of his Father, as the Word-which-he-was ever more profoundly enlightened his human mind and heart by new contemplative graces.

In this living, deepening experience of God his Father, he worshipped the Father in the Jewish liturgy with the infinite profundity of his divine heart, he brought to the religious attitudes of his people a depth which these had never had before.

Thus, in participating in the liturgy of his people, the growing Jesus experienced ever more deeply and understood ever more fully what it means for man, son of God, to live in religious obedience to the Father in heaven. He daily deepened the "reverent submission" (Heb. 8:5,c) which he brought to supreme perfection in his acceptance of the chalice in the agony in the garden. What Yves Congar has said of the obedience of Jesus to Mary and Joseph in the home of Nazareth is true also of his submission to the Father in the liturgy:

Jesus learned obedience not only through what he suffered, as the letter to the Hebrews (5:8) tells us, but also from his life as a child in his home at Nazareth. It was in the practice of the fourth commandment that Jesus began, in his human soul, the practice of filial obedience which he had to give to his heavenly Father. . . .

Yes, his loving obedience to his Father in heaven was first formed in his human consciousness by his child's attitudes at Nazareth. . . .

All the filial obedience of Jesus is summed up in his passion, by which our salvation is effected. He had practiced it throughout his life and by this very practice he had humanly better understood and deepened it.[1]

In his reverent submission on Calvary, he brought all liturgy, all religion, to its fulfillment. In participating in the liturgy of his people and in meditating upon their Scriptures in the consciousness of his sonship, Jesus came to realize ever more explicitly that he himself was the fulfillment of all the things spoken of in the law and prophets and celebrated in the liturgy. For if the answer to the question, "How does the Son of God live as a man," is learned in the very experiencing of authentic human life, the answer to the more specific question, "What is his precise mission in living this human life?" is found in the divine revelation given in the history, Scriptures and liturgy of his people, as well as in the course of events as enlightened by these.

1. Congar, *op. cit.,* pp. 56, 54.

Through the Scriptures, the liturgy, the course of events, his experience of human life, his interaction with his fellowmen, Jesus came to this deeper self-understanding only because he was enlightened above all by the Word which he was, "the true light that enlightens every man"—every man, including Jesus, and especially Jesus.

Jesus, Source of All Contemplation

In speaking of our blessed Lord's need for his hidden life at Nazareth, we have chiefly tried to show how these years were necessary for his personal growth, that he might become *the man that he had to be*. Perhaps we have overemphasized this element. Let us, therefore, try to restore the proper balance by considering some words of Father Yves Congar, who puts the chief emphasis on how these years helped Jesus become the man he had to be *for us*.

Congar studies the contribution to his mission as Savior and revealer of divine truth "which was made by the knowledge Jesus acquired during his human life, whether by education, experience, relationships with other men, or finally, by his human reflection about the world, men and God."[2]

Though he was God and brought a divine message, Jesus was a man speaking this message to men. Whatever infused knowledge Jesus received directly from the Word concerning his person and his mission, had to be communicated to men in human language. He had to speak with human words and needed to share in the human experience which gave rise to this human vocabulary. He had to reflect, he had to know men, he had to know the human and religious concepts of his people.

Jesus had to reveal the religious relationship in its full truth. To do this, he had to reveal something of the mystery of God and the true condition of man as well as the state to which he is called. He did this by drawing unceasingly, not only from the treasury of human knowl-

2. *Ibid.,* p. 52.

edge and language, but also from the experience which he acquired
from things and from men . . .

He who had come to make the name of God known to men (Jn.
17:6, 26) did not cease to think about his mission as he looked at
things and learned their names and properties as he walked among
men. Unceasingly, he sought and found in things all the power they
possessed to signify what he had to make known. He bent with ardor
over the chalice of all the flowers to draw out the signifying elements
of the thought of God which is to be found in the heart of things, and
which must somehow be brought out.[3]

If our Lord's experience of human life and of the world about
him helped him to conceptualize and deepen in a human way his
self-understanding, as well as his appreciation of the truths he had
to reveal in human language, he always saw infinitely more perfectly into the meaning of everything than any mere man could
have done, because of his own interior intuitive contemplation of
the mystery of God.

For example, his experience of St. Joseph's paternity in the little
home of Nazareth, helped him to conceptualize in a human way
his intuitive experience of God as his personal Father whom he
must reveal as the one who wished to be father of all men by the
grace of divine adoption. At the age of twelve he articulated his
consciousness of God his Father in no uncertain terms: "Did you
not know that I must be in my Father's house?" (Lk. 2:49).

Jesus could have this word only from his Father and from the
certitude that he was the only Son, but he could formulate it only in
the language that he received from Mary and Joseph and only from
the experience that he drew from his surroundings.[4]

Yet, though he formulated his consciousness of God's paternity
in terms of his human experience of Joseph's paternity, his experience of Joseph's paternity, on the other hand, was enlightened by
the intuitive knowledge which he possessed of the mystery of God
his Father. There is a mutual influence of the two sources of knowl-

3. *Ibid.*, pp. 59, 60.
4. Guillet, *op. cit.*, p. 392.

edge, and both are necessary. "The contribution of man and his experience, and the contribution of God who reveals something of his mystery, correspond in a kind of dialogue and condition one another to form the *Christian* understanding and judgment."[5]

The light coming directly from God, however, holds the primacy, and is definitive in giving ultimate meaning to all things:

If Jesus had not had knowledge received immediately from God of the full truth which he had to reveal, he would not have known with the necessary fullness and assurance the signifying value of the human notions and words of which he had experience. If he had not known the Holy Spirit, he would not have known that water is a powerful symbol of him. . . . It was necessary that there be some irruption in him of the light of the creative Word for him to know, at the level of his human consciousness, the revelatory value, the power to reveal God, possessed by the images of which he had experience with us.[6]

Truly, in the light of his own self-awareness as Son of God, Jesus deeply penetrated the true meaning of everything. His deep experiential understanding of himself as a man who is truly Son of God gave him a profound understanding of all men as image of God destined to be divine sons by grace. Only in his light do we have the fullness of meaning of ourselves and of everything else.

Jesus knew the truth of human nature in a firm and total way. The same was true of all his words, in which is to be found the source of eternal life, of absolute life and truth (cf. Jn. 6:68). . . . He knows the import and infinite value of his words and his deeds; yes, of his words and deeds *as man*. He knows this by that knowledge directly communicated from God and by that direct vision which, in consummating his human knowledge, makes him the perfect prophet.[7]

His fullness of knowledge, acquired by divine revelation and human experience, "was to be the measure of all that the Church, following the apostles, would understand and communicate in her

5. Congar, *op. cit.*, p. 57.
6. *Ibid.*, p. 64.
7. *Ibid.*, pp. 64–65.

tradition. . . ."[8] All the divine understanding possessed by the people of God, all Christian contemplation, is a participation in our Lord's own contemplation. It is a sharing in the fullness of light which his own human mind reached in his process of growth through his living experiencing of the truth of man—of man who is true only when he is a son of God contemplating his heavenly Father.

Our Lord's authentically human living of his divine sonship is the continuing cause of our living of the divine sonship in him: "He learned obedience through what he suffered; and being made perfect, he became the source of eternal salvation to all who obey him" (Heb. 5:8-9).

He personally enlightens each one of us with the fullness of the light which he himself had acquired in his process of contemplation. In our contemplative process, he leads us into the light and obedience and full reality of the divine sonship which he himself had experienced in a fully human way. For only in him are we sons of God. By Baptism, our grace of divine sonship, he lives his divine sonship in us and we live it in him. In our contemplative process, he personally brings us to an ever deeper awareness of what we are by his grace—sons of God in the Son!

8. *Ibid.*, p. 62.

5

What Jesus Saw
in the World and in Men

What We Do Not See

Modern man is not finding God in creation or in his fellowmen.

God has revealed himself in the things he has made. All creation proclaims his glory. Why, then, cannot modern man find him in his creation? Why is atheism more widespread than ever before in history? Why, in our times, is atheism worldwide, socially constituted, militant, considering itself something to be taken for granted? God, it would seem, has not been very successful in revealing himself.

Mankind was made in the image and likeness of God. Human relationships should, therefore, be a revelation of the intimate relationships existing among the three divine Persons. But how can envy and dissension, war and hatred, riots and bitterness, reveal a family of God, a people participating in the family life of the Trinity? Do not the people of this twentieth century, torn by one world war after another, say with justice: There is no God of love! or even: There is no God!

If there is so much talk these days about finding God in the cosmos and in one's fellowmen, no doubt it is because our times have failed so miserably in doing so. Seemingly, it is no easy task.

Why is the task so difficult? Why have we lost the ability to find the true meaning of all that God has made, when all things speak their meaning so clearly?

> The heavens are telling the glory of God
>> And the firmament proclaims his handiwork.
>
> Day to day pours forth speech
>> and night to night declares knowledge.
>
> There is no speech, nor are there words;
>> their voice is not heard;
>
> Yet their voice goes out through all the earth,
>> and their words to the end of the world (Ps. 19:1–4).

There are perennial reasons for the difficulty in finding God, reasons as old as mankind itself, reasons spoken of in the Scriptures. But because of his special mentality, modern man has an added difficulty. The search for meaning is especially critical in contemporary society. Vatican II speaks of the dulling of the contemplative and sapiential faculties of modern man and his consequent confusion concerning his own meaning (*GS* 56). This dulling is due in no small degree to the tendency of the modern scientific mentality to take a narrow view: "Today's progress in science and technology can foster a certain emphasis on observable data and an agnosticism about everything else" (*GS* 57).

One of the urgent problems of the times, says the Council, is how to "preserve among men the faculties of contemplation and wonderment which lead to wisdom" (*GS* 56). The search for meaning is a contemplative process. But man today seeks *the useful, not the meaningful*. God, indeed, gave man dominion over the world that he might master it and use it in providing for his temporal necessities. But he gave man the world for a far more wonderful reason: that it might be a revelation of God himself, a manifestation of his presence.

That is the *meaning* of the cosmos: to him who has eyes to see, it reveals the Lord who made it and upholds it. It would not be there if the Lord were not there giving it existence. Modern man, intent only on mastering and using the world, and ignoring its meaning as pointing to the transcendent, has lost the ability to understand it, interpret it, contemplate the Lord who is revealed in it.

This special modern obstacle to finding God is really not so modern after all. Jesus spoke of it in the Sermon on the Mount: Do not be so set on using the world that you lose sight of the kingdom of God, God's presence in the midst of his people: "Do not be anxious, saying 'What shall we eat?' or 'What shall we drink?' or 'What shall we wear?' For the Gentiles seek all these things; and your heavenly Father knows that you need them all. But seek first his kingdom and his righteousness, and all these things shall be yours as well" (Matt. 6:31–33).

Jesus is really warning against the danger of sin, which is the cause of man's difficulty in finding God. "You cannot serve God and mammon; therefore I tell you do not be anxious about your life, what you shall eat or what you shall drink, nor about your body, what you shall put on" (Matt. 24–25). We can become so preoccupied in mastering and using the world that we make it our god, and are blinded to the living God.

There is much talk these days, we said, about finding God in nature and seeing him in our fellowmen. However, we often get the impression from this talk that in seeing God in nature and in the people with whom we live, we are to forget about trying to see God in himself. The transcendence of God seems to be denied.

We must, indeed, learn to find God in the creation and in our fellowmen, but not in such a way as to identify God and his creatures.[1] We must learn from Jesus the right way of contemplating God in the cosmos and in our fellowmen. We must see men and things as Jesus saw them, respond as he responded. The pagan world had lost the knowledge of God; the Son of God came to restore this knowledge.

St. Paul was insistent that the pagan world could know God:

---

1. We noted in our preceding volume, *Prayer, the Search for Authenticity* (New York: Sheed and Ward, 1969) that many contemporary Christians under the influence of atheistic humanism have fallen into this trap.

"Ever since the creation of the world his invisible nature, namely his eternal power and deity, has been clearly perceived in the things that have been made" (Rom. 1:20).

Those pagans, however, who did discover the God revealed in creation, had only an obscure knowledge of him; not the full light, but "a ray of that Truth which enlightens all men" (*NA* 2). With the help of the witness to himself given by God in nature, says St. Paul, man gropes for the full light (Acts 17:26–27).

The good news about Jesus proclaimed by the Apostles is the answer to the gropings of all mankind: "What, therefore, you worship as unknown, this I proclaim to you" (Acts 17:23). Nature as a witness to God starts us groping for him, but we find him fully revealed only in Jesus Christ his Son.

And once we have found God in Christ, then nature itself takes on a new luminosity. We begin to see it in the way Jesus saw it when he was on earth, as a sign of the heavenly Father's love for his children. And only when, with Christ, we have found the Father can we begin to understand our fellowmen as destined to be his children and our brothers in Christ. Only in Jesus do we learn to see all creation and all our fellowmen as a revelation of the invisible Father. To see what Jesus saw, we must participate in his light, we must share in his vision of the Father.

What Jesus Saw

Because Jesus was ever experiencing the Father's love for him as Son, and was ever contemplating his plan to bring all men into that sonship, he could see evidence of his Father's love everywhere. His joy in the Father overflowed as a joy in all things, for he saw all things as the gifts and signs of the Father's love for men. In the beauty of the fields, in the singing of the birds, he saw the Father's provident love for his children: "Look at the birds of the air! They neither sow nor reap nor gather into barns, and yet your heavenly Father feeds them. Are you not of more value than they? Consider the lilies of the field, how they grow; they neither toil nor spin; yet

I tell you, even Solomon, in all his glory, was not arrayed like one of these. But if God so clothes the grass of the field which today is alive and tomorrow is thrown into the oven, will he not much more clothe you, O men of little faith?" (Matt. 6:26, 28–30).

Jesus sees all creation, then, as the gift of the Father to his children, as the revelation of his love for them. And he sees these children as destined to behold the Father as he himself beholds him, and thus overflow with his own joy in the Father.

In the silently growing seed in the field, Jesus contemplates the Father's word planted in the hearts of men, the word of life by which he begets them as his children.

In the blind, Jesus sees the opportunity of glorifying the Father by giving them his own divine insight; in the crippled, he sees the chance to give them power to walk all the way to the eternal mountain of God. This man was born blind, he says, "that the works of God might be manifest in him" (Jn. 9:23); in curing the cripple on the Sabbath, he says, "The Father is working still, and I am working" (Jn. 5:17). That is, Jesus sees the Father at work not only in the lilies of the field and in the birds of the air, but even more in the hearts of men, enlightening them concerning a life transcending this world, and giving them power to attain it.

He sees himself as doing this work of the Father, and is ever conscious of the Father working in him and through him: he commands the cripple to walk, and the cripple does so; he tells the blind man to see, and the man sees Jesus as Son of God! (Jn. 9:35–38).

And every time Jesus contemplates a human heart, even the heart of a sinful Samaritan woman, he sees that its infinite depths are capable of receiving the Holy Spirit, "a spring of water welling up to eternal life" (Jn. 4:14).

He sees the little ones as destined to see the Father, as entrusted to angels who will bring them to the vision which they themselves enjoy (Matt. 18:10). Thus, in the eyes of every little child, he contemplates the reflection of the Father in heaven upon whom they gaze in wonderment.

Just as Jesus was the first man to see the Father, so, too, he was the first man to see the Father in men. For if the Old Testament speaks of men as sons of God, it never does so in the full meaning which Jesus gives to this title. When the Old Testament calls the just man a son of God, it means only that God treats him *as if* he were a son; the Old Testament has not yet arrived at the concept of man being raised to a participation in God's very own life.

It is only when the Son of God comes and shares fully in man's life that man understands at last that he is called to share fully in God's life. Christ's own experience of his divine sonship convinces him of God's will to adopt men as his sons. Jesus was the first to experience this truth in love, and only he could reveal it. Only "he who descended from heaven, the Son of Man who is in heaven" (Jn. 3:13) could make the stupendous revelation of divine sonship which met with the uncomprehending resistance of Nicodemus: "Unless a man is born from above, he cannot see the kingdom of God" (Jn. 3:3,j).

Nicodemus said, "How can a grown man be born? Can he go back into his mother's womb and be born again?" (3:4,j). Until the Son of God revealed it, it was unheard of that man, born of woman, could be born anew of God. Only Jesus, contemplating his Father in heaven, could see his fellowmen as destined to become children of the Father. These things could not be seen by contemplating the cosmos. Nor could we ever have dreamed of them merely by looking at our fellowmen.

To see creation and our fellowmen in the way the New Testament would have us see them, we must participate in Christ's own contemplation of the Father and in his experience of the Father's love. Christian contemplation, we said, is always a participation in Christ's own inner light and love. Jesus has caught us up into his own contemplation. In speaking eloquently of his Father in heaven and of his love for his children, and giving us at the same time his own interior light in the Holy Spirit, Jesus has given us his own vision, so that with him and in him we can see what he sees. "We have the mind of Christ. . . . We have received . . . the Spirit which is from God that we might understand the gifts bestowed on us by God" (1 Cor. 2:16,12).

Every apostle has to be contemplating the Father in heaven with Jesus if he is to succeed in catching others up into the contemplation of Jesus; if he is to enable others to see what Jesus saw in the Father, in men and in the world. An apostle has to have the vision of Jesus himself.

An apostle is like the guardian angels in two ways. First, both "angel" and "apostle" mean "one sent." That is how Jesus loved to describe himself. He is the apostle of the Father, "the one whom the Father has consecrated and sent into the world" (Jn. 10:34). Secondly, the guardian angel is able to recognize the likeness of the heavenly Father in the face of the little ones confided to him, because he ever sees the face of the Father in heaven (Matt. 18:10), just as Jesus was ever contemplating his heavenly Father.

And so it has to be with every apostle. He can recognize Christ and the Father in his fellowmen only because he is so familiar with the face of the Father which he has contemplated in Christ, image of the Father. An apostle, according to St. Mark's definition, is one who must be *with Jesus,* and be *sent by Jesus:* "He called to him men of his own choosing . . . that they might be with him and that he might send them forth to preach" (Mk. 3:13–14,c). With Jesus and in Jesus, the apostle contemplates the Father; and is sent by Jesus to bring his fellowmen to see the Father.

6
"Lord, Show Us the Father!"

Jesus taught us to contemplate the heavenly Father at work in nature, "making his sun rise on the evil and on the good, and sending rain on the just and the unjust" (Matt. 5:45), providing good things for all his children; for good and evil alike are called to be his children. Thus, our Lord taught us to see all our fellowmen as children of the Father in heaven.

And he showed us how the Father works in the hearts of his children, planting his word there like a seed and carefully nurturing it with the sunshine of his love and with the waters of his grace till it bears a full harvest in life everlasting.

But it is not enough for us to see the Father at work in all things. Nor is it enough for us to see the Father imaged in his children. We soon desire to see the Father himself. Just as a man is not content to contemplate the image of his wife in their children but loves to look directly upon her and speak intimately with her, so the lover of God cannot be content with seeing God and serving him only as reflected in men. He must gaze upon him and speak directly with him in prayer and contemplation.

Jesus spoke so much about his Father—this Father whom he was ever contemplating—that his disciples soon had an ardent desire to see the Father together with him. "Lord, show us the Father," said Philip, "and we shall be satisfied" (Jn. 14:8).

Scholars sometimes interpret Philip's request to see the Father as a petition to see some spectacular manifestation of the divine glory, similar to the salvation deeds of the Old Testament in which God had manifested his saving presence. This may indeed have been the point of Philip's request when it was originally presented; "Jesus, show us the glory," may have been the way he phrased his petition. Our Lord's response seems to indicate that this is what Philip meant. The reply, "Philip, he who has seen me has seen the Father," means that, if the glory of God was manifest in the salvation deeds of the Exodus and in other saving events of the past, the glory is now to be seen in the person of Jesus and in the salvation event of his death and Resurrection. "We saw his glory, the glory that is his as the only Son of the Father!" (Jn. 1:14,j).

However, in reporting this conversation for a later Christian audience, the Evangelist rephrases Philip's request, interpreting it to make it meaningful for the lives of Christians, making it truly a request to see God in Person: "Lord, show us the Father, and we shall be satisfied." In his response, Jesus shows the only way we can come to such a vision of the Father.

Can we blame anyone for the desire to see the Father, since Jesus was always speaking about that Father? The whole purpose of the Son in coming into the world was to reveal the God whom no man had ever seen. His disciples' desire to see the Father shows that Jesus had done his work well.

Why, then, in the Evangelist's reinterpretation, is there a gentle rebuke in our Lord's response to Philip? "Have I been with you so long, and yet you do not know me, Philip? He who has seen me has seen the Father; how can you say, 'Show us the Father?'" (Jn. 14:9).

Was our Lord telling Philip and the rest of us that we will have to be content with seeing the Father only in Jesus, his image? Was our Lord's response to Philip pretty much like Yahweh's response to Moses when Moses said, "Do let me see your glory?" Philip's request is phrased in a way which reminds us of the request of

Moses, and no doubt the Evangelist sees a relationship between the two requests. Are we to conclude that as Moses was refused the vision of the face of Yahweh, so we are refused face to face vision of the Father?

Not at all. In his Gospel, St. John contrasts Moses and Jesus: "The law was given through Moses; grace and truth came through Jesus Christ" (Jn. 1:17). What Moses was not granted to see, Jesus has seen; and more than that, he reveals it to us: "No one" —not even Moses—"has ever seen God; the only Son, who is in the bosom of the Father, he has made him known" (Jn. 1:18).

If Jesus meant that we would never see the Father except as reflected in his own glorified humanity, why would he have aroused desire to see the Father? Had he not declared only a few moments before that he would have said so if there were no place for his disciples in his Father's house? Certainly to dwell in the Father's house is to see the Father:

> One thing I have asked a hundred times,
>   this, O Yahweh, do I seek:
> To dwell in Yahweh's house
>   all the days of my life,
> Gazing upon the loveliness of Yahweh,
>   awaking each dawn in his temple (Ps. 27:4,a).

Jesus promises the fulfillment of the psalmist's desire: "In my Father's house there are many rooms; if it were not so, would I have told you that I go to prepare a place for you? And when I go and prepare a place for you, I will come again and will take you to myself, that where I am you may be also" (Jn. 14:2–3).

"Where I am . . ." Jesus knows the Father even as the Father knows him (Lk. 10:22). To be where Jesus is, then, is to know the Father with Jesus and in him; it is to be in the bosom of the Father; it is to be with Jesus where he has been glorified in the full presence of the Father (Jn. 17:5).

Nor will it be merely a seeing of the glory of the Father as reflected in the glorified humanity of Jesus, his image. For already in this life there is a spiritual, interior manifestation of Christ and the Father who are dwelling in us: "He who loves me will be loved by my Father, and I will love him and manifest myself to him. . . . We will come to him and make our home with him" (Jn. 14:21,23). Certainly this spiritual seeing of God even now foreshadows a more wonderful spiritual seeing of God in the next life which is more than merely seeing the glorified humanity of Christ.

Our Lord, then, is not refusing the vision of the Father as Yahweh had refused Moses the vision of his inner glory. Rather, the parallel between the request of Moses and that of Philip suggests that what Moses had asked is somehow to be granted in Jesus.

He Who Sees Me

If our Lord is not denying a future face to face vision of the Father, what then does he mean in saying, "He who has seen me has seen the Father"?

He is telling us that only they will be able to come to the Father's house to see him face-to-face who now see the Father at work in Jesus in his paschal mystery. Jesus had just said, "No one comes to the Father but by me" (Jn. 14:6). Considering the whole context of these words in the Last Supper discourse, we have to interpret them in this way: "No one comes to the Father except *through me in my paschal mystery,* through me in my sacrifice." Likewise, his answer to Philip has to be interpreted, "He who has seen *me in my paschal mystery* has seen the Father." The only way to God is by faith's penetration into the meaning of the paschal mystery and by true participation in that mystery.

The whole theme of the Last Supper discourse in St. John's Gospel is our Lord's paschal mystery, his sacrifice in which he passes out of this world to the Father (Jn. 13:1). His death, his going away, is no mere death; it is his going to the Father. No one can come to the Father except through this sacrificial death. *In his sacrifice,* Jesus is "the way and the truth and the life" (Jn. 14:6). Therefore, when Jesus says, "He who has seen me has seen the Father," he means that one must see Jesus in the sacrifice of the cross as the only way to the Father. Jesus, lifted up on the cross, is the Father's supreme salvation deed, the greatest revelation of "the glory." If, as originally spoken, Philip's request, "Lord, show us the Father," was a petition for some marvelous manifestation of God akin to the manifestations of "the glory" in the salvation deeds of the Old Testament, then our Lord's words of rebuke, "Have I been with you so long, and yet you do not know me, Philip?" would mean: Have you not understood even now that the salvation I bring is of a different order than the Old Testament salvation deeds and in a different manner than those glorious divine interventions of the past? You are to see the saving glory of God at work not in miraculous signs and wonders like the passage through the Red Sea nor in the flaming fire of Mount Sinai, but in the humiliation of the Son. You are to see God saving his people in the humble obedience of his Son. In his sacrifice, you will see the new Exodus, the new Passover; you will see salvation in the new Paschal Lamb.

"He who has seen me has seen the Father." In Jesus on the cross one must see the Father carrying on his salvation work; one must see Jesus as Son of God, one with the Father even in his death by crucifixion.

"How can you say, 'Show us the Father?' Do you not believe that I am in the Father and the Father in me?" (Jn. 14:9–10). That is, even if you see me nailed to the cross, you must see in faith that even then I am one with the Father and the Father is with me. I am his true Son. Both my words and my works, Jesus continues, are the Father's: "The words I speak to you I do not speak as from myself: *it is the Father, living in me, who is doing this work.* You must believe me when I say that I am in the Father and the Father is in me" (Jn. 14:10–11,j).

"It is the Father, living in me, who is doing this work." In this work, my sacrificial death, the Father is accomplishing his work of salvation. Jesus had expressed the same thought on another occasion:

> When you have lifted up the Son of Man,
> then you will know that I am he
> and that I do nothing of myself. . . .
> He who sent me is with me,
> and has not left me to myself,
> for I always do what pleases him (Jn. 8:28–29,j).

Even when Jesus is lifted up on the cross, the Father works with him. He does not leave Jesus to himself, who does nothing of himself. The sacrifice of Jesus is God's work of salvation.

Of his miracles, Jesus had said, "My Father goes on working, and so do I" (Jn. 5:17,j). Now he says the same of his work on the cross: "It is the Father, living in me, who is doing this work" (Jn. 14:10,j).

It was not enough, then, for Jesus to show us how to contemplate the Father at work in nature, in the lilies of the field and in the birds of the air. Jesus teaches us to contemplate the Father above all as revealed in the paschal mystery. That is his supreme salvation act, the supreme revelation of his love: "For God so loved the world that he gave his only Son" (Jn. 3:16). We must see the Father's saving love revealed and given to us in the Son's sacrifice.

Christian contemplation has always focused its attention chiefly on this paschal mystery. For short of the face-to-face vision of heaven, this mystery is the truest revelation of the Father for what he really is. "God is love. In this the love of God was made manifest among us, that God sent his only Son into the world, so that we might live through him. In this is love, not that we loved God, but that he loved us and sent his Son to be the expiation for our sins. . . . So we know and believe the love God has for us" (1 Jn. 4:8–10,16).

God is manifest, then, in Christ's sacrifice. There, above all, while we are on earth are we to contemplate our God; there he is most clearly revealed to men still in this life. Such are the things we contemplate daily in the eucharistic sacrifice.

Contemplation and Involvement
in the Paschal Mystery

Our reaction to such contemplation, the fruit of such contemplation, is involvement in the paschal mystery through love of neighbor: "Beloved, if God so loved us, we also ought to love one another. . . . He who does not love his brother whom he has seen, cannot love God whom he has not seen" (1 Jn. 4:11,20). The contemplation of God's love revealed in the crucifixion enables us to contemplate our fellowman as "the brother for whom Christ died" (1 Cor. 8:11), the brother for whom we therefore spend ourselves and are spent.

The contemplating of Christ in our neighbor is what we might call "contemplative action," or "active contemplation." It is contemplative action, for the action of loving and serving neighbor *precisely as one for whom Christ died* presupposes that we have contemplated God's love for us in Christ crucified. Service of neighbor springs forth as the fruit and continuation of this contemplation. It is active contemplation, for seeing Christ in neighbor is no mere gazing; it is "practising the truth in love" (Eph. 4:15,c). It is "faith working through love" (Gal. 5:6). Convinced, through contemplation of the paschal mystery, of God's love for us, faith responds to that love in loving service of neighbor.

Seeing Christ in neighbor, then, is not some sort of mere knowledge. It is existential involvement; it is a living of the truth. It is Christian faith and love seeing what is to be done, a seeing in love which moves to doing. That is why we called it contemplative action; it is action springing from the contemplation of Christ in neighbor, "the brother for whom Christ died."

But how can we see neighbor as the brother for whom Christ died if we have not seen Christ dying for him? The contemplating of God in neighbor does not dispense us from directly contemplating God in Christ crucified, for only the contemplation of Christ himself gives rise to this contemplative action on behalf of neighbor.

The two contemplations are, indeed, one. They are contemplation of two aspects of one same mystery. They are two elements in one same movement of love, the love in which we give ourselves to God, the love in which we give ourselves to neighbor.

For we have not really contemplated Christ crucified unless in our vision we see also those for whom he was crucified—ourselves, and those of our brethren who are here and now in continuing need of his redemption.

If faith's insight into God's love revealed in Christ crucified gives rise to effective love of neighbor, this service of neighbor in turn opens us to receive a deeper insight into God's love for us. It is a perfect disposition preparing us to receive infused contemplation. Service of neighbor is not infused contemplation, but when it springs from truly self-sacrificing love it is a disposition to receive the gift of infused contemplation.

There are many incidents in the lives of the saints illustrating this truth. Men like St. John Bosco, spending themselves and being spent in the service of the needy, found themselves wonderfully filled with contemplative graces when they turned from their labors to explicit prayer. Their lives were a spiralling circle of one same love of God and neighbor, turning ever from prayer to action and from action to prayer, and back again.

Thus, while still a student at the University of Paris, Blessed Jordan of Saxony was on his way one night to the church of the Friars Preachers to join in the singing of Matins. He met a half-clothed beggar along the way, to whom he gave some of his clothing. As he entered the church, Jordan was overwhelmed with the grace of a new and profound experience of Christ, who appeared to him crucified and wearing the items with which Jordan had clothed the beggar. When we have seen Christ in neighbor, in the sense of effectively serving neighbor for love of Christ, then we are open to receive a deeper contemplation of God himself.

Jordan was speaking from deep personal experience when, some years later as successor of St. Dominic, he wrote to the Friars

Preachers that only he who abides in the love of neighbor is granted the grace of seeing God:

It remains, beloved sons, that before all these things you must have a constant mutual charity among yourselves, for it cannot be that Jesus will appear to those who have cut themselves off from the unity of the brotherhood: Thomas, for not being with the other disciples when Jesus came, was denied sight of him: and will you think yourself more holy than Thomas. . . . One will not see Jesus unless he has more zeal for that charity which seeketh not her own.[1]

Moreover, the only sure proof that we have seen God in some degree of contemplation, is our gift of self to God and to neighbor. This is one of the meanings in our Lord's answer to Philip's request, "Lord, show us the Father." We see the Father and the revelation of his love in the sacrifice of his Son. But we have not really seen the Father if we have not also seen ourselves as a sacrifice offered with Jesus for our brothers. "He who does not love does not know God" (1 Jn. 4:8). He who does not love his brother has not really experienced the Father.

On the other hand, we have not really seen Christ in neighbor; we have not seen neighbor as the brother for whom Christ died if we have not seen ourselves as a sacrifice in service of brother. In saying, "Greater love has no man than this, that a man lay down his life for his friends," Jesus was calling for our imitation of his own self-giving (Jn. 15:13), the love of neighbor which opens us to a new experience of the Father's love for us. "For this reason the Father loves me,"—filling me with his glory—"because I lay down my life for the sheep" (Jn. 10:17,15).

1. Gerald Vann, *To Heaven with Diana* (New York: Pantheon Books, 1960), p. 157.

7

"Beholding the Glory
of the Lord"

In a very revealing paraphrase of the words of Genesis, "Let us make mankind in our image and likeness" (Gen. 1:26,c), St. Paul says: "Man is the image and *glory* of God" (1 Cor. 11:7).

The glory of God was a term used in the Old Testament to signify the brightness and overpowering intensity of the divine presence. It was God himself revealing himself in all his holiness and power and majesty. It was God as present to men and communicating himself to them more and more, in a process reaching its fullness in Messianic days: "And the glory of the Lord shall be revealed, and all flesh shall see it together" (Isa. 40:5).

All this is fulfilled in Christ. "We saw his glory, the glory that is his as the only Son of the Father" (Jn. 1:14,j). The Son, in whom God has spoken to us in these last days, is "the brightness of his glory and the image of his substance" (Heb. 1:2–3,c).

In the grace of his conversion, St. Paul had personally experienced the glory of God present in Christ, and had come to realize that every man is called to participate in this glory. "For it is the God who said, 'Let light shine out of darkness' who has shone in our hearts to give the light of the knowledge of the glory of God in the face of Christ" (2 Cor. 4:6). "And we all, with unveiled face, beholding the glory of the Lord, are being changed into his likeness from one degree of glory to another" (2 Cor. 3:18). Thus, through the contemplation of the Lord Jesus in faith, man becomes ever more fully "the image and glory of God."

How Man Is God's Image and Glory

Every man has been created and redeemed to be the image and glory of God, the reflection of the divine majesty, the temple and sign of his presence.

Man is God's *image* precisely by reason of his capacity to receive God into his heart in a mutual exchange in knowledge and love.[1] He is image inasmuch as his very nature as created by God is open to receive God's presence, open to receive God's own life and self-revelation.

And man is the *glory* of God by reason of his actual possession of God, his participation in the very life of God, when Father, Word and Spirit make their home in him and manifest themselves to him, and are embraced in man's awareness of them in knowledge and love. Like Moses, of whom it is written, "The skin of his face shone because he had been talking with God" (Ex. 34:29), man becomes the glory of God when he lifts his face to God, and God shows his face to him in intimate friendship. "For the glory of God is living man, and the life of man is the vision of God," says St. Irenaeus.[2]

Hence, the traditional theological interpretation of Genesis 1:26: Man, the image of God, is fully the likeness of God only in possessing the Glory, the divine presence, as in a living temple. He is fully like God only through sharing in God's own inner life. "For we are the temple of the living God" (2 Cor. 6:16).[3]

1. *Eo ipso imago ejus est, quo ejus capax est:* Man is the image of God by the very fact that he is capable of receiving him. St. Augustine, *De Trinitate* (Book 14, Ch. 8).
2. *Adversus Haereses,* IV, 20:7.
3. See Henri de Lubac, The *Mystery of the Supernatural* (New York: Herder & Herder, 1967), p. 119. This explanation comes more from the living experience of Christians, who experienced that glory dwelling in

"*Do Let Me See Your Glory!*"

As image of God made to receive the glory of God—God's own presence—man's very nature is a cry for this glory. The prayer of Moses, "Do let me see your glory!" (Ex. 33:18,c) and the request of Philip, "Show us the Father, and we shall be satisfied" (Jn. 14:8) are indeed the request of every man. Each man's nature cries out for the glory implicitly; the repentant sinner begs for it explicitly; the lover of God calls for it still more ardently and urgently.

Thus, recognizing the implicit cry of his nature, the psalmist makes the cry explicit: "My heart has said of you, 'Seek his face!'" (Ps. 27:8,j). Another psalmist, a sinner, cries in his repentance, "Wash me thoroughly from my iniquity and cleanse me from my sin . . . Cast me not away from thy presence, and take not thy Holy Spirit from me" (Ps. 51:2,11). Still another, a friend of God who used to enjoy his intimacy, but from whom God now seems to be hiding his face, is burning with desire to experience his presence again: "As a hart longs for flowing streams, so longs my soul for thee, O God. My soul thirsts for God. When shall I come and behold the face of God?" (Ps. 42:1–2).

"*His Countenance Fell*"

To sin is to turn one's face from God. When Cain was envious because God seemed to favor Abel more than himself, "Cain was very angry, and his countenance fell" (Gen. 4:5). Like a stubborn child, who will not look up at his mother when she is trying to correct him, but looks at the earth; so Cain would not look at God, though God entreated him and rebuked him in kindness: "Why has your countenance fallen? If you do well, there is lifting up"; that is, you can lift your face to God without fear or shame (Gen. 4:7

them, than from a scientific exegesis of Genesis. Therefore, this explanation is not to be rejected on grounds that contemporary exegesis sees man as image of God because of his dominion over the world.

von Rad).[4] Cain stifled the voice of God which was thus speaking to his conscience and by murdering his brother "went away from the presence of the Lord" (Gen. 4:16).

"His countenance fell" has sometimes been interpreted as a disfigurement in Cain's appearance.[5] Cain was, indeed, disfigured. The likeness of God in him was distorted, for when he turned his face away from the Lord the glory of God could no longer shine upon it. God could no longer dwell in him.

A face turned from God cannot reflect his glory. It cannot receive his indwelling Presence. All sinful mankind, like Cain, "went away from the presence of the Lord" (Gen. 4:16). "Both Jew and pagan sinned and forfeited God's glory" (Rom. 3:23,j).

"The Skin of His Face Shone"

The glory of God shone on the face of Moses whenever Moses was in communion with God: "The skin of his face shone because he had been talking with God." When Moses came out from speaking with God to relay the Lord's message to his people "the people of Israel saw the face of Moses, that the skin of Moses' face shone" (Exod. 34:35). Moses was thus a "glory of God," a presence of God with his people.

Whenever Moses would finish speaking with the people, he would put a veil on his face (33). The veil, says St. Paul, indicated the imperfection and the temporary character of the glory manifested in Moses, "who put a veil over his face that the Israelites might not see the end of the fading splendor" (2 Cor. 3:13). A greater glory of God was to come in the person of Jesus.

Jesus came with "the glory that is his as the only Son" ever beholding the face of his Father (Jn. 1:14); "In the beginning was the Word, the Word was in God's presence" (Jn. 1:1,a). Jesus the Man is the image and glory of God because, even as man, he was

4. von Rad, Gerhard, *Genesis* (Philadelphia: Westminster, 1961), p. 101.

5. *Ibid.*

ever the Son contemplating the Father, and thus reflected the
Father's glory to his fellowmen.

The Look of Jesus

There must have been something extraordinary about the look of
Jesus—his way of looking at the Father in heaven, his way of
looking at people. His disciples noticed this look, the Evangelists
repeatedly speak of it:

And Jesus *lifted up his eyes and said,* 'Father, I thank thee that
thou hast heard me'" (Jn. 11:41). "And *looking around on those*
who sat about him, he said, 'Here are my mother and my brothers!'" (Mk. 3:34). "He *looked up to heaven,* and blessed and
broke . . ." (Lk. 9:16). "And the Lord turned and *looked at
Peter.* And Peter . . . went out and wept bitterly" (Lk. 22:61).

He raises his eyes to look at the Father in prayer; he lowers them
to look lovingly on men. In contemplating the Father his face
catches the reflection of the Father's glory, and he turns to relay the
glory to us: "He who has seen me has seen the Father" (Jn. 14:9).

The look of Jesus is sometimes a countenance of wrath: "And
he looked around at them with anger, grieved at their hardness of
heart" (Mk. 3:5). Most of the time, however, it is a look of love,
a turning of the face in the sense of bestowing divine favor: "And
Jesus looking upon him loved him" (Mk. 10:21).

But the rich young man upon whom he looked with love, re-
sisted the face of God. "His countenance fell"—all the joy went
out of it—"and he went away sorrowful, for he had great possessions" (10:22). Jesus then looked all the more intensely upon his
disciples (10:23,27). His longing heart did not want to lose them,
too!

"The Image and Glory of God"

Truly, Jesus is the image and glory of God. "He is the image of
the invisible God" (Col. 1:15) in whom once again God shows

his face to sinful mankind. In biblical thinking, an image was no mere copy or likeness; it was a presence and manifestation of him whose image it was.[6] The message of the apostles, says St. Paul, is "the gospel of the glory of Christ who is the image of God" (2 Cor. 4:4,c). For Paul has received "enlightenment concerning the knowledge of the glory of God shining on the face of Christ Jesus" (*ibid.* 6).

The glory of Jesus, however, is no mere reflection of God's glory as was the glory on the face of Moses. Jesus possesses the glory by nature; the glory is his personal divinity: "We saw his glory, the glory that is his as the only son of the Father" (Jn. 1:14,j).

"From Glory to Glory"

When Jesus turned the face of divine favor upon the rich young man—"and Jesus looking upon him loved him"—and presented the requirements for loving in return, the countenance of the young man fell; his eyes avoided the eyes of Jesus.

But what about the man who has the courage and the generosity to meet the gaze of Jesus and look at him steadfastly face to face? He who contemplates Jesus regularly is transformed into his likeness! "And we all, with faces unveiled, beholding the glory of the Lord, are being changed into his likeness from one degree of glory to another; for this comes from the Lord who is Spirit!" (2 Cor. 3:18).

They who contemplate the divinity of Jesus in faith "with face unveiled" are transformed into his likeness "from glory to glory," that is, from one degree of glory to another. The formula "from glory to glory" (the literal Greek) emphasizes the continuing process and intensification of the transfiguration of those who persistently contemplate the Lord. It is a process of growth in his image and glory.

6. Ceslaus Spicq, *Théologie Morale du Noveau Testament* (Paris: Gabalda, 1965), p. 689.

The transfiguration is accomplished in the believing man by "the Lord who is Spirit." Man repeatedly turns his face to Christ in faith. The Lord gives it his own glory.

The interpreters of the Scriptures have always found the phrase "the Lord who is Spirit" very difficult. "The Lord," of course, is the risen Christ. "Spirit" expresses the divinity or spiritual nature of the risen Christ. The Lord of glory is the source of a spiritual power which exerts its transforming efficacy upon believers; this power is identical with "the Spirit who gives life" (2 Cor. 3:6), the Holy Spirit. Thus, the transformation of the believer is the united work of Christ and the Holy Spirit, who are but one principle of action in their sanctifying work.[7]

The Lord Jesus, then, as giver of the Spirit, spiritualizes, divinizes, glorifies his own, transforming them in his own likeness from glory to glory. The incessant "beholding the glory of the Lord with unveiled face," the persistent looking toward him in contemplation is a steadfast openness to the Lord in faith, an openness to his Spirit and power. For it is the Lord himself who impresses his likeness upon those who contemplate him.

And the likeness and glory is a participation in the very life of the Holy Trinity, we said: Father, Word and Spirit make their home in man and manifest themselves to him when man embraces them in faith and love.

Such is Christian contemplation. Though the transformation from one degree of glory to another is "the work of the Lord who is Spirit," effort is required on the part of the Christian as well, the effort to be ever open to the Spirit, the repeated turning to the Lord Jesus to behold him in faith: "Behold the Lamb of God!"

7. *Ibid.*, p. 743, note 2.

8

The Cross and Transfiguration

"Beholding the glory of the Lord with faces unveiled" does not restrict us to the contemplation of Jesus in his resurrection, ignoring his passion and death and the rest of his lowly life on earth. Rather, to behold the glory of the Lord is *to see that Jesus is God* at every stage of his life on earth.

Indeed, St. Luke pointedly calls Jesus "Lord" again and again, beginning with the miracle of the raising of the son of the widow of Naim: "When *the Lord* saw her, he had compassion on her" (Lk. 7:13). "*The Lord* appointed seventy-two others" (10:1). "*Lord,* teach us to pray" (11:1). "Why are you untying the colt? *The Lord* has need of it" (19:33–34). Luke would not have us forget the divine nature of the one who was entering Jerusalem to die; just as he says that the infant wrapped in swaddling clothes is Christ *the Lord* (Lk. 2:11).

The apostles may not have been clearly aware of the divinity of Jesus until after his Resurrection and his exaltation as Lord. This does not mean that *we* are to look upon Jesus only as man until his Resurrection. "Even though we once regarded Christ from a human point of view, we regard him thus no longer" (2 Cor. 5:16).

Since we ourselves are transformed by stages from one degree of glory to another, so we must contemplate Jesus, the Lord, in the various stages of his journey to the glory of the Resurrection. It is not enough to see him only in the glory of his Transfiguration, putting exaggerated emphasis on his Resurrection to the neglect of the other mysteries of his life.

In fact, the risen Lord is meaningful for us only in the context of his earthly life, passion and death. The vision of Jesus "transfigured before them" (Mk. 9:2) makes sense only in the total context in which the Evangelists place it.

All three Evangelists who tell the story of the Transfiguration are careful to note the amount of time which elapsed between this event and the one of which they had just written, thus indicating that they see a definite connection between these events. The Transfiguration is to be understood in the light of the earlier event, namely, the prediction on the occasion of Peter's confession of faith of Christ's journey up to Jerusalem to suffer and to die and to rise again, and the teaching that every Christian must take up his cross and follow Jesus on this journey.

Moreover, in St. Luke's account, the topic of conversation among Jesus, Moses and Elijah during the Transfiguration is this journey of Jesus, "his departure which he was to accomplish at Jerusalem" (Lk. 9:31). In the Greek, the word translated as departure is "*exodus.*" The journey of Jesus up to Jerusalem and by way of the cross to the Father in heaven, is the new Exodus, the fulfillment of the Israelite Exodus from Egypt to the Promised Land.

Just after the Transfiguration, Jesus begins the journey: "he set his face to go to Jerusalem" (Lk. 9:51).

The Transfiguration, in other words, makes it possible for us to understand the way of the cross, the journeys of Jesus into the glory of the Father.

Peter's Confession and the Suffering Messiah

Peter has no sooner confessed his faith in Jesus as Messiah—"You are the Christ" (Mk. 8:29)—than Jesus begins to instruct the disciples concerning the kind of Messiah he really is. He is the Suffering Servant of Yahweh: "And he began to teach them that the Son of Man must suffer many things, and be rejected by the elders and the chief priests and the scribes, and be killed, and after three days rise again" (Mk. 8:31).

Although "he said this plainly" (8:32), "Peter took him and began to rebuke him." Peter could not understand a suffering Messiah.

But turning to his disciples with that look of his (8:33), Jesus rebuked Peter: "Get behind me, Satan! Because the way you think is not God's way but man's" (8:33,j). Your vision is too earthbound! You are blind to the things of God. That is why you, too, must go the way of the cross—you must deny yourself; you must die to your own narrow viewpoint if you wish to see God! There is no contemplation, no seeing of God, without self-sacrifice.

"And he called to him the multitude with his disciples and said to them, 'If any man would come after me, let him deny himself and take up his cross and follow me'" (8:34). Not only must Jesus go the way of self-denial, but all his disciples must follow him in this. There is no other way to glory. One cannot walk in the necessary way of the cross unless he contemplates Jesus walking in that same way; nor will he have the courage to follow, unless he sees this Suffering Servant as Son of God and Lord of Glory.

Therefore, Jesus gives them a vision of his glory. Six days afterwards Jesus took Peter and James and John up a high mountain apart by themselves and was transfigured before them (9:2). And the Father introduces his Son precisely as Suffering Servant, and as New Moses, leader in the New Exodus, thus backing up emphatically everything that Jesus had just proclaimed. "There came a voice from the cloud, 'This is my Son, the Beloved. Listen to him'" (9:7,j).

These words of the Father clearly echo two passages from his Sacred Scriptures.

"This Is My Son, the Beloved"

"Behold my servant, whom I uphold, my chosen, in whom my soul delights" (Isa. 42:1). St. Luke's and St. Matthew's versions make the words of Isaiah echo even more clearly than does Mark's: "This is my Son, my chosen" (Lk. 9:35); "This is my Son, my Beloved, with whom I am well pleased" (Matt. 17:5).

In Isaiah he is introduced as servant (Isa. 42.1), and the fourth Servant poem describes his sufferings (Isa. 52:13–53:12). But at the Transfiguration he is introduced as Son, so that even in the intensity of his sufferings and in the reality of his death we will see him as the divine Person, the Son of God. Just as we must never let our knowledge of his divinity blind us to the reality of his suffering humanity, neither must we let his sufferings hide from us his divinity. We must contemplate the total mystery; we must not "divide" Jesus (I Jn. 4:3,v): "Every spirit that confesses that Jesus Christ has come in the flesh is of God; every spirit that severs Jesus is not of God" (1 Jn. 4:3).

In the fourth Servant poem, the people conclude that the Suffering Servant is one who is rejected by God. Sufferings, they think, are the sign of God's anger: "We esteemed him stricken, smitten by God" (Isa. 53:4). So, too, as Jesus hangs upon the cross, his enemies interpret his sufferings as a sign that he is not of God: "He trusts in God; let God deliver him now, if he desires him; for he said, 'I am the Son of God' " (Matt. 27:43).

But God at the Transfiguration had forestalled this interpretation when he insisted that the suffering servant *is* his beloved Son.

Jesus, too, foretelling his crucifixion, reasserts his divine sonship and his full conviction of his Father's love and approval: "When you have lifted up the Son of man, then you will know that I am he. . . . He who sent me is with me; he has not left me alone, for I always do what is pleasing to him" (Jn. 8:28–29). The sign of the truth of these words is the glory which transfigures Jesus while the Father declares, "This is my Son, the Beloved."

The glory fades away, and Jesus stands before the three disciples in his helpless humanity, ready and able to suffer and die: "Who, though he was in the form of God, did not count equality with God a thing to be grasped, but emptied himself, taking the form of a servant, being born in the likeness of men. And being found in human form, he humbled himself and became obedient unto death, even death on a cross" (Phil. 2:6–8).

The same pattern has to be followed in all the adopted sons of God. If we are to be transfigured in his likeness from one degree of glory to another, we must empty ourselves with him, in humility, obedience, penance, patient suffering. We must contemplate Jesus in his humility, in his passion, on the cross and not just in the glory of his Resurrection. We must see and live the sufferings of the Son of God. We must be deeply involved in every stage of his mystery. The reality of the Lord's Resurrection, far from removing self-denial from Christian life, imposes it upon us.

"Listen to Him!"

Therefore, the voice from the cloud at the Transfiguration not only echoed Isaiah, but it quoted Deuteronomy as well. The Father repeats words he had spoken some 1400 years before through his prophet Moses. As he was nearing the end of his life, Moses had said, "A prophet like me will the Lord, your God, raise up for you from among your own kinsmen; *to him you shall listen*" (Deut. 18:15,c).

God had once spoken to Moses from a bright cloud on Mount Sinai; from the bright cloud on the mountain of the Transfiguration, a voice says, "This is my Son, the Beloved. *Listen to Him!*" He is the new Moses. Follow him, just as your ancestors followed Moses in the desert. Listen to him when he says, "Follow me in the way of the cross."

Moses is there to testify that this is the prophet like himself— and greater than himself—whom God said he would raise up. Moses and Elijah, the great prophets of old, fade away, and the disciples see *only Jesus* (Mk. 9:8), the only guide thenceforth: "No one comes to the Father but through me" (Jn. 14:6).

Thus Peter, who had rejected the idea of a suffering Messiah, who had been told by Jesus that his way of thinking was not God's, is told by the Father himself to listen to Jesus when he says: "If any man would come after me, let him deny himself and take up his cross and follow me" (Mk. 8:34).

The words Jesus had spoken to Peter—"Get behind me, Satan! Because the way you think is not God's way but man's" (Mk. 8:33,j)—are strangely contemporary in their applicability; for in our times, too, the role of the cross is rejected. "Christ is risen," they say, "so penance is useless, unnecessary!" Some would remove the crucifix from our altars and replace it with a portrait of the risen Christ. They miss the point of St. John who shows us the glory of God in the crucified Lord: "When you have lifted up the Son of Man, then you will know that *I am he*" (Jn. 8:28). In a variety of ways, John shows the glory shining forth in Jesus in his serene majesty at the Last Supper and in the Passion: "Whom do you seek?" They answered him, "Jesus of Nazareth." Jesus said to them, "*I am he!*" The glory of the name Yahweh—"I am he"— overpowers them. "When he said to them, 'I am he,' they drew back and fell to the ground" before the majesty of the one whom they would crucify (Jn. 18:4–6).

After the Transfiguration, the journey of Jesus begins: "He set his face to go to Jerusalem" (Lk. 9:51). At the very outset of his account of this journey, St. Luke presents three vocation stories (Lk. 9:57–62) in each of which the theme is self-denial: "I will follow you wherever you go. . . . The Son of Man has nowhere to lay his head" (9:57–58). "Leave the dead to bury their own dead" (v. 60) and follow me in the new life of the children of God. Follow me in my attitude toward sufferings—follow me in my obedience, follow me in my love of the Father expressed in obedience. Obedience without love is worthless; sufferings without love do not make you beloved sons of the Father; sufferings and obedience with love do.

The Transfiguration and the Agony

The necessity of contemplating the Lord of glory in the sufferings of the Passion is implied by St. Luke with his usual artistic finesse.

He draws a striking parallel between the account of the Transfiguration and that of the Agony in the Garden (Lk. 9:28–36; 22:39–46).

In either case, Jesus goes up a mountain to pray, and on both occasions he takes with him the same three witnesses, Peter, James and John. It seems that it is night both times, for the disciples can scarcely keep awake; and it is "the next day" in the morning when they come down from the Mount of Transfiguration.

On the Mountain of Transfiguration, Jesus receives assurance of his Father's love for him as Son, though he will have to suffer; on the Mountain of the Agony, the Father keeps his pledge and sends his angel to console Jesus: "There appeared to him an angel from heaven strengthening him" (22:43).

The witnesses fall asleep each time, but awaken the first time to see his glory, and the second time to see his sweat of blood. The Lord of glory in a bloody sweat, the Son of God in agony!

Such is the mystery which all Christians must contemplate. Christian contemplation is not an oriental technique for escaping in Nirvana the hard realities of life. In contemplating Christ, the Christian faces up to the reality of life, takes up the cross with Jesus and finds the true life in him who is lifted up. "As Moses lifted up the serpent in the wilderness, so must the Son of man be lifted up, that whoever believes in him may have eternal life" (Jn. 3:14–15). "We see Jesus who for a little while was made lower than the angels crowned with glory and honor because of the suffering of death, so that by the grace of God he might taste death for everyone" (Heb. 2:9).

9

They Were Not Listening

After the glory of the Transfiguration—in the midst of which the Father had said concerning his Beloved Son, "Listen to him"— Jesus begins his journey to Jerusalem, announcing at the outset the purpose of the journey:

And as Jesus was going up to Jerusalem, he took the twelve disciples aside, and on the way he said to them, "Behold, we are going up to Jerusalem; and the Son of man will be delivered to the chief priests and scribes, and they will condemn him to death, and deliver him to the Gentiles to be mocked and scourged and crucified, and he will be raised on the third day" (Matt. 20:17–19).

No sooner has he said this than James and John send their mother to Jesus with a request: "Command that these two sons of mine may sit, one at your right hand and one at your left in your kingdom" (20:20).

The request is so directly opposite the whole tenor of what Jesus had just been saying that we can only conclude that these two disciples were not listening when Jesus spoke. Their minds were too occupied with instructing their mother to put in their request. They were so busy forwarding their personal ambitions that they could not pay attention to Jesus. Even if they heard his words, the words made no impression in their hearts.

James and John knew that great things were afoot. Very recently they had seen Jesus in all his glory in the Transfiguration, and now everything is astir as Jesus begins his journey to Jerusalem. The two have concluded: He is going up to the capital city to exert his power and establish himself as messianic King. We had better act fast and insure glorious positions for ourselves in his kingdom!

The kingdom they envisage, however, is an earthly one, with worldly splendor and power. And they are very self-seeking; they are concerned chiefly about their own glory in the kingdom. That is why they do not really hear what Jesus says. They miss the point of his instruction concerning the true nature of his kingdom, in which one comes to heavenly glory only through suffering and service on earth. So he repeats for them even more emphatically that he is a suffering Messiah, and they must share in his suffering: "Are you able to drink the cup that I am to drink? . . . . Whoever would be great among you must be your servant . . . even as the Son of man came not to be served but to serve, and to give his life as a ransom for many" (22:26–28).

We are all like James and John—and like Peter when he chided Jesus for speaking of suffering—in our inability to understand the ways of God. Though we hear the word of God again and again in the sacred liturgy, it has so little effect upon us that it seems as though we weren't even listening when Jesus spoke to us; for Jesus is truly present in the liturgy, speaking to us in the proclamation of his word (*SC* 7).

The spiritual deafness of James and John on this occasion gives the clue to our deafness. James and John were so concerned about themselves, so intent upon making a place for themselves in the earthly splendor of the kingdom, that they were blind to the spiritual realities involved.

Each one of us is likely to be blinded by some form or other of self-interest: we are busily concerned about riches or pleasure, vanity or bodily comfort, or the lust for power and position; and so we receive little light from the word of God.

That is why we must go the way of the cross. That is why we must deny ourselves. Otherwise we will not see God but only ourselves.

The contemplation of God, the experience of his love and presence, is impossible to the unmortified who are concerned only about self. They do not listen when God speaks his word of invitation to them; they do not understand his call to great intimacy with him; they ridicule the idea that the contemplation of God is the normal development of the baptismal vocation and grace. They do not know how blind they are. As Peter rejected the idea of a suffering Messiah, so they reject the need of self-denial in their own lives.

Who Was the Blind Man—Jesus, or His Disciples?

Each time Jesus speaks of his suffering and death, the Evangelists take care to note that the disciples did not understand what he was saying. "They understood none of these things; this saying was hid from them, and they did not grasp what was said" (Lk. 18:34; cf. Mk. 9:32). Certain contemporary writers interpret the disciples' inability to understand as an indication of Christ's lack of clarity and articulation in declaring who he was, and therefore as a sign that Jesus himself did not know very clearly who he was. Certainly, they say, the disciples would have got the point if Jesus had declared unequivocally that he was the Messiah and Son of God!

This is not the point the Evangelists are making! They are not trying to indicate any ignorance on the part of Jesus! They are trying to make a point concerning the Christian audience for whom they are writing. They underscore the apostles' lack of understanding chiefly to bring home to all Christians how easily we are blinded to the things of God by our excessive self-concern.

The ambition of James and John, Peter's concern for his own skin, the pride of the disciples in seeking to be greatest, the rich young man's attachment to his possessions, the jealousy of John concerning the pseudo disciple who was casting out devils in the name of Jesus—all of these are recounted by the Evangelists in connection with our Lord's journey to Jerusalem, his prediction of his sufferings, and the inability of the disciples to understand Jesus as a suffering Messiah and the true nature of his kingdom. Each is an example of self-concern blinding men to the ways of God. The Evangelists are telling us that any Christian who desires to possess the kingdom in the fullness of understanding must enter upon the way of the cross, the way of voluntary self-denial.

Let us not blindly miss the point and attribute the ignorance to Jesus rather than to ourselves. We had better take seriously this theme of lack of understanding and blindness, not trying to make out that Jesus did not know who he was, but realizing that it is we who do not know who we are. The blinding effects of self-concern and self-indulgence are only too much with us. He who would see the light needs careful self-discipline.

There is no evidence in the Scriptures that Jesus was undisciplined and self-centered. In his concern for the honor of the Father and for the salvation of his fellowmen he was totally open to the Father and to the light and love of God.

It is not Jesus who is presented by St. Mark as questioning and doubting and hesitating. From the very beginning everyone is impressed that he speaks with authority (Mk. 1:22). Everyone but he is doing the questioning: "What is this? A new teaching!" (Mk. 1:27); "Who then is this?" (4:40); "Where did he get all this? Is not this the carpenter?" (6:2). The entire first part of Mark presents everyone as asking questions about Jesus, leading up to a climax in Jesus' own question to his disciples, "Who do you say that I am?" and Peter's profession of faith, "You are the Christ!" (8:29).

Jesus himself clearly knew what he was about: "He taught them as one who had authority" (Mk. 1:22), "with authority he commands even the unclean spirits, and they obey him" (1:27); with authority he declares, "My son, your sins are forgiven" (2:5). He makes himself "Lord even of the Sabbath" (2:28); he unhesitatingly puts himself above the Law, bringing it to a new spiritual perfection: "You have heard it said. . . . But I say to you" (Matt. 5:21,27,31,33,38,43).

A young priest was recently arguing that priests should not try to be so holy, but should be sinners among sinners. Jesus, he said, was just another man among men. Why should priests try to be better than he?

If Jesus had been just another man among men, he would have passed unnoticed. Though he was like us in all things except sin, he had something which made him stand out among others, something besides his humanity which drew all men to him: "And they were astonished at his teaching, for he taught them as one who had authority, and not as the scribes" (Mk. 1:22). "Many who heard him were astonished saying, 'Where did this man get all this?'" (Mk. 6:2).

Where did he get his unhesitating self-assurance? How can anyone see him as a man of uncertainty, a man doubting who he was? The Evangelists attribute to others the lack of understanding and the blindness.

Service, the Remedy for Self-concern

As a remedy for the ambition and self-concern of James and John, Jesus says, "Whoever would be great among you must be your servant . . . even as the Son of man came not to be served but to serve, and to give his life as a ransom for many" (Matt. 22:26–28). Service of others will bring us out of our selfishness and open us to the light.

Of course, the same self-concern which blinds us to the word and light of Jesus, blinds us to the opportunities to be of service to our fellowmen. We must deliberately look for these opportunities and act upon them. The asceticism of self-sacrifice in the service of others will open us to the understanding of the word of God; it will prepare us for the contemplative lights.

And we must pray for the light—"Lord, that I may see!"—not

only for the divine light itself in which we see God, but for light to see what blinds us, what sort of selfishness closes us to the light.

In his telling of Christ's prediction of his sufferings and death, and of the failure of the disciples to understand, St. Luke immediately adds the story of the blind man of Jericho whose prayer to Jesus is, "Lord, that I may see!" (Lk. 18:42,c). The blindness of the disciples concerning the mystery of Jesus is retold to suggest to us that we, too, are blind for the same reasons. Luke would have us pray, like the blind man of Jericho, "Lord, that I may see!"

And Jesus said to him, "Receive thy sight; thy faith has saved thee."

Who then was the blind man? Was it Jesus who gave sight to the blind man or was it the disciples?

Contemplation is for all Christians. But so few attain to it because so few will pay the price; so few are willing to undergo the thorough and persistent mortification of the self-centeredness which blinds us. Our prayer does not become very profound and interior because we live too much on the sense periphery of life. Instead of using our senses as the windows of our heart, opening upon a beautiful creation in which God is present and manifest, we use them to indulge our desire to experience every possible pleasure. And so we see God neither in his creation nor in our fellowmen, and still less in our heart, the place where man most intimately meets God.

It has become fashionable these days to claim that all mortification of the body is the product of an un-Christian dualism which thinks that the body and the spirit are in opposition. Moreover, it is argued that since God made all things good, and since the Son of God has consecrated all things by entering this creation and becoming part of it, we should therefore enjoy every lawful pleasure; self-denial is unnecessary and even un-Christian.

Christianity has always insisted that everything God made is good, and that God made the body as well as the soul and put them together as one existing thing. But it has also insisted that

Christ's consecration of all things is a continuing process to be completed by us through our mortification of the old self and continuing renewal in the Spirit: "Put off your old nature . . . and be renewed in the spirit of your minds and put on the new nature" (Eph. 4:22–23).

We cannot rightly claim, then, that because God made everything good we should play down the idea of the cross and should enjoy every lawful pleasure. " 'All things are lawful for me,' " says St. Paul, quoting the claim of the Corinthians, but adding, "but not all things are helpful. 'All things are lawful for me,' but I will not be enslaved by anything" (1 Cor. 6:12). Guardianship of the exterior and interior senses and mortification of the body are as necessary as ever for anyone who would experience the closeness of God in prayer and infused contemplation.

There is a beautiful passage in which St. Augustine presents Jesus to us as the Creator of all things, and yet mortifying himself in the use of these same good things which he himself has created. Commenting on the words of Jesus, "If any man wants to come after me, let him deny himself, take up his cross and follow me" (Matt. 16:24), Augustine places the following words on the lips of the divine Savior:

This is the way: walk through humility so that you may come to eternity. I have given you an example: I was hungry, I thirsted, I was exhausted, I slept, I was captured, I was scourged, crucified, killed. . . . I who created all things became poor, lest anyone who believed in me should dare to be proud in earthly riches. . . . I who feed all creatures was hungry myself; I who created all drink was thirsty—I who am spiritually the food of the hungry and the fountain of the thirsty.[1]

Yes, God created all things good, but they must be redeemed again from the effects of sin and reconsecrated to God by our using them in the way the poor and suffering Jesus used them: each

1. Quoted by Pope Paul VI, "Religious Life and Aggiornamento," *The Pope Speaks,* X (1965), p. 330.

one of us, like him, denying self in the use of these good things in the spirit of the evangelical counsels. "The world cannot be transformed and offered to God," says Vatican II, "without the spirit of the beatitudes" (*LG* 31).

" 'All things are lawful for me,' but not all things are helpful" (1 Cor. 6:12).

II

Christian Contemplation: A Fullness of Baptism

Introduction

The test of any happening in the Holy Spirit is Christ, the living
Gospel. For the Holy Spirit gives his gifts only from Christ, "in
whom are hid all the treasures of wisdom and knowledge" (Col.
2:3). "He will glorify me, for he will take what is mine and
declare it to you" (Jn. 16:14).

If Christ is the norm, it follows that baptismal grace is the norm,
for we are all baptized into Christ as one body with him. Every
spiritual phenomenon must be judged in the light of the basic
Christian reality which is bestowed upon all Christians in Baptism.
Authentic Christian contemplation measures true to this norm.

Contemplation is a function of baptismal grace. It is an essential
part of the full response to faith and Baptism, and, therefore, is a
happening completely in the line of ordinary Christian grace. It is
as deeply rooted in Baptism as is the mission to apostolic action: "It
is of the essence of the Church," says Vatican II, "that she be . . .
fervent in action and at leisure for contemplation. . . . Whatever
is of action is ordered toward contemplation and is subordinate to
it" (SC 2).

Contemplation can be very much misunderstood if it is considered
out of this total context of Christian life and if it is not seen as the
very warp and woof of Christianity. Christian life is a blending of
grace and nature, an ever more complete merging of the two. By
his very nature man was created as openness to God, as image which

receives the divine likeness from one degree of glory to another by the work of the Lord who is Spirit. The divine intervention in the life of a Christian through the gifts of the Holy Spirit in ever more frequent and intense graces of light and love is of the very essence of Christian life as rightly lived.

These graces of light and love received in the openness of faith, hope and charity are in the order of contemplation. They are either infused contemplation or are ultimately ordered to it. They are a continuing and deepening of the initial enlightening granted in Baptism.

Indeed, contemplation is baptismal dynamism at its best, for without it faith and Baptism cannot reach their full fruitfulness. In early Christianity, Baptism was called the Illumination, the Enlightening. The baptismal character, the incorporation into Christ, is a receptivity to ever fuller enlightenment. One is united to Christ the Head that he might see with the eyes of Christ and love with the heart of Christ, and that he might have ever more fully "the mind of Christ" through the light of the Holy Spirit, who searches "everything, even the depths of God" (1 Cor. 1:16, 10).

Thus, a return to the ancient Christian concept of Baptism as the enlightening, the receiving of Christ the Light of the World, would help restore contemplation to its rightful place in our concept of Christian living. The initial enlightening of Baptism reaches its earthly fullness in the graces of infused contemplation.

Moreover, as an essential development of baptismal grace and as a dynamic response to it, contemplation, like every other development of Baptism, plays an indispensable role in building up the Body of Christ, the Church. Indeed, according to Vatican II, the Church is not fully built up in a locality where there is no contemplative community: "The contemplative life belongs to the fullness of the Church's presence, and should therefore be established everywhere" (*AG* 18). The contemplative communities are specialists and leaders in an essential element of every Christian's life.

Contemplation, then, is a function of baptismal grace, the grace of the Holy Spirit as operative in faith, hope and charity. In what follows, we shall show how faith, hope and charity are inevitably contemplative. Contemplation is but an intense experiencing and living of the basic Christian baptismal reality.

10
Contemplation: A Fullness of Charity and Hope

Contemplation: Joy in the Lord

The basic Christian reality is participation in Christ's sonship. In Baptism we are born again of water and the Holy Spirit as sons in the Son. The first effect of the Holy Spirit in our hearts is the cry "Abba, Father!"

Sonship in Christ brings us into the Lord's own joy in the Father. We have seen how Jesus thrilled with joy in the Holy Spirit and thanked the Father for giving him the mission of revealing the Father (Lk. 10:21–22). His purpose in revealing the Father is to bring us into his own joy in the Father: "These things I have spoken to you that my joy may be in you and your joy may be full" (Jn. 15:11).

This revelation, we said, is an interior one, given only by the indwelling Spirit of Jesus poured into our hearts. The grace of adoption as sons and the grace of revelation of the Father are one and the same grace. When we cry "Abba" in recognition of God as our Father, "it is the Spirit himself bearing witness with our spirit that we are children of God" (Rom. 8:15–16). And in this sonship we rejoice. Joy is the fruit of the Holy Spirit, joy in the possession of God as our Father. "The kingdom of God does not mean food and drink, but righteousness and peace and joy in the Holy Spirit" (Rom. 14:17).

Contemplation is a profound living of these basic realities of Christian faith. In the obedience of faith, we open ourselves ever more fully to the Lord's revelation of the Father; we surrender to the Holy Spirit who alone, by his personal presence in us, can lead us into this revelation. Contemplation is but a functioning of the gifts of the Holy Spirit, especially wisdom and understanding perfecting our faith and love in which we experience God's fatherly love and presence.

Contemplation is thus joy in the Lord, a participation in Christ's own joy in his loving contemplation of the Father and experience of his love. As a fruit of the baptismal grace of adoption as sons, it is of the essence of Christianity; it is inseparable from a truly dynamic living of our adoption as sons of the Father.

Contemplation is therefore inevitably apostolic. For anyone who thrills with joy in the Holy Spirit because he is a son of the Father rejoices, like Jesus, in bringing others into this same joy. What we have seen, writes St. John, we proclaim to you that you may have fellowship with us in our fellowship with the Father in Jesus his Son. We write this that our own joy may be complete (cf. 1 Jn. 1:1-4).

Though contemplation is joy in the Lord, it is also sorrow in the Lord, for it always involves us deeply in our Lord's total paschal mystery—in his dying as well as in his Resurrection.

Contemplation: Mutual Presence in Love

Joy is the fruit of love. Once a person has tasted the joy of loving the Father in Christ, his love can only desire to taste it more deeply. The desire for contemplation is thus a normal characteristic of fervent Christian love.

By its very nature, love seeks the presence of the beloved—presence in its full meaning of intimate communion, of deep mutual awareness and exchange in love. It is a conversation, not just on a superficial level of words, but from the very depths of one's being and into the depths of the other.

Such loving communion with God, such full presence with him
is possible only in the Holy Spirit who proceeds from the deep
heart of God and from our heart cries back to the Father in response. Contemplation is nothing else than profound communion
with God in ardent love in the Holy Spirit. Love is the beginning
of contemplation, and love is its fruit. It is an intense living of
the basic Christian reality of fellowship with the Father in the
Son through the Holy Spirit. It is the indwelling of the Holy
Trinity in a marvelous fullness, a fullness of dynamic presence. A
normal fruit of this love and joy in God is praise and thanksgiving:
gratitude for what God has done for us in revealing himself, and
joy that he is what he is!

Thus it is obvious that Christian contemplation is no mere intellectual exercise; it is not an idle gazing at beauty or truth as it
is sometimes accused of being. It is condemned as the privilege of
the man of leisure who has nothing else to do; it is censored for
being the selfish pastime of the uncommitted.

Contemplation: Love's Involvement
in the Paschal Mystery

On the contrary, authentic Christian contemplation involves one
intensely; it commits one totally; it draws one dynamically into
Christ's sonship; and this means into unreserved participation in
the complete paschal mystery, into Christ's dying for his fellowmen as well as into his resurrection in the Spirit. One cannot contemplate the crucified Christ without desiring to spend oneself and
be spent for the salvation of one's fellowmen.

Vatican II defines contemplation as "adhering to God with mind
and heart" (*PC* 5); it is a beholding with the intelligence and
an involvement in love, an impetus toward the Father in the Son's
own Spirit. It is "knowing" God in the biblical sense of the term,
a knowing which includes loving and serving. The human spirit and

heart are profoundly engaged: "He who cleaves to the Lord is one spirit with him" (1 Cor. 6:17).

Because it involves one deeply in the paschal mystery, contemplation is "incarnational." The contemplative by his suffering with Christ in deep faith and love "fills up what is wanting to the sufferings of Christ for his body the Church" (Col. 1:24). Christ's sufferings become "incarnate," as it were, in the world today in the sufferings of all who suffer with Christ. But to suffer with Christ is a contemplative function; anyone who suffers truly *with Christ and in Christ* is living the basic contemplative reality. For one suffers in profound union with Christ only when one's faith and love are truly enlightened and alert, bringing one into dynamic union with the Lord in the loving acceptance of life's difficulties and love's burdens. The loving and joyful acceptance of "the work of faith and labor of love and steadfastness of hope in our Lord Jesus Christ" (1 Thess. 1:3) requires the contemplative insight and loving understanding received from the Holy Spirit, which are a continuing and deepening of the baptismal enlightenment.

Contemplation and Eschatological Hope

The norm of any happening in the spiritual life, we said, is Christ in his paschal mystery. But this norm can be applied from both ends. We can judge the happening not only from the point of view of its baptismal roots, its correspondence with the basic baptismal reality, but also from the point of its heavenly fulfillment. At the time of the final accounting, the faithful servant is told, "Enter into the joy of your Lord" (Matt. 25:21); enter fully into the life of the Trinity, and, therefore, fully into their joy.

For contemplation is eschatological as well as incarnational. It is a dynamic thrust in hope toward the future. Because it involves us deeply in Christ's paschal mystery, the whole thrust given to a Christian in contemplation is toward the building up of the Kingdom, which is "righteousness and peace and joy in the Holy Spirit" (Rom. 14:17). For to the extent that one has experienced joy in the Spirit, he thirsts for the fullness of the Spirit for himself and for his brothers in Christ, just as Christ thirsted at Jacob's well and on the cross for the living waters, the Holy Spirit, that he might pour him into our hearts.

St. Ignatius of Antioch, hastening to his martyrdom, exclaims, "Now at last I begin to be a Christian!" He explains this ardent desire for martyrdom, this thirst for full participation in the paschal mystery, saying, "The living waters within me cry, 'Hasten to the Father!' "

The thirst for the Father in heaven is the baptismal thirst. He who has tasted the Spirit thirsts for more. The thirst for the Father is intensified through participation in the other sacraments. "For by one Spirit we were all baptized into one body . . . and all were made to drink of one Spirit" (1 Cor. 12:13). Exegetes dispute as to whether "drinking of the Spirit" refers to Baptism or to the other sacraments, especially the Eucharist. Certainly we drink more deeply of the Spirit in each of the sacraments, since each of them is a new participation in the paschal mystery and so brings a new mission of the Holy Spirit, fruit of that mystery. This is especially true of eucharistic participation.

The only explanation of our ardent desire and hope for the fullness of the Spirit, the only explanation of our homesickness for the Father in heaven, is the fact that we have already tasted of the Spirit. The eschatological longing, the thirst for God aroused by the Spirit who has been given to us, is not a thirst for the totally unknown but for something which has already been tasted, something which one already really possesses in some degree. As St. Gregory expresses it in the Homily in Matins of Pentecost: "Whoever desires God with a sincere heart is already in real possession of the one whom he loves." And St. Augustine said, in the Homily of the day before: "We cannot love God unless we already have the Spirit of God."

For although man, as spirit, is openness to God, and his very being is a natural desire to see God, that desire remains ineffective until the Holy Spirit touches a man's heart. Only tasting of the Spirit can arouse an effective desire and a confident hope of fully possessing God.

The Christian's tasting of the Spirit is not a mere passing tasting. For the Holy Spirit is given in Baptism that he might dwell permanently in the Christian: "You know him, for he dwells with you and will be in you" (Jn. 14:17).

For he is the Spirit of promise and, therefore, the source of our hope for the full possession. His very presence in us is the pledge of a fuller presence if we open ourselves to this presence.

Therefore, to desire to drink daily more deeply of the Spirit is not presumption. It is a well-founded hope and lawful desire. The Christian should become drunk, not with wine, but with the Holy Spirit—the new wine of the Spirit given to us in the eucharistic chalice.

The full tasting of the Spirit can only be through the gifts of the Spirit, for which we open ourselves in faith, hope and love. "O taste and see that the Lord is good" (Ps. 34:8). The tasting is love experiencing the Lord through the gift of wisdom.

The more we taste the Lord, the more we hunger and thirst for more. Those who have the deepest felt need for prayer are those who have already experienced prayer. It is by praying and deepening the experience that we learn to pray and are drawn more and more to prayer.

Hence, our Lord's insistence on persistence in prayer. If there is one thing he teaches about prayer, it is perseverance in asking the Father for all sorts of things, but especially for the Holy Spirit (Lk. 11:13).

If we wait till we are in the mood to pray before we try to pray, soon we will be praying less and less. We have to make efforts to put ourselves into the mood, and these efforts should be made at frequent intervals. By bringing prayer into the living rhythm of our lives, we can more easily foster the prayerful mood and remain in it.

For it is they who experience the Holy Spirit in prayer who are most thirsty for the fullness of the Spirit. The experience of the Spirit in contemplation gives us a dynamic thrust toward the full eschatological presence of the Lord.

11
Faith Is Necessarily Contemplative

The experience of the Holy Spirit in prayer, leading to thirst for the Father, is but a normal functioning of faith as perfected by the contemplative gift of understanding.

Indeed, the gift of understanding is necessary for the full functioning of faith. Without the gift of understanding, we are not very much at home with divine things. Understanding, however, makes the things of God as it were connatural to us; it gives us a ready and easy familiarity with them.

Since faith concerns the unseen realities of God the intellect experiences a certain restlessness concerning them. It cannot lay hold of them, no matter how much it would love to. And so the Holy Spirit of understanding must come to our rescue. "For the Spirit searches all things, even the deep things of God. For who among men knows the things of a man save the spirit of the man which is in him. Even so the things of God no one knows but the Spirit of God. Now we have received the Spirit that is from God that we may know the things that have been given us by God" (1 Cor. 2:10–15).

The gift of understanding is necessary for the full functioning of faith because by Christian faith we do not believe in mere statements about God, such as creeds and dogmatic formulations. Rather, we believe the divine realities expressed in these formulations. The reality believed is the personal God revealing himself to us. The same holds true for the symbols and words in the Scriptures and the liturgy. We must not stop at the words and symbols. We must penetrate deeply into the divine realities expressed in them.

This we do by the simple intuitive perception given in the gift of understanding. The divine realities infinitely surpass human concepts and language. They are just too big for words. And hence, faith which accepts them needs the divine aid of the gift of understanding to penetrate with a simple gaze, a direct intuition in the light of the Holy Spirit, the reality of God revealing himself. Such understanding is possessed only by those in whom the Holy Spirit actually dwells, revealing himself to their open hearts by his very presence.

This divine manner of understanding the realities of God is in contrast to the natural mode of human knowledge, which is by way of concepts, discursive reasoning, analysis and synthesis, and so on. In the Scriptures, in the liturgy, in homilies, in theology, the divine truths are expressed in this natural mode of thinking.

But homilies and liturgy and formulas of faith and scriptural passages are meaningless to us unless the Spirit himself teaches us the divine realities expressed in them. Any insight into divine realities received in a sermon or in a reading or in interior prayer, any insight resulting in a new surge of love for God, comes from the working of the gifts of wisdom and understanding.

St. Luke, in his story of the Lord's Resurrection, tells us how Jesus appeared to his unbelieving disciples and "opened their minds to understand the Scriptures" (Lk. 24:45). Thomas Aquinas cites this passage in asserting the necessity of the gift of understanding in penetrating the words and symbols of scripture and liturgy.[1] Any penetration of the mysteries of faith in hearing the word of God or in interior prayer and meditation requires that Jesus by his Holy

1. Thomas Aquinas, *Summa Theologica,* trans., Fathers of the English Dominican Province, 1st complete American ed. (New York: Benziger, 1947), 2a, 2ae, Q. 8, a. 2.

Spirit open one's mind to understand. Faith is always an obedience, a surrender to Christ. *Credo ut intelligam:* I believe so that I may understand. I believe so that I may be led by Christ into all the truth through his Holy Spirit.

Urs von Balthasar writes:

There is certainly also the way of simple faith which embraces the mystery of the Incarnation (or any mystery of faith) in a single sentence, a plain formula, and is humbly content to do so. But that is not contemplation, which only begins at the point where the mystery begins to reveal itself to the believer and to enlighten him in his depths.[2]

He continues: "Mystical prayer is simply the experimental knowledge of the same mysteries of faith that the ordinary person of prayer lives in the darkness of faith."[3]

And yet any true insight of love into the divine mysteries, any loving insight received even by the person of most simple faith, as for example when he listens to the word of God, is essentially in the same order as the fullness of contemplation, for it is a fruit of the gift of understanding.

Faith as Understanding

Indeed, the gift of faith is itself an initial gift of divine understanding. Faith's continuing efforts to understand, in an ever deeper penetration of the mystery, rests upon the initial understanding which is faith itself, the interior light of grace which is God's personal testimony to this human person.

All deeper understanding acquired in homilies, in listening to the word, in interior prayer, in the reflections of conscience is but an unfolding of the initial understanding which comes in the gift of faith itself. "So long as we have not somehow understood every-

2. Urs von Balthasar, *Prayer* (New York: Sheed & Ward, 1961), p. 127.
3. *Ibid.*, pp. 75–76.

thing even before it is explained to us, we have understood nothing in Christianity."[4] Even the words of Jesus himself were grasped in their divine meaning only by those in whom the Holy Spirit was working: "No one can come to me unless the Father who sent me draws him . . . It is written in the prophets, 'And they all shall be taught by God' " (Jn. 6:44–45).

St. Augustine, in rhetorical amazement that the repentant thief, crucified with Jesus, could understand what the priests and scribes who knew the Scriptures could not understand, questions the thief: "While you were carrying on your thievery, did you meditate the Scriptures on the side?" And the thief replies: "Jesus looked at me, and in his look, I understood everything."[5]

In the Scriptures, for God to look upon man, for God to turn his face to him is to breathe his Spirit into him; it is to give him his own life. Understanding comes only in God's gift of himself.

Faith: the Perception of God-with-Us

For the divine realities which we perceive in varying degrees of faith and understanding are not just truths *about* God. Nor are they merely the reality of God in himself. The reality perceived in faith is *God given to us*—"God-with-us" in the Incarnation and in the Church, God offering himself to each one who will believe, God dwelling in those who do believe, God *experienced* by those in whom he dwells.

This experience is possible only in faith perfected through understanding. The full object of faith is the personal God living in us, God as revealed to us in the very giving of himself to us, God as experienced in the interior revelation which is his very presence. This presence is experienced through love uniting us directly to God, love tasting God in the Gift of Wisdom.

4. Bernard Bro, O.P., *The Spirituality of the Sacraments* (New York: Sheed and Ward, 1968), p. 8.
5. *Ibid.,* quoted.

Certitude and Joy: Fruits of Understanding

The result of the penetration of the divine realities through the gift of understanding is certitude of faith and fullness of joy. These are the fruits of the Holy Spirit corresponding to the gift of understanding.[6] When we commit ourselves to Christ, the Truth, in the obedience of faith, the Spirit of Truth, through the gifts of understanding and love, leads us into the whole truth, the truth which is Jesus himself, the First Truth, the divine Person whom we embrace in faith and love in a personal relationship. Dwelling in us, the Word reveals the Father to us, and our joy in him is made full.

To the extent that the Spirit of understanding gives us this direct intuition of the Truth, we are "in the Truth" (3 Jn. 3:3,j). We live in Christ; he lives in us. He enlightens us by his presence, taking us to the Father in his own Spirit of love. When we thus live "in the Truth" through faith perfected by understanding, our faith has a certitude which no attacks against it can shake, no reasons alleged against it can cause to doubt.[7]

The Pure of Heart See God

Through this understanding we have the beatitude of the pure of heart who see God (Matt. 5:8). St. Peter attributes purity of heart to faith perfected by the Holy Spirit. Speaking of Cornelius and the pagans to whom he preached at Caesarea, Peter declares: "God . . . giving them the Holy Spirit . . . cleansed their hearts by faith" (Acts 15:8–9).

The believing heart is progressively purified in a number of ways, as the gift of understanding becomes increasingly operative in it. It is cleansed of inordinate affections which it had followed previ-

6. *Summa Theologica,* 2a, 2ae, Q. 8, a. 8.
7. "I write this to you about those who would deceive you; but the anointing which you have received from him abides in you, and you have no need that anyone should teach you . . ." (1 Jn. 2:26–27).

ously in spiritual blindness (like the blindness of James and John when they still sought earthly glory at the right hand and left of Jesus). In the light of understanding, the heart perceives the divine values and pursues them. The believing heart is cleansed also of doubt and grows in divine certitude (like the once doubting Thomas who was able to say at last in the fullness of joy "My Lord and my God!").

Faith is also cleaned, through the gift of understanding, from excessive attachment to signs and symbols and human formulations of truth, whether in doctrine or in prayer and liturgy. Such faith does not stop at the signs or the formulation. It penetrates with pure insight into the reality of God himself, God revealing himself to the pure heart in which he dwells. Faith is purified also from excessive reliance upon the customs and institutions and life-styles through which man strives to live his faith. With the insight of understanding, one no longer identifies the faith with this way or that way of expressing it in life, in word, in worship. In a crisis, such as the present one in the Church, the man whose faith is purified by understanding is not upset when he is deprived of the "good old ways" of liturgy, of instruction, of life, of religious observances. His faith is primarily a deep personal relationship with the person of Christ, who guides him securely by his Holy Spirit.

Faith enlightened by the gift of understanding is purified also of willful personal opinion and prejudice. There is a pseudo faith which is nothing more than personal opinion, a will to believe what suits one's desires and self-love. A heretic is one who chooses what he wants to believe, and rejects as irrelevant what does not suit his fancy or convenience. Opinionated people of this sort often claim to have the Holy Spirit and fanatically attempt to force their ideas upon others. Much of the current rejection of authority in the Church appeals in this way to the Spirit: "We have the Spirit," they claim, implying that others do not. We sorely need to apply the criteria for "testing the Spirit" (1 Thess. 5:21). Where the Spirit's gift of understanding is really at work, faith is purified of opinionated willfulness.

Faith should, therefore, be a dynamic openness to the Holy Spirit of understanding, an everliving surrender of one's own mind to him in the humble obedience of faith, to be led into the truth which is Christ. This surrender to the Word and Spirit is the basic contemplative attitude. It is the basic Christian attitude. It is openness to God in hope for his self-giving. It is receptiveness to him in love that he may accomplish in us the purposes of his love, his purpose to adopt us as his sons in revealing himself to us as Father.

As we have seen, the basic Christian reality which we experience in faith and contemplative understanding—the grace of adoption as sons—is actually a grace of interior revelation of the Father. "No one knows the Father except the Son, and he to whom the Son wills to reveal him" by giving him the Holy Spirit of adoption, who leads him into this truth. Only when the Spirit is poured into our hearts can we cry "Abba!" Only in the Holy Spirit of love do we recognize and experience God as Father, for only in the Spirit do we experience God's own life in us. Only in the Spirit are we "in the Truth," that is, in the Son. "The Spirit himself bears witness with our spirit that we are children of God" (Rom. 8:16).

In the following chapters, I will consider in some detail how we experience God as our Father in this witness of the Holy Spirit.

12
Coming to Self-awareness through Prayer

The Holy Spirit puts the Son's own prayer into our hearts. "Because you are sons, God has sent the Spirit of his Son into our hearts, crying, 'Abba, Father!' " (Gal. 4:6).

We pray thus because the Spirit has revealed to us what and who we really are. "When we cry 'Abba, Father,' it is the Spirit himself bearing witness with our spirit that we are children of God" (Rom. 8:15–16). By this witness, the Holy Spirit leads us to self-awareness as God's children.

Man is a mystery, and only the Holy Spirit can reveal to him what he really is. Only the Spirit can give him the answer in his search for meaning; the Spirit alone can help him solve his identity crisis. Man is mystery incomprehensible to his own unaided powers, for he was created to transcend himself. He was created as openness to the Infinite and can be fulfilled only in the possession of the Infinite. But he cannot even know that this is so until he has experienced the witness of the Spirit calling him to divine sonship, to personal communion with God as Father, not just his need for something beyond himself.

Only by the witness of the Holy Spirit is man able to possess himself in complete self-awareness. Only in prayer—in the experience of the Holy Spirit and in response to him—can he understand and become his true self. Indeed, as we shall see, only in the higher prayer of infused contemplation can he attain the full self-awareness in which alone he can be fully himself as son of God. It will be evident that contemplation is the fulfillment not merely of baptismal grace. It is necessary for the accomplishment of our human nature itself, which, according to Vatican II, was created for communion with God:

The most sublime element in human dignity consists in the call of man to communion with God. By the very manner of his origin man is invited to converse with God: for he exists only because he has been created by God out of love and is ever preserved by that love, and does not live fully according to the truth unless he freely acknowledges that love and commits himself to his Creator (*GS* 19).

Just how does the Spirit bear the witness by which alone man can come to awareness of himself as son of God? How does he bring us to an ever fuller consciousness of this divine sonship and prayerful acceptance of it? Surely it must be by giving us a living awareness of our life in God—of our relationship to the Father and of our brotherhood in Christ—and by leading us to reflect upon this experience; just as any man grows in self-awareness through reflection upon his experience of life.

We have seen how even Christ came to full self-awareness not only through reflection upon his immediate experience of his human existence as a man among men, but especially through reflection upon his contemplative experience of his divine Sonship and his Father's love for him. So, too, the rest of us, if we are to come to full self-awareness as sons of God, must reflect not only upon our experience of our existence in the world of men and things; we must reflect also upon the experience of our existence in God as adoptive sons in the Holy Spirit; we must prayerfully meditate.

Prayer is nothing else than this becoming aware of and accepting the basic Christian reality of one's adoption as son of God. It is experiencing ever more deeply what one is by God's gift—son or daughter in communion with the Father.

Nor is it enough to become *aware* of what we are by grace. We must also accept and *affirm* and deepen it by living it deliberately, prayerfully, expressing it by acting as children of God, doing always what is pleasing to the Father, and thus experiencing our sonship more fully.

Self-awareness in Freedom

Man's consciousness of himself and his world arises through the exercise of his various powers: his senses and his emotions, his reason and his will. Only in the use of his faculties is he alive to himself. His self-awareness reaches its high point in his free act; he experiences just what it means to be himself when he possesses himself in freedom, exercising self-determination in freedom of choice. Not in any act of choice, however, does he experience himself to the full, but only in the highest act of freedom: the giving of himself in love in a personal relationship. For we possess ourselves in freedom only that we may give ourselves in love. Freedom is the power to love, and love is the giving of self. Love cannot be forced; it is not love unless it is given freely. Man most fully possesses himself in freedom, then, in giving himself in love. It is then that he is most fully himself; it is then that he most truly experiences what it means to be himself.

And yet he is most fully himself not in any and every personal relationship, not in any gift of self to any person whatsoever. He is supremely himself only in the gift of self in Christ to God, his Creator and Father. In this gift of self to God, he most fully affirms, most fully experiences, his divine sonship.

For man is either ennobled or degraded by what he loves. If he gives himself totally to something beneath himself, such as the pursuit of riches, he is dragged below his personal dignity. But if he gives himself totally to Someone above himself in a mutual relationship of love, then he is ennobled by that communion in friendship.

Without the invitation and witness of the Holy Spirit, we said, man could never even have dreamed of aspiring to a personal friendship with the Lord of the Universe. He could, indeed, have had a marvelous awareness of his personal dignity by giving himself in the freedom of love to his fellowmen. But this would not yet be an awareness of himself in his highest possibilities. This would not yet be to experience himself in his full living capacity as a person made for infinite love, a person whose capacities can be fulfilled only in the love and possession of God.

Only in the actual experience of friendship and communion with God, only in the free gift of himself to God in response to God's gift of self to him, does he possess himself in complete self-awareness, knowing himself for what he really is: son of God, image and glory of the Father.

For this was he made, only in this is he truly himself. This is the mystery of man; and he could not have dreamed of its possibility if he had not experienced it in some way, if the Holy Spirit had not borne witness of it to him personally by giving him at least some sort of initial experience of this communion in love, an experience giving rise to the cry, "Father!"

Full Self-awareness in Contemplation

Something is best known, of course, only when it is experienced at its fullest perfection. A child, for example, cannot fully know himself, for he has not yet experienced himself in the fullness of his powers. Whatever self-awareness he has may be quite accurate as far as it goes, but he has many marvelous discoveries concerning himself still ahead of him.

So, too, from the earliest days of his experience of the divine life, the Christian may very accurately cry "Father!" through the initial witness of the Holy Spirit. And yet full self-awareness and self-possession can come only in full communion with God. The fullness of the Spirit's witness consists in the fullness of communion with God as experienced in infused contemplation.

Prayer, then, is a growing awareness of one's true self, one's self as communion with God. We can say that one's true self *is* communion with God, since a person can be fully himself only in the communion of love with another. And the Other with whom man must be in communion to be most fully himself is God.

Forgetting Self in the Awareness of God

Though prayer is at least implicit awareness of one's self as communion with God, the focus of attention is God rather than self. As love and communion with God are perfected, one more and more comes out of self and into the Beloved and is aware primarily of him. One becomes more explicitly aware of him and only implicitly aware of self. As the ancient teachers of prayer tell us, he prays best who does not even know he is praying. Excessive self-consciousness can destroy prayer.

For example, how often a praying person stands aside, as it were, to admire his own holiness. Or again, (and our "experience-conscious," "happening-happy" contemporaries are especially prone to this), we are so concerned about *experiencing* prayer as a "happening" that we are distracted from the God we should be experiencing. We shall speak more of this later. Or again, the praying one can get so wrapped up in his personal problems, his ambitions, his bodily comfort, or the like, that his meditation degenerates into self-concern. He is concerned not so much about God or about his true self as son of God, but about his false self, his pride, his pleasure, his comfort.

Jesus said to St. Catherine of Siena, "Be concerned about me, and I will be concerned about you." The same thought is expressed in various ways in the Scriptures. "Cast all your anxieties on him, for he cares about you" (1 Pet. 5:7). "Draw near to God, and he will draw near to you" (Jas. 4:8). Paradoxically, in the very concern about God and forgetfulness of self, one finds one's true self. "Whoever loses his life for my sake will find it" (Matt. 16:25).

If in one's efforts to pray one discovers that invariably he ends up thinking about himself, then he must meditate upon self to discover just why he is so self-centered. What sort of selfishness keeps bringing his attention back to self? Is it vanity, ambition, lust, gluttony or what have you? He must die to this false self if he is to find his true self in unhampered communion with God.

One of the most effective killers of the selfishness which hinders communion with God is true community with one's fellowmen. The self-sacrifice necessary for community living helps kill the excessive self-centeredness which makes praying difficult. On the other hand, prayerful communion with God gives rise to the love which attentively and generously engages in self-sacrificing service of neighbor. Obviously, interior communion with God and self-sacrificing communion with neighbor are mutually helpful.

Mental Prayer

Interior communion with God, we said, is a dynamic living of the basic baptismal reality, our divine sonship. This requires a lively awareness of God's ever-present offer of himself to the man of faith, and a ready acceptance of the offer. We recall St. Teresa's simple definition of mental prayer: it is nothing else than being on terms of intimate friendship with God, conversing frequently with him in the secret of our heart, because we know he loves us.[1]

The Lord is ever present in the hearts of those he loves, dwelling in them by baptismal grace, giving witness of his presence through the inspirations of his Holy Spirit. If we are to come to mature self-awareness as sons of God, if we are to come out of ourselves and into God in the loving cry, "Father!", we must live in attentiveness to the interior witness of the Spirit.

In the following chapters we will examine some of the many manners in which the Spirit gives this witness, this experience of our divine sonship and of God's Fatherhood.

1. E. Allison Peers, trans, and ed. *The Complete Works of St. Teresa of Jesus* (New York: Sheed and Ward, 1944), Vol. 1, p. 50.

13
The Nature of the
Spirit's Witness

Faith and Personal Divine Witness

The initial witness of the Spirit to our spirit is the graces preparing for faith and the gift of faith itself.

Faith is the willing acceptance of divine revelation. Through this acceptance, communication is effectively established between God and man. As communication, revelation and faith are a relationship between persons. In revelation, the personal God personally reveals himself to a human person.

This can only be by grace, an intensely personal grace from God to *this* human person, *this* believer. Any man's faith is always a response in grace to a grace of personal revelation to him. For that which is revealed in divine revelation and accepted in faith is no mere indifferent impersonal message, no mere instruction on how to do something or even on how to live a human life. What is revealed is God himself as a personal God, and the whole purpose of the revelation is the establishment of personal relationships with man in the communion of mutual love and self-giving. In divine revelation, God gives himself.

If the purpose of revelation were merely to instruct man on what to do, it could be given in an impersonal way and could be passed on from one man to another even in human words. God could give instructions on bridge-building, on child-bearing in this impersonal way—but not his self-revelation!

Divine revelation is, therefore, ineffective unless the personal God personally reveals himself to each human believer in an interior grace, the gift of faith, an interior witness from the Holy Spirit.

The initial witness is (along with certain preparatory graces) the grace of faith, the grace without which God's personal self-revelation cannot possibly be received. The initiative comes entirely from God.

The grace of faith is first of all something in God and then something in man (though the two aspects are simultaneous in time). As something in God, the grace of faith is God himself in his gracious personal approach to a man in the desire of giving himself to this man. God, present in all things as their creator and conserver, but in a hidden way because of his divine transcendence, by a mysterious interior witness manifests his presence to this human person in the gift of faith. This grace is his mysterious presence to this person inviting him to personal communion with himself. For what is really offered in the grace of faith is the further gift of uncreated Grace, that is, God's gift of himself to be possessed by this man through personal communion with God.

Thus the grace of faith on God's part is God himself present to a person, offering himself in self-revelation. The grace of faith in man is man's willing, personal response to this mysterious interior witness from God, this mysterious personal offer of self-revelation through self-giving. The personal, willing response of man is itself the grace of faith on man's side; for the very response is possible only by God's gift. "Man cannot say 'Yes' to God until God gives him the 'yes' to say."[1] The grace which is faith moves a man to

---

1. This sentence is the comment of Sr. Mary Henry Soniat, O.P., when reading the original manuscript. She intended it to bring out clearly that man's free response to God in faith is itself the gift of God's grace.

surrender willingly to the truth of God revealing himself; it moves him to give willing assent to God revealing and God revealed.

Nor is it a once-and-for-all revelation. It is rather a continuing self-manifestation by God in frequent interior lights to which man ought to live in perpetual attentiveness. By its very nature, living faith is contemplative.

When man believes, when by God's gift of faith he responds to God's offer of personal communion by giving himself to God in the surrender of faith, then God responds to him by the gift of himself, pouring out his love into the heart of the believer in the personal gift of the Holy Spirit (Rom. 5:5). The initial witness of the Spirit, the offer and the giving of the grace of faith, is perfected by the Spirit's witness to our spirit that we are now sons of God, a witness giving rise in our hearts to the prayer of the Son, "Father!" Our communion with the Father in faith is sealed in the Holy Spirit in our love's response to his love.

In its deepest essence, then, faith is ordered toward personal encounter with God, toward lasting communion with him. The revelation accepted in faith is not primarily a set of truths expressed in human words (though this articulation of the revelation in human concepts is necessary if man is to respond to the revelation in a human way). The revelation is God himself, God revealing himself, lovingly giving himself in the very gift of faith and charity, in the desire for personal communion with man.

The Witness of the Spirit in Contemplation

Man's communion with God in faith and love is deepened and perfected by God's continuing and ever fuller self-revelation through self-giving to this man. The Lord communicates himself especially through the workings of the Holy Spirit's contemplative gifts of wisdom and understanding by which faith and love are brought to their perfection. If man's faith has its origin in God's grace of interior witness and man's response in this grace, and if faith has an initial perfecting through another grace, God's gift of himself in the pouring of his love into this man's heart by the giving of the Holy Spirit, and in man's response of love in this grace, so, too, all subsequent perfecting of man's communion with God in faith and love can come about only through God's further graces of ever fuller self-communication and man's ever fuller response in the more perfect giving of himself to God.

That is why we say that faith is a continuing grace; it is a direct union with God in the Spirit through Christ so that by the working of the Spirit God gives man the experience of his fatherly love and presence.

Only in the fullness of communion with God, we said, can man be fully aware of himself in his deepest reality, his divine sonship. And this fullness of communion is attained in the prayer of contemplation which, through the gifts of wisdom and understanding, perfects man's faith, hope and charity. Thus in infused contemplation the Holy Spirit gives us the supreme experience (short of the beatific vision) of our divine sonship, the supreme witness that we are sons of God in Christ.

But let us consider now this witness as given on lower levels than infused contemplation, the levels of beginnings in the life of the Spirit.

Interior Witness and Exterior Word

The grace of faith—the acceptance of God's self-revelation and offer of continuing and deepening communion with him—is deeply interior. As divine revelation, it is too big for unaided human understanding to grasp in mere human ideas and words. It comes as an inexpressible interior "word" or grace, and at first operates in man in a largely prereflective way. However, if man is to respond in a human way and in daily human life to God's self-revelation, he must reflect upon what God is accomplishing in him. He must understand it in practical human concepts.

Therefore, God presents his revelation to man not merely in the personal interior witness which is the grace of faith; he presents it also in human words and signs. He sends his prophets and preachers who articulate his message in human language. The supremely perfect presentation of his revelation in a human way is the very person of his Son, the Word made man. He is the revelation of what man is called to be as son of God.

However, a man grasps the divine revelation expressed in human words and signs and above all in the person of Christ, only because at the same time God gives him that personal interior witness, the interior "word" of faith; which is, indeed, a participation in the eternal Word, "the true light which enlightens every man." Through reflection upon the word of faith as preached in human words, and above all through reflection upon Christ the Word, man comes to an ever fuller understanding of God's interior revelation to him, his interior experience of God and of his own adoptive sonship. This continuing, deepening enlightenment requires continuing interior witness from the Holy Spirit and attentive listening and response to him, so that what man experienced prereflectively at first is brought to ever fuller awareness through reflection. Thus man ever more clearly knows himself as son of God.

For our divine life in Christ, like our human life, is not endowed with instinct. Therefore, religious reflection or meditation in openness to the Holy Spirit is indispensable for Christian living. Only the Holy Spirit, we said, can lead us to the understanding of ourselves as children of God, since our divine sonship transcends the whole order of creation and surpasses all merely human experience and understanding. Our life as God's children can be experienced and understood only by the grace of the Holy Spirit working in our human reflection. "He will guide you into all the truth" (Jn. 16:13).

The Instinct of the Holy Spirit

In Baptism, the Holy Spirit comes to dwell at the very ground of our being at the deepest roots of our existence. He gives us something which resembles instinct, a kind of divine instinct for the things of God. Commenting on Romans 8:14—"All who are led by the Spirit of God are sons of God"—St. Thomas Aquinas writes: "The man of the Spirit is led to do something, not principally from the movement of his own will, but from the instinct of the Holy Spirit."[2] For the man in whom the Holy Spirit dwells, the man who lives by fervent Christian love seems to know instinctively the right thing to do. His love has a remarkable ability to know the things of God, even though these things infinitely surpass mere human discernment.

We say that this guidance of the Holy Spirit resembles instinct, because although we are still in the darkness of faith concerning the things to which the Spirit is leading us, and they are infinitely beyond our understanding, yet by the grace of the Holy Spirit the conscientious Christian unerringly chooses the right thing. And yet this divine "instinct" is not an unreasoning instinct like that of animals which have no freedom of choice. For although the guidance of the Holy Spirit does surpass our full human understanding, it is nevertheless received by us in a human way, granting us at least a minimum of human understanding; and it results in free choice of the right course of action. Under the inspiration of the Holy Spirit, it is really we ourselves who direct our lives in freedom. For if God's life in us is to be lived humanly in keeping with our freedom as persons, the interior "instinct" of the Holy Spirit working in us at first in a prereflective way needs to be ever more clearly articulated in our human thought and understanding so that we can respond in full intelligence and freedom to the invitations of God.

For example, when a baptized person is still a child or an adolescent and sincerely seeks always to do the things pleasing to God, then the Holy Spirit dwelling in him will give him a sure "instinct" for the good. By this grace, at first he will choose and do the good prereflectively without a fully reasoned-out understanding of the reason why his choice is good. More advanced Christians are often able to testify that this is, indeed, what had happened to them

2. Sti. Thomae Aquinatis, *In Omnes S. Pauli Apostoli Epistolas Commentaria* (Taurini, Italia: Marietti, 1925), p. 112.

in their youth, for example, when they found themselves in a difficult situation such as a serious occasion of sin. Though they were still lacking in full understanding of right and wrong, though they were still incapable of judging on their own the right thing to do in the difficulty, instinctively they recognized and rejected evil. They firmly chose the good, though they did not clearly recognize the reasons for doing so. Reflecting on this in later years, they realized with gratitude that it could only have been by the instinct of the indwelling Holy Spirit who preserves the sincere of heart that they were saved from doing things which could have ruinously changed the course of their lives.

However, what we do at first instinctively or prereflectively under the inspiration of the Holy Spirit we must learn to do with ever fuller awareness under the same Holy Spirit. For it is a mark of human maturity to do everything in freedom and self-possession, knowingly and willingly making the right choice. The inspirations of the Holy Spirit have to be translated into our own free choice guided by intelligent faith and inspired by enlightened love. We must know how to detect and interpret the interior graces of the Spirit. We must know how to live reflectively, meditatively, in openness to him. We must learn to act in the full awareness of our freedom as children of God. For our Father in heaven respects the freedom he has given us, and he awaits our enlightened choice of him in love.

Thus we become fully spiritual persons, no longer the infants and sensual persons spoken of by St. Paul (1 Cor. 2:14–3,4). We no longer live chiefly under the influence of the emotions. We live in the Holy Spirit of love conscientiously seeking, understanding and generously fulfilling the true will of the Father. What the sincere child does prereflectively under the instinct of the Holy Spirit, the truly mature Christian does reflectively guided by a well-formed conscience in the full light of adult responsibility.

He can come to this full self-awareness in his divine sonship, we said, only through attentiveness to the repeated witness of the Holy Spirit, who testifies again and again with our spirits that we are children of God, bringing us to the awareness of our dignity, and teaching us to act accordingly. The mature Christian conscience is ever alert to the continuing witness of the Holy Spirit, so that the functioning of his conscience is first of all a prayer of listening to the Spirit, seeking to know the will of the Father.

The mature Christian conscience, then, acts with reflection and understanding, with enlightened and responsible choice.

In another sense, however, the most enlightened and most mature conscience works more than ever by the seemingly blind instinct of the Holy Spirit. For when one has long been faithful to a carefully cultivated Christian conscience and has always chosen deliberately to do the things that please the Father, the Holy Spirit leads him ever more intimately into the mystery of God, "even the depths of God" (1 Cor. 2:10), inspiring him to reach for things surpassing all human understanding.

"For in hope we were saved. Now hope that is seen is not hope. . . . The Spirit helps us in our weakness; for we do not know how to pray as we ought, but the Spirit himself intercedes for us with sighs too deep for words" (Rom. 8:24,26), and guides us infallibly by his divine "instinct" to this hope. In the freedom and intelligence of the sons of God, we surrender ourselves totally to the Spirit's witness to these things unseen. And with certainty and assurance, we find our way through the darkness.

Alertness to the Spirit's Witness

The "instinct" of the Holy Spirit, we have tried to make clear, is no mere instinct, no matter how prereflectively it may seem to work in beginners, and no matter how totally the mystic may seem to surrender to it. For only the truly conscientious child of God is really open in responsive faith and love to receive this inspiration. In the freedom of the sons of God, he willingly gives himself over to the inspiration of the Spirit. He does not "quench the Spirit" by indifference, negligence or downright rejection.

The Spirit, of course, in his mercy can still lay hold of a sinner's heart and convert him. The Spirit blows where he wills (Jn. 3:8). However, there is a "blasphemy against the Spirit" (Matt. 12:31), "a sin unto death" (1 Jn. 4:16,c), a progressive callousness to him which resists him unto total rejection of the life of divine sonship.

If, then, we are ever to come to our full freedom and self-possession as sons of God, we must develop a profound attentiveness and responsiveness to the witness of the Spirit. Let us, therefore, consider further the ways in which the Spirit gives his witness of our sonship in our very response to the grace of his presence.

14

Experiencing a Divine Person

"The Spirit Joins With Our Spirit" (Rom. 8:16)[1]

"When we cry 'Abba, Father,' it is the Spirit himself bearing witness with our spirit that we are children of God" (Rom. 8:15–16). *With our spirit;* that is, he bears his witness in our human spirit, in the action of our spirit praying to the Father in love, or (as is evident in other scriptural passages which we shall examine later) in the action of our spirit in living our lives as true children of God. "The Spirit does not give witness to the ears of men by an exterior voice, but gives his testimony through the effect of filial love which he causes in us."[2] We "hear" the Spirit not by directly experiencing the very person of the Spirit, even though his personal presence is truly in us. Rather, we experience his presence, we receive his witness, through his effects in our spirit, through the action "in the Spirit" which he produces in us, our action as true sons of God.

He is really dwelling in us, but because he is the infinitely transcendent God we can know his presence in this life only "in a mirror dimly" by faith (1 Cor. 13:12). We do not have the direct

1. Jos. A. Fitzmyer, trans. *Jerome Biblical Commentary* (Englewood Cliffs, N.J.: Prentice-Hall, Inc., 1968), Vol. 2, p. 316.
2. Sti. Thomae Aquinatis, *In Omnes S. Pauli Apostoli Epistolas Commentaria,* p. 113.

experience of his very person now. That will be possible only in
the face-to-face vision of eternal glory. And yet his presence is
manifested to us in the effects he causes in us, in the God-like
activity as sons of God which he produces in us conjointly with
our human spirit. The divine life in us, truly a participation in the
Spirit's own life, is the sign and proof of his presence. And in these
signs, in this God-like activity, in a manner we experience the
Spirit himself.[3]

St. Thomas teaches that through the mission of a divine Person
to a man, the man can know that Person in a kind of experience
of him. He knows the Person in a gift of grace which brings about
a personal union with God in the manner proper to the divine
Person who is sent.[4] The Person sent conforms the man to himself
in such a way that the man in his personal union with God is in the
likeness of that divine Person. "Because the Holy Spirit is love, the
soul is assimilated to the Holy Spirit by the gift of charity: hence,
the mission of the Holy Spirit is according to the manner of charity.
. . . The Son is sent in the manner of intellectual enlightenment
which breaks forth into the affection of love. . . . For the Son is the
Word, not any sort of word, but one who breathes forth love."[5]

In this union with God in love, or in enlightenment with love,
the man knows the divine Person who is sent to him. In a way, he
experiences the divine Person. Thus, the Holy Spirit is experienced
in the Christian's love for the Father. "We cry 'Father' not so
much by the sound of the voice as by the intention of the heart,
which because of its intensity is said to be a cry. . . . The greatness
of this intention proceeds from the affection of filial love which
the Spirit causes in us."[6]

3. St. Thomas calls it an "as it were" experience of the Spirit: *quasi-
experimentalis. Scriptum super libros Sententiarum Petri Lombardi*
(Parisiis: Lethielleux, 1929), Vol. 1, d. 14, q. 2, a. 2, ad 3.
4. *Commentaries on the Sentences,* in the place referred to in note 3.
5. *Summa Theologica,* I, Q. 43. a. 5, ad 2.
6. St. Thomae Aquinatis, *In Omnes S. Pauli Apostoli Epistolas Commentaria,* p. 112.

The mission of a divine Person, then, is manifested in the likeness of himself in his relationships with the other divine Persons which he causes in a man. Sometimes in the grace of infused contemplation the likeness is so vivid, and the union with the divine Person is so close that the Christian seems to be experiencing directly the very Person of the Holy Spirit or of the Son, and he is intensely aware of his own filial relationship with the Father in the Son through the Holy Spirit. This is not to be wondered at, since the Christian life is truly a participation in the life of the Holy Trinity.

Even though we do not "see" God the Father, there is some kind of awareness of him as distinct from the Spirit and the Son. And it *is* a *kind* of seeing. For one says "I see" when he understands. There is a real sense of light, almost like real light, like a brightness which fills one's whole self.

Most Christians most of the time, however, experience the Holy Spirit and his witness prereflectively, acting as sons of God, but not realizing that this very life as children of God is the Spirit's witness to their sonship. Since they fail to reflect prayerfully on what the Spirit is accomplishing in them, they do not come to a very deep awareness of themselves as children of God, nor of the divine Persons in whose life they participate.

Thus the verse of St. Paul: "It is the Spirit himself bearing witness with our spirit that we are children of God," can be explained at seemingly opposite poles: on the level of beginners in the spiritual life or on the level of mystical experience. In reality, there is no opposition between these explanations. It is one same experience, but on widely differing levels.

The grace of our adoption as sons, prereflective at first, operates more and more on the level of explicit consciousness as we mature in the divine sonship. Through reflection or meditation we begin to interpret it in terms of human words and concepts and more consciously and willingly we begin to live as sons of God. Eventually, if we are painstakingly faithful in devoted responsiveness to the

Spirit, the grace works more and more on the level of full mystical experience.

The mystical experience of our divine sonship in infused contemplation, however, does not need to wait until we are fully mature in the Christian life. It can come often, though very briefly and less intensely, even in the early stages, especially if our spiritual life is developing in a healthy Christian environment of people who are really living as God's children. Even children will be contemplative when they live among deeply prayerful people!

On all the levels and in all the manners in which the Spirit bears witness to our divine sonship, then, the graces of contemplation can already be working at least in a fleeting way. Our part is to learn to live in faithful attentiveness to the witness of the Spirit. In the next chapter, therefore, we shall consider the following manners, indicated in the Scriptures, in which the Spirit by his witness works to bring us to an ever fuller awareness of our divine sonship:

He gives his witness by inspiring our *prayer*, "Father" (Rom. 8:16); by giving us an ever-deepening *faith in Christ* as God's own Son (1 Jn. 4:13–15); by leading us to *live* truly as sons of God (Rom. 8:14), especially in our *love* for one another (1 Jn. 3:14, 24). In all these ways we experience God as our Father and we grow in awareness of our divine sonship.

15

Various Manners of the
Spirit's Witness

The Witness of the Spirit in our Prayer,"Father!"

In the ordinary daily praying of the Lord's Prayer in the Holy
Spirit, we can have a nonmystical experience of God as our
Father (which, however, helps open us for the mystical experience
when he sees fit to give it to us). For example, through the repeated
asking for our daily bread, for all the necessities of life, we experience ever more that God *is* our Father. By inspiring the faith
and hope in which we say, "Father, give us this or that good thing
we need," the Holy Spirit bears witness with our spirit that we are
children of this Father.

In the tenth chapter of St. Luke, Jesus rejoices in the privilege
of revealing the Father to us; in the eleventh chapter he teaches
the Lord's Prayer. It is in our perseverance in praying this prayer
that the Lord ever more clearly reveals the Father to us. The mystics
love to comment on the Lord's Prayer; it is the model for even the
highest stages of prayer.[1] Hence, the need of perseverance in this
prayer so that this experiencing of the Father may be daily deepened.

That is why immediately after teaching the Our Father, Jesus

1. The last section of this book will be a continuation of the commentary on the Lord's Prayer which we begin in this chapter.

goes on to give two lessons in persistence in praying. If evil men give good things to their children, the Father in heaven will all the more give good things to those who ask him. But above all, he wishes to give the Holy Spirit (Lk. 11:13) who gives us increasingly the mystical experience of our Father making us ever more perfectly sons in the Son.

Contemplation is thus somewhere between the initial understanding which is faith, and the full revelation of the Father in heaven, not in the sense that the dark manner of faith is removed in contemplation, but in the sense that contemplation is a dynamic functioning of faith, vividly experiencing the presence of God. Though, by comparison with the face-to-face beatific vision, this contemplation is still "in a mirror darkly" (1 Cor. 13:12). For the grace of adoption, we said, consists in God's interior manifestation of himself to us in his indwelling Word and Spirit sent into our hearts. Obviously, the grace of adoption is perfected only in the beatific vision, the full manifestation, the full inheritance of the sons of God.

The Spirit's Witness

Every grace of witness from the Holy Spirit is intended to deepen our faith and to perfect the communion with God in Christ which is the whole purpose of faith. Hence, St. John tells us that acceptance of Jesus as Son of God is the sign of our divine sonship and is the work of the Spirit's witness in us: "If anyone acknowledges that Jesus is the Son of God, God lives in him and he in God. . . . We can know that we are living in him, and he is living in us because he lets us share his Spirit" (1 Jn. 4:15,13,j).

Just as the Spirit bears witness to our divine sonship through the effects of filial love which he causes in us, so he bears this witness through the effects of faith in the divinity of Christ which he causes in us. For, indeed, our filial love is a participation in Christ's own love of the Father, and only through faith in his divine Sonship can we be sons of God in filial love. "This is the testimony: God has given us eternal life, and this life is in his Son; and anyone who has the Son has life; anyone who does not have the Son does not have life" (1 Jn. 5:11–12,j).

Faith in Christ's divinity, then, as source of our divine life in communion with the Father, and the contemplative gift of understanding which perfects faith are the fruit of the witness of the Spirit. "When the Counselor comes, whom I shall send to you from the Father, the Spirit of truth who proceeds from the Father, he will bear witness to me. . . . He will glorify me for he will take what is mine and declare it to you. All that the Father has is mine; therefore, I said that he will take what is mine and declare it to you" (Jn. 15:26; 16:14–15).

In other words, he will declare the divinity of Jesus, showing that the Father's divinity is Christ's, too. "By this you know the Spirit of God: every spirit which confesses that Jesus Christ has come in the flesh is of God, and every spirit which does not confess Jesus is not of God. This is the spirit of antichrist" (1 Jn. 4:2–3).

The widespread contemporary denial of the divinity of Christ is the work and sign of the spirit of anti-Christ. The sign of the presence of the Holy Spirit, on the other hand, is a great love of Jesus as true Son of God, and loving contemplation of him, especially in his paschal mystery. For Jesus is the revelation of the Father: "No one has ever seen God; the only Son, who is in the bosom of the Father, he has made him known" (Jn. 1:18). The Spirit, leading us to the contemplation of Jesus as only Son, teaches us to be sons in the Son. Only they who "believe in his name" (that is, in his divinity), have "power to become children of God" (Jn. 1:12).

If Jesus is not God, Son of the eternal Father, then neither are we sons; and verily, the witness of the Spirit of Truth is a lie!

The Spirit's Witness

We experience God as Father not only in praying for the daily necessities of life through Jesus Christ his Son, but also through *living* as sons of the Father, by doing his will in the paschal obedience of Jesus, who experienced and revealed his sonship precisely in this filial obedience: "he learned obedience through what he suffered" (Heb. 5:8). Our prayer to the Father in the Spirit, "Father, thy will be done on earth as it is in heaven," is a prayer that we may enter into Christ's obedience, that our experience of God as Father may bear fruit in our living as his sons.

In this very living of our sonship we experience more deeply his Fatherhood and his love for us.

All of us, no doubt, claim that we believe in God's love for us. Or do we believe in it? Are we sometimes tempted to doubt it, especially when, by his will, it is necessary for us to suffer hardships? Rejecting his will when it is hard to take is like rejecting our sonship. It is a refusal to act as sons in filial obedience; and is, therefore, a rejection of his fatherhood, a refusal of his love. We doubt his love because it asks difficult things of us.

Perhaps we say, "Yes, God so loved the world that he gave his only Son; yes, the crucifixion reveals his love for all mankind. But what about his love for me personally? How can I be sure that the love of Calvary is for me personally unless I can truly experience it in a personal way?" We do not doubt a love when we are actually experiencing it.

We experience God's love for us in a personal way by experiencing the Holy Spirit within us in the effects he produces in us. "The love of God," that is, God's love for us "has been poured forth into our hearts by the Holy Spirit who has been given to us" (Rom. 5:5,c). In response to this gift of the Spirit, we turn to God in love, crying, "Father!" We could have no real love for God as Father unless at least in some minimum way we had experienced the presence of his Spirit in us and thus had experienced his love for us. The initial gift of faith with the initial gift of understanding which it brings is some sort of intuition of God's personal love for us; it is God witnessing to his desire or communion with us. Even if he confronts us as sinners, it is for the sake of winning our repentance and reconciliation with him in love. Faith is, therefore, ultimately faith in divine love; it is a response to God's mysterious witness to his desire for friendship with us.

Therefore, anyone who really has faith has had some sort of experience of God's love for him; he has received an invitation to divine friendship. If the believer has forgotten this experience, if he now seriously doubts God's love for him, is it not because he has failed to reflect frequently upon the favors he has received from divine love? Is it not because he has not responded deeply enough in appreciation, in thanksgiving?

Above all, is it not because he has failed to affirm his sonship by *living* it, and thus deepening his awareness of it? The surest sign of God's love for us and our divine sonship is our really living as his sons, experiencing our sonship like Jesus in loving obedience to the Father. The person who is not doing God's will, who is not living as a child of God, and feels sorry for self because he or she is not experiencing God's love, has only self to blame. Such a one has rejected God as Father by an unloving unwillingness to shoulder the burden of doing his will. In self-pity, he or she has failed to esteem self highly as a child of God's love, one who gratefully and courageously does the Father's will in response to his love.

Always the sincerest response to God's love is the filial return of love which expresses itself in doing his will. It is such a one who experiences ever more fully God's love for him; for to such a one the Lord manifests himself: "He who has my commandments and keeps them, he it is who loves me; and he who loves me will be loved by my Father, and I will love him and manifest myself to him" (Jn. 14:21).

If the cry "Abba!" in prayer results from the experiencing of God's love for us in giving us his Spirit, even more a *life* which cries "Father!" results from the experiencing of God's love. We translate into life the prayer "Father!" which the Spirit of the Son inspires in our hearts by acting as sons of God in everything we do, doing always, as Jesus did, the things that please the Father (Jn. 8:29).

If we do always the things that please the Father precisely *because* they please him and because we love him as a Father, this very love of ours for him is some sort of experience of his love for us, for it is the sign and effect of the presence of his Spirit in us— his own love for us poured into our hearts. Just as we cannot say "Father" in prayer except in the Holy Spirit, so we cannot do always in life the things that please the Father except in that same Holy Spirit. Thus, in the very living of our sonship in filial obedience to his will we experience ever more deeply his fatherly love.

Especially when the doing of his will is very difficult, our very desire and effort to do it—"not my will, but thy will be done"—is a sign of our true sonship, a sign of his love for us and of the presence of his Spirit in us. His Spirit "helps us in our weakness . . . he intercedes for us with sighs too deep for words" (Rom. 8:26), inspiring our calls to the Father for help in our darkness of faith, in our difficulties and in our temptations. We experience his fatherhood in the fatherly help he gives us in response to this prayer, a help which comes in the form of the Spirit's gifts of fortitude and consolation. The Spirit enables us to say courageously with Jesus, "Abba, Father, all things are possible to thee; remove this cup from me; yet not what I will, but what thou wilt" (Mk. 14:36).

Experiencing God's Love

Unless the Word through his Spirit speaks an interior word to my heart, none of the other words expressing God's will are really meaningful to me. Ordinarily, of course, I perceive the interior word of grace only as clothed in other words or signs of his will by which the Lord speaks to my conscience. For example, when I hear the word of God in preaching or in the liturgy, in reading the Scriptures or in words of counsel from my fellowmen, and so on, I hear it as a compelling personal appeal of God to my conscience because it is accompanied by an interior word of grace to my heart. A mature conscience is ever alert and responsive to these interior invitations of divine love.

We all more or less expect that God will speak thus to our hearts in his scriptural and liturgical word and in explicit prayer, but we are not as convinced as we should be that the interior word of grace, the invitation of divine love, comes clothed also in the providential circumstances of daily life.

The life situation in which I am involved, such as a relationship with my fellowman—his need for my help, his right to justice, his appeal for love—each life situation is a call to my conscience, and so a word from God. In every situation of conscience there is an invitation from God, an offer of divine love and grace. The situation in which a Christian finds himself thus enters into the very texture of his contemplation of God and the purposes of his love.

Because nothing escapes the government of Divine Providence, every such situation somehow manifests the saving will of God. The scriptural teaching on Divine Providence must not be misinterpreted in the old pagan way or in the Mohammedan way as a blind and passive submission to inexorable fate or to a sheerly arbitrary whim of God. For the Christian, or for any truly conscientious man, the providential situation is always a call to responsible, creative action; it is a word from God somehow indicating to my free responsibility the call of his love. Trust in Providence is not a mere passive surrender, nor is it an abdication of responsibility. It is a taking hold of the love and grace of God offered in the situation and putting it to work in the form of free and responsible action dictated by enlightened conscience. Love's response to each providential situation (and every situation is providential) is expressed in the creative action called for by the situation. Man comes to fulfillment and to salvation by the grace of God offered in each situation and by his own creative action which is the fruit of this grace.

True enough, there are exceedingly difficult situations when everything seems completely beyond our control and power to act, and all we can do is endure in patient waiting. But even this patience is not passivity. For the true Christian, it is an active participation in the paschal mystery of Christ through living faith, hope and charity. It is not always easy to see whether a situation calls for patient suffering or for creative action. "God gives us serenity to accept what cannot be changed, courage to change what should be changed, and wisdom to distinguish one from the other."

This correspondence of conscientious human freedom with the providence of God should be operative in every situation of life. We should not limit our thoughts of God's providence only to those cases when everything is going badly, and so we try desperately to make an act of trust in providence. Nor should we think of him only when everything turns out wonderfully well, and we express amazement at the loving wisdom of providence. Nothing at all escapes the powerful control of God's wise and loving care. And only in the conscientious response to every life situation can God's Word and Spirit become fully effective in our lives.

Whoever lives in this conviction that God is present with an offer of love and saving grace in every detail of life, and who, therefore, seeks always to respond to God in the way that pleases him in each situation, will receive the special help of the Holy Spirit of Counsel in those difficult situations when human reason is baffled, or whenever the Lord wishes to give a new direction to his life which he would not have thought of himself.

Faith's contemplative ability to see the loving providence of God working in each situation, and love's ready response to this providence brings a deep peace and serenity, a participation in the serenity of Jesus as he said, "Father, into thy hands I commit my spirit." This peace is another form of the Spirit's witness that we are sons of God; it is a way of experiencing the Father's love for us. "We know that in everything God works for good with those who love him, who are called according to his purpose" (Rom. 8:28).

The Spirit's Witness

Another good sign that we have experienced God's love for us is our watchful attentiveness to the Holy Spirit and our eager openness to his inspirations. Because God has manifested his love for us, we respond in a desire to please him, a desire to follow his inspirations. Even more, we desire his presence. This desire and expectation for the fullness of the Holy Spirit is a movement of love in response to his love, an effect of the presence of the Spirit in us. Lack of eagerness for God, indifference toward him, would seem to indicate that we have not experienced God's love for us. Where is the fault? Is it on God's part? Has he no love for us?

When God pours his love into our hearts in the giving of his Spirit of adoption as sons, he means that we should be his children forever. He desires that we come into ever fuller communion with him. Why, then, are we not always in a more active relationship with him? Why are we not more fully in communion with our Father, more ardent in our desires for him?

Is it because we have forgotten our past experiences of his love for us? Is it because we have not responded adequately to these experiences? Is it because we have not kept alive in our consciousness the memory of what he has done for us and have not been grateful enough for his favors?

Mindfulness of the Lord's personal favors to us in the past is of great importance for a fervent life in the Spirit. For when we are still comparative beginners in a serious spiritual life, our experiences of God's personal love for us may be rather brief and infrequent and not very profound. In between these experiences, we tend to forget God's love for us, and especially if we have been negligent in meditation and interior prayer. In times of real hardship we are even tempted to doubt his love for us. It is then that grateful recalling of what his love has already done for us is of the greatest importance.

One of the favorite biblical verses of St. Teresa was, "*Misericordias Domini in aeternum cantabo*" ("The mercies of the Lord I will sing forever") (Ps. 88:2,d). Undying grateful remembrance of the divine favors given her personally was a cardinal point in her spirituality.

The favors of the past are always a pledge of greater favors to come, for God does not give his grace in vain. "The gifts and the

call of God are irrevocable" (Rom. 11:29). The graces of the past
are the seed of future graces. They will be given to us when we
are open to them, when we are ready for them through our response to former graces, and when God's plan for us provides that
they be given. Grateful mindfulness of the favors of the past inspires fidelity in the present and saves us from the darkness of
discouragement in God's seeming absence. It also gives rise to hope,
desire and expectation of favors to come.

To respond to God's love for us in the past by expecting further
favors in the future is not presumption (unless, of course, we have
forfeited what we had by sinful infidelity to grace). Rather, our
love for God feels bound in conscience to respond to his love in
this eager expectation, this watchfulness for his further inspirations.
Our love feels that it owes it to him to let his love have its way in
accomplishing all the purposes of his love. Our love owes it to his
love to welcome all his graces with joy, because it pleases him to
give them, even when these graces bring the need for being "con-
formed to the Son" in his crucifixion (cf. Rom. 8:29).

Our eager watchfulness for the Spirit and our vigilance for his
self-bestowal in ever new graces is a movement of love in grateful
response to our experience of his love for us. This vigilance or
openness to his inspirations is itself a sign of the presence of the
Spirit, for it is the experience of his love which wakes us to the
longing for his greater love. And only the vigilant will continue
to experience his love. The negligent, the indifferent are not open
to love if it should come.

The sincerity of our gratitude for his love, of course, is manifest
in our seeking to do always the things that please the Father who
so loves us. This doing of his will guarantees that our expectation
of his further love will not be presumptuous. Cultivating a conscience which ever sincerely seeks and does the things that please
the Father will open us still more to receive the Holy Spirit so that
we will be led ever more completely by him, the true light of our
conscience. "For all who are led by the Spirit of God are sons of

God" (Rom. 8:14). Truly, in the very living of our sonship through doing the will of the Father in the paschal obedience of Jesus, we experience that God is our Father who has poured his love into our hearts in the gift of his Spirit. Not the least sign of his love is his allowing us to bear in our persons the likeness of his Son's own sufferings for our personal salvation and for that of mankind:

"God is treating you as sons; for what son is there whom his father does not discipline?" (Heb. 12:7).

"For while we live we are always being given up to death for Jesus' sake so that the life of Jesus may be manifested in our mortal flesh. So death is at work in us, but life in you" (2 Cor. 4:11–12).

A life expressing the mystery of Jesus, Christ incarnate in our everyday life, Christ incarnate in our bearing of hardships lovingly, presupposes contemplation; that is, faith penetrating the mystery of Jesus with a conviction which expresses itself in the sonship of doing God's will. "Thy will be done on earth as it is in heaven."

Experiencing God as Father

We experience our divine sonship most commonly by living as brothers in Christ for this is the will of the Father. St. John writes: "By this we know that we have passed out of death into life, because we love the brethren" (1 Jn. 3:14). We have passed out of death into life; that is, we have participated in the paschal mystery, Christ's death and resurrection. We have died to sinful selfishness to live in the Spirit as sons of God. The proof that we are sons of God is our love of our brothers.

John seems to be saying that our love of our brothers is an experience of divine sonship. For in John's biblical vocabulary, to know means to experience, that is, to know something in the very living of it. When John says that we *know* by our love of the brothers that we have passed from death to life, he means that in

fraternal charity we experience the life in the Spirit, the life we
have received from the Father in the Resurrection of the Son. Is not
this in some way to experience God as our Father?

The section beginning with the words, "We know that we have
passed out of death into life because we love the brethren" (1 Jn.
3:14) closes with the words, "By this we know that he abides in us,
by the Spirit which he has given us" (1 Jn. 3:24). Thus, the fraternal love in which we experience our divine sonship—the love
which the indwelling Spirit inspires in us—is another form of the
witness of the Spirit with our spirit. "God himself has taught us by
his Holy Spirit to love one another" (1 Thess. 4:9).

Brotherly Love as Prayer

Obviously, filial love of the Father and fraternal love of one another are expressions of one same faith and love in the Spirit, and
whatever springs from the love can in some sense be called an
expression of the prayer "Father!" Our life is fully life only when
it is prayer—that is, awareness in living faith of our divine sonship,
lovingly affirmed sonship expressed in the prayerful effort to do
always the things that please the Father. So, too, our relationship
with our fellowmen is fully and divinely fraternal only when it is
also prayer; that is, when our fellowmen are consciously and lovingly accepted as brothers in Christ.

This "horizontal prayer" can only be a sort of divine awareness
in living faith and eager charity, and it is necessarily contemplative,
or at least rooted in some minimum of contemplation. When love
of neighbor is easy, when it costs us little, possibly we can love
neighbor in a prereflective way without very much contemplative
awareness. But to love neighbor when he injures us, or when
service in love requires great self-sacrifice, this requires an awareness of our Father in heaven or a consciousness of Christ our
crucified brother.

Therefore, Jesus taught us to turn to the Father in the Lord's
Prayer to obtain the grace of love of neighbor when a neighbor

has harmed us: ".... as we forgive those who trespass against us."
For consciousness of God, we forgive our brothers; we bear wrongs
patiently. "This is indeed a grace, if for consciousness of God anyone endures sorrows, suffering unjustly" (1 Pet. 2:19,c). To aid us
in this heroism in brotherly love, the true test of our love, Peter
at once recommends prayerful reflection on Jesus, the Suffering
Servant: "Unto this indeed you have been called, because Christ
also has suffered for you, leaving you an example that you may
follow in his steps" (1 Pet. 2,21,c).

Thus, love of neighbor as "horizontal prayer" is rooted in "consciousness of God," in direct prayer to the Father and in lively faith
in the Suffering Servant. Someone has said that love of neighbor is
the privileged form of prayer. There is some truth in this; not in the
sense that it replaces all other prayer, but in the sense that it is a
certain fullness of our relationship with the Father and is a necessary expression of it.

16

The Witness of the Spirit in the Eucharist and in Penance

The Experience of God's Love in Eucharistic Participation

One of the ordinary ways of deeply experiencing God's love for us is eucharistic participation. "In the liturgy, especially in the divine sacrifice of the Eucharist, the work of our redemption is being accomplished" (SC 2). To say that in the liturgy the work of our redemption is being accomplished is to say that in the liturgy Jesus is communicating to us his Holy Spirit, the fruit of his paschal sacrifice, the Spirit in whom we call God Father and live as his children, the Spirit in whom we love one another as brothers and sisters in Christ. Only through the working of the Holy Spirit in our hearts is the paschal mystery fruitful in us; and this very working of the Spirit in us is an experiencing of God's love for us.

Jesus in his paschal mystery is the supreme revelation and communication of divine love, and that revelation and giving of love is made intimately personal for each one of us in the eucharistic mystery. "God so loved the world that he gave his only Son" (Jn. 3:16); the Son loved his own to the utmost (Jn. 13:1), giving himself *for* us on the cross, giving himself *to* us in the Eucharist: "This is my body which will be given up for you; this is the cup of my blood which will be shed for you and for all men."

The gift of his body and blood to us is no mere external sign of love. It contains the very reality it signifies: the transcendent God really giving himself. The outward signs of this self-giving, the eucharistic signs, have to be accompanied by the interior witness of the Holy Spirit, for the God who is given infinitely surpasses human understanding and our ability to perceive him. By the interior witness, the Holy Spirit testifies to the reality of God's gift of himself. The supreme signs of God's love—the visible self-giving of Jesus on the cross, and his visible self-giving in the eucharistic signs—would be meaningless to us without the interior personal witness of the Spirit given in the eucharistic signs. This witness testifies that Christ's dying on the cross is love for us personally. It is not merely love for the Twelve at the Last Supper, not merely for the Mother of Jesus and for John at the foot of the cross, not merely for Dismas who died in friendship with Jesus.

It is normal, then, that we should experience God's love for us in a special way in Holy Communion. The outward sign communicates to us the interior grace or witness of the Holy Spirit, giving us an experience of intimate union with God. An outpouring of the Holy Spirit into our hearts is the normal fruit of eucharistic participation, for the giving of the Holy Spirit is the fruit of our Lord's sacrifice. But the normal effect of the pouring of the Holy Spirit into our hearts is deeper faith and more fervent love. Therefore, the most immediate witness of God's love for us experienced in the eucharistic participation is the very faith and fervor of love which we experience in the actual participation and for some time afterwards.

Would the Eucharist really be a sign of God's love, as it is intended to be, if it did not give this interior experience of his love? It is meant to give this experience; and if the experience is profound, it will not pass quickly away. A deep awareness of the presence of God will continue for some time.

The speed with which many Christians depart from the Eucharistic celebration would seem to indicate that they do not experience

God's love very deeply in their Holy Communion. If they did, they would linger in attentiveness to the God whose love is embracing them.

If eucharistic participation is meant to be an experience of God's love, why do we not experience it more deeply? Is it because we have not sharpened our powers of spiritual perception? "You need milk, not solid food; for everyone who lives on milk is unskilled in the word of righteousness. Solid food is for the mature, for those who have their faculties trained by practice to distinguish good from evil" (Heb. 5:14). The faculties, enlightened by faith, must be trained by practice in spiritual perception.

The perception of the experience of the divine love in the Eucharist and openness to their experience involves much more than mental concentration and alertness to the realities of faith at the time of participation. It requires a purification of the heart, of the senses, the emotions, the intellect, the will, the memory and imagination and the other interior powers.

The unspiritual man does not perceive the gifts of the Spirit of God, for they are folly to him, and he is not able to understand them because they are spiritually discerned. . . . But I, brethren, could not address you as spiritual men, but as men of the flesh, as babes in Christ. I fed you with milk, not solid food; for you were not ready for it; and even yet you are not ready for it, for you are still of the flesh. For while there is jealousy and strife among you, are you not of the flesh and behaving like ordinary men? (1 Cor. 2:14; 3:1–3).

Though Paul is speaking here of the Corinthians' inability to perceive the deeper wisdom which he had to offer them through his preaching, his words concerning spiritual dullness apply also to our lack of spiritual perception in our participation in the Eucharistic mystery. We are "still of the flesh . . . behaving like ordinary men."

The heart must be more and more purified of all sorts of selfishness, not just that which leads to strife and jealousy, but also of the other kinds of self-indulgence which blunt the spiritual faculties.

He who indiscriminately indulges in every pleasure even though they be lawful ones will not develop his powers of spiritual perception, and he can scarcely expect to receive a profound experience of divine love in prayer or in liturgical participation. " 'All things are lawful for me,' but not all things are helpful" in living the life in the Spirit (I Cor. 6:12).

The heart must be thoroughly disciplined concerning even lawful pleasures if it is deeply to perceive the divine presence. It must be trained by practice to give full attention to spiritual realities. An undisciplined heart has little power of concentration on these realities, little alertness to the Spirit. Its attention is scattered and lacks the recollection necessary for receiving the more subtle and profound witness of the Spirit.

It is important that we do not misunderstand the manner in which we are to experience God's love in the Eucharist or in the other forms of prayer and meditation. We have said that the Spirit is experienced chiefly in the deep faith and steady love which he causes in our hearts. This is not necessarily manifest in the emotions. It can glow in our heart as a profound peace and serenity, an unshakeable certitude of faith, and a steadfast love which goes forth into daily life and does the will of God in all things, especially in loving and serving neighbor.

There are many people who participate frequently in the Eucharist who experience this profound peace and security of faith without reflecting explicitly that this, "the peace of God which surpasses all understanding" (Phil. 4:7), is truly an experience of God's love and presence.

It is well to remember that the gift of infused contemplation often comes as an exceedingly delicate and subtle grace which can be extinguished by too much exteriority in our manner of praying, or by rushing about distractedly in various activities. This delicate grace of peace in the divine presence should be a rather normal effect of Holy Communion. Therefore, a more or less prolonged period of silence after Holy Communion should be encouraged so

140 Dynamic Contemplation

that the faithful may learn to perceive this sign of God's love and presence. Fortunately, liturgists and theologians are once again recommending such quiet thanksgiving.[1]

The people who claim that they "get nothing out of the Mass" are not "tuned in" to these delicate interior graces which come to those who have their faculties of spiritual perception trained by practice to receive them.

A Caution Concerning Spiritual Experience

All that we have said concerning the experiencing of God's love for us evokes the perennial danger about which experts in the spiritual life have always warned us: mistaking mere feeling in prayer and illusory spiritual satisfaction for signs of deep love for God.

In any other era of Christianity, spiritual writers would play down spiritual experience and speak more about the darkness of faith. However, we have spoken so much about experiencing God because contemporary man is avid for exciting experience of every kind, and it is important to convince him that God really can be experienced. If man today has not experienced something, then he tends to deny its existence or even its possibility. So he will not put much effort into the search for it, and he wants to experience a thing here and now; otherwise, he is not interested in it.

And his experience has to be "a happening." It has to be novel, exciting, fast moving. For that very reason his experiences are often very superficial. He develops no sharpness of spiritual perception and no ability to discern the more subtle interior graces of the Holy Spirit. So, of course, he tends to deny their existence, and he rejects the importance of infused contemplation. His superficial experiences may seem great to him, but they are like a shallow brooklet, bubbling and gurgling noisily, which seems to be a real brook. A real brook however, eventually becomes deeper and deeper and it carries a greater and greater volume of water. Then it be-

1. Cf. Otto Semmelroth, "The Unity of Rite and Reflection in the Eucharistic Celebration," *Theology Digest* 16 (Spring, 1968), pp. 35–38.

comes calm and quiet, hardly seeming to move. "Still waters run deep."

Superficial human experience, however, does not necessarily become deeper through repetition. It grows in depth only through the effort to reach the more profound realities of life. Going through "a happening" deepens one's life only to the extent that one has insight into the deeper realities which may be involved in the event.

"Experiencing God" vs. "the God Experienced"

Too many people who are interested in prayer are so intent on trying to *experience* prayer that they are distracted from the *God experienced*. It is like being in love with love rather than with a person loved. They are so concerned, for example, about making each liturgical celebration a brand new "happening" that they never penetrate to what is really happening, God's giving of himself in spiritual grace. Or they are so concerned about expressing the whole man—body and emotions as well as mind and heart—in their prayer and liturgy that they sometimes end up expressing less of man. Their excessive concern for the manner of external expression keeps them on the superficial level, and it distracts them from the interior heart of prayer, from the God who should be embraced in prayer.

We need, therefore, to educate ourselves to pay less attention to "the experience" so that we may concentrate our whole being on the God experienced. We should become so wrapped up in God in simplicity of heart that we forget ourselves and our feelings or lack of them. This, we noted earlier, is one of the effects of the Spirit's gift of understanding: purification of the heart from undue attachment to externals and forms of expression. When our prayer has become deeply interior, we are relatively unconcerned about whether "forms of prayer" are new or old. We can pray well either way, and with or without the forms.

In our prayer we must become ever more like the Incarnate

Word, who was ever "toward the Father," intent upon him and his glory, and never standing aside, as it were, to admire himself for being so good at prayer! In prayer, says Urs von Balthasar, "all that takes place must be in the truth, so that the person praying rests, not in his own feelings, but in the Lord."[2]

"The Peace of God Which Surpasses All Understanding"

The experiencing of God's love in the Eucharist (or in any other kind of prayer), then, does not have to be a bubbling celebration, a new and exciting "happening" each time. It can, and ordinarily should be, a profound peace surpassing all understanding.

Thus, there is the Christian (and there ought to be a multitude like him) who in simplicity of heart very profoundly experiences God's nearness in the Eucharist, but he is so wrapped up in God that he scarcely realizes that it is he himself who is experiencing God. His chief attention is not on himself or on the experience, but on the God he experiences. His is indeed a deeply authentic and pure experience of God, pure of the dross of excessive self-concern. He needs no superficial "happening" to "get something out of the Mass."

He is astounded to hear people say that they get nothing out of Mass, and yet he is at a loss to describe what he himself gets out of it. The daily eucharistic celebration in which he participates may be very ordinary in its externals, austere and quiet in its sense-perceptible and emotional overtones, and yet it offers him something indescribably rich. When he is questioned about what the Eucharist means to him, he merely says that he could not live without it. That is why he returns to it daily, not in empty routine, but in a living rhythm of life, like the regular filling of the lungs with life-giving oxygen. The Eucharist is as necessary to him as breathing, and just as quiet and peaceful.

Just as calmly and quietly as the growing and fruitful tree soaks

2. *Op. cit.,* p. 106.

in the warm sunshine and air and drinks in the waters and chemicals from the soil, so he peacefully absorbs the light and love and life of God as he returns day after day to the eucharistic Lord. "Without me you can do nothing," says Jesus in the eucharistic context of the Last Supper. "As the branch cannot bear fruit by itself unless it abides in the vine, neither can you, unless you abide in me" (Jn. 15:4–5). Jesus, the vine, is present in the fruit of the vine, the consecrated wine, that we may live in him, imbibing the fullness of his life and fruitfulness.

On the surface the life of such a Christian may appear very ordinary indeed, and to himself he does seem very ordinary, for he does not analyze the deeply sanctifying effect of God's presence with him. One cannot be in the intimacy of God, however without absorbing the holiness of God, anymore than one can walk in the sunshine without experiencing its light or warmth.

He seems very ordinary to himself, moreover, because he is still characterized by many human failings. For God's own righteousness or holiness which is communicated to him in the Eucharist infinitely surpasses mere human ethical perfection and can coexist with human faults.

When I was a child, we had a coal-burning stove in our kitchen, which used to glow red-hot on a cold winter morning. One of the stove lids had a tiny crack in it. When there was no fire in the stove, the lid was cold and black, and the crack could not be seen. But when the fire was blazing, the lid became hot and brilliant like the fire itself, absorbing all the qualities of the fire while still remaining iron. And the crack became clearly visible.

So, too, when the Spirit of God dwells in a man, the man absorbs the life and qualities of God himself. He is spiritualized and divinized. Yet he retains for a long time many of his human defects, which become all the more noticeable to him in the divine light.

So he can consider himself a very ordinary man, and even a sinner, though he is aglow with divine life. "We have this treasure in earthen vessels, to show that the transcendent power belongs to God and not to us" (2 Cor. 4:7). God prefers to dwell in defective vessels that the glory may be his and not ours. He knows only too well that if his own beauty in us shines forth too soon or too brilliantly, we may fall down in idolatry of self, mistaking "the image and glory of God" for God himself. God must guarantee our humility and simplicity throughout the process of our progressive transfiguration "from glory to glory."

And, of course, because of a Christian's faults, his fellowmen may express shock when they see him approach the eucharistic Lord, and they may mock him in disbelief when he claims he does get a wonderful but inexpressible benefit from the Eucharist. How can so ordinary a person as he be experiencing the ineffable God?

And yet, it is his very ordinariness and sinfulness which impels him to go frequently to the Lord for life and healing. He does not approach the Eucharist in self-righteousness, but in profound humility, knowing that he cannot live life apart from Christ, his life.

He does not concentrate all his efforts on acquiring human ethical perfection, complete and perfect virtue, "a righteousness of his own" acquired by his own power. He lives ever in openness to receive an ever fuller participation in God's own righteousness which is granted to him in faith (Phil. 3:9–10).

He is not upset by hurt pride when his failings reveal to him his human sinfulness. He does not stay away from the Lord in false humility. He hastens to him, praising and thanking the merciful Lord who will receive him and clothe him in his own holiness. He comes to the Eucharist in a wonderful mixture of humility and audacity, confessing that he is a sinner but confessing also the goodness of the Lord whom he knows will receive him in compassion because he comes in repentant faith and hope.

The Spirit's Witness in the Confession of One's Sinfulness

No matter how pure his heart is, no matter how free it is of the consciousness of guilt, nevertheless, as one who has been redeemed and is still in the process of being redeemed, he goes to the Father only in Jesus; for "in the liturgy, especially in the sacrifice of the Eucharist, the work of our redemption is being accomplished" (*SC* 2).

He realizes that "God is greater than our hearts" (1 Jn. 3:20). Our heart may blame us, perhaps because of its sinfulness, but he who is greater than our heart can enlarge it by his sanctifying presence. Thus, just as we experience God as Father in praying, "Give us this day our daily bread," so, too, we experience his love in praying, "Father, forgive us our trespasses as we forgive those who trespass against us."

The very ability to say this in sincerity and truth is a witness of the Spirit in our heart, a witness that the Father loves us. For the supernatural contrition which is necessary for forgiveness, inspired by divine faith and hope, can come only from the inspiration of the Holy Spirit. Indeed, the honest recognition of guilt even before contrition is already some sort of encounter with God whose voice sounds in conscience. The consequent fear of the Lord which is the beginning of repentance is the work of the Holy Spirit.

And the granted forgiveness is clearly an experience of God's love for us, for it comes only in an outpouring of the Spirit himself into our hearts. "You yourself are the forgiveness of sins," we pray to the Holy Spirit in the Postcommunion prayer of Pentecost Tuesday. The deep peace of heart which is the fruit of the sacrament of Penance is the Spirit's own witness that God loves us.

The witness of the Spirit and the experience of the Father's love is all the more profound when to the petition, "Forgive us our trespasses," we add, "as we forgive those who trespass against us," forgiving someone who has really harmed us. The sincerity and truth of the forgiveness of neighbor is already the sign that we ourselves have been forgiven, for it is a witness to the presence of the Spirit in our heart, and his presence is the remission of sin.

This, no doubt, is the meaning of St. John's statement, "By this" —love of neighbor—"we shall know that we are of the truth and reassure our hearts before him whenever our hearts condemn us"

(1 Jn. 3:19–20). If we are impelled in the consciousness that we are sinners to say, "Forgive us our trespasses *as we forgive those who trespass against us,*" "God is greater than our hearts, and he knows everything" (1 Jn. 3:20). He knows that a heart which can forgive others in full sincerity is "of the truth," is a son of God in the Son. The sign that we are "of the truth" and are growing in the perfect love "which casts out fear" (1 Jn. 4:18) is love of neighbor (1 Jn. 3:16–19). The surest test that we love neighbor and are children of God is the forgiveness even of enemies: "Love your enemies . . . that you may be children of your Father who is in heaven" (Matt. 5:44–45).

If we have such love of one another, God will acknowledge us as his children in spite of our immaturity, our imperfections, our occasional falls. For the divine life in us is not yet strong enough to avoid all failures. We are still in the process of growth; we are in the process of being redeemed. The interior peace which assures us we are children of God springs from our God-given ability to love neighbor. It is the sign that we are the begotten of God. "Love is of God, and he who loves is born of God, and knows God" (1 Jn. 4:7).

Our very confession that we are sinners needing forgiveness through Christ, our very prayer, "Father, forgive us our trespasses," inasmuch as it is a participation in the prayer of Jesus, "Father, forgive them," is a witness from the Holy Spirit that God loves us in his Son.

Contemplation in Ordinary Christian Living

Certainly all the ways in which we experience God's love in the Holy Spirit, such as the confident hope with which we ask the Father's forgiveness when we have offended him, the ability to live courageously as sons of God in times of trial and when love of neighbor involves great cost to self, the perseverance in asking God for our daily needs especially when he does not seem to be answering our prayers, certainly all of this presupposes some spiritual understanding of our divine sonship. Faith perfected by at least some minimal degree of the contemplative gifts of understanding and wisdom, some intuitive insight into the reality of God sharing his life with us, some loving union with the Father dwelling in us are evidences of our divine sonship. That is why every element of Christian living includes some measure of contemplation. Faith cannot fully achieve its purpose without this understanding, this intuition of the divine reality of God-with-us. Faith is necessarily contemplative.

Hence, St. Thomas Aquinas writes: "Although every Christian in the state of salvation does not come to the perfect state of contemplation, he must nevertheless participate some way in contemplation. The command is given to all: 'Pause a while and *know* that I am God' (Ps. 46:10). This is also the purpose of the third precept of the Law."[3] In other words, everyone is commanded by God to be a contemplative at least on Sunday.

3. *III Sent.,* d. 36, a. 1, ad 5. The word "know" in the Psalm quoted is to be understood in the biblical meaning of experiential knowledge in love.

III
The Apostolate
of Contemplation

Introduction

The whole apostolate of Jesus on earth was to lead his fellowmen into communion with the Father in contemplation and love: "I made known to them thy name, and I will make it known, that the love with which thou hast loved me may be in them, and I in them" (Jn. 17:26). "This is eternal life, that they may know thee the only true God, and Jesus Christ whom thou hast sent" (Jn. 17:3).

Such, too, is the mission of the Church. "It is of the essence of the Church that she be fervent in action and at leisure for contemplation. . . . Her action is ordered to contemplation and is subordinate to it" (*SC* 2).

In this section, we shall consider some of the ways in which Christians help one another and all their fellowmen to the contemplation of God. We shall see, also, further examples of contemplation in ordinary daily life.

17

Coming in Community
to Contemplation

Mental prayer, says St. Teresa, is nothing else than being on terms of intimate friendship with God, conversing frequently with him in our hearts because we know he loves us.

We know he loves us, because his Spirit dwelling in our hearts gives continuing witness, convincing us that God is our Father and repeatedly offering us deeper communion with him. Living in this communion requires a continuing awareness of God's ever-present offer of himself and a ready acceptance of the offered communion.

Communion with God in the Community of His People

This offer of communion with us is made in keeping with our nature, in human words and signs as well as by interior grace. And, therefore, the offer of communion is made to us in the community of men, the Church: in the real presence of Christ speaking to us in a human way in the words of the Scriptures and in the words of the liturgy, and giving himself to us in the sacraments of the liturgy. The interior witness of the Spirit to each individual is interpreted in human thoughts with the help of these words and signs given in the community of God's people.

The response to the divine witness and grace thus given in this human way is an ever deepening communion with God as we gradually discover our sonship and brotherhood, as we discover that we are in God and he in us by this mutual presence in awareness and love.

Thus, in community one learns to pray. If prayer is such a problem for so many people today, no doubt it is because the Christian community is not praying as fully as it ought.

For a person comes to supernatural Christian awareness in the same process in which he comes to psychological self-awareness. Only in community with persons can we be persons. Therefore, just as a child comes to understand his humanity and develops his human personality only by living among human beings in personal relationships, so the child of God comes to understand his divine sonship by living among true children of God.

At first the baptismal cry "Father!" is in the heart of the child in an inarticulate way, as a kind of spiritual instinct planted in his heart as a prereflective grace. This interior instinct of the Holy Spirit comes to reflective awareness, however, in the midst of other *lives* which are already the cry, "Father!"—that is, lives which authentically interpret and translate into Christian word and action the interior grace of divine sonship.

Since full Christian self-possession in awareness and liberty is possible to the extent that the prereflective beginnings in grace become more and more fully conscious and voluntary, progressive instruction and enlightenment in the word of God must accompany the interior baptismal grace.

However, the word of God is best understood and accepted when it is seen at the same time in the witness of lives, when it is seen incarnate in those with whom we live.

The word as heard and as seen in lives is accepted and loved because somehow it has already been understood through the interior witness of the Holy Spirit. And on the other hand, the interior witness of the Spirit, too big for human words and thoughts, is brought to human understanding with the help of the word as lived by others. Furthermore, the holiness of life of those who live the word is a sign to us, reassuring us of the reality of the interior word of faith. For God's interior witness, to which we respond in faith, is always confirmed by some sort of sign.

Thus our life in the Spirit is interpreted for us by other truly Christian lives. By accepting this interpretation, we come to our self-understanding as sons of God. We become ever more consciously and willingly like the Word of God—incarnations of the word, as it were, and epiphanies of that word to others.

For when Christ is the light of our conscience, the light directing our life, then Christ shines in our life. When one grows up in the midst of lives shining with Christ, the growing life becomes an incipient prayer, an implicit cry, "Father!" which will spring ever more easily into explicit prayer.

By measuring true to our divine sonship, "doing the truth in love" (cf. Eph. 4:15), we are ever more open to receive new missions of the persons of the Word and his Spirit, in whom we more and more profoundly experience the divine reality of sonship in Christ. Our prayer becomes the explicit cry "Father," and our lives shine more brilliantly with the likeness of Father and Son.

Witness Presupposes Contemplation

The witness given to others by the more mature sons of God requires a more profound and certain experience of these divine realities. "If the trumpet give forth an uncertain sound, who will prepare for battle?" (1 Cor. 14:8,c). If the father of a family, the mother, the elder children, the elders in a religious community or in a parish, are inconsistent in their Christian living, the younger members will be confused.

The elders will be inconsistent to the extent that their experience of the inner light and grace of adoption is still shallow. For perfect witness can be given only by one who is fully led by the Holy Spirit—"whoever are led by the Spirit of God, they are the sons of God" (Rom. 8:14,c)—because only the gifts of understanding and knowledge give the interior certitude and joy of an unwavering faith which is shaken by no crisis of faith and which can solve every problem of life in the light of faith.

Vatican II, speaking of the remedies for atheism, gives a definition of the Christian witness which has to shine in the integral life of the Church and her members, a life which makes the Holy Trinity "present and in a sense visible. . . . This result," says the Council, "is achieved chiefly by the witness of a living and mature faith, namely, one trained to see difficulties clearly and master them" (*GS* 21).

The life of the Trinity shines forth in the lives of Christians, in other words, in practical everyday living, in the solution of life's problems in the light of a mature faith.

The process by which one comes to this certitude of faith, this clarity and sureness in making a Christian judgment of a situation, is really a contemplative process, whether the one who goes through the process realizes this or not. For only faith as perfected by the gifts of understanding and knowledge has the unwavering certitude and the clear insight into the divine meaning of earthly realities which is necessary for mastering life's situations in the fully Christian way and thus bearing witness to the Holy Trinity. If such Christian living manifests the Holy Trinity, as the Council says it does, it must be because the Holy Trinity is living in the man so solving the problems of his times.

The Council attributes this Christian witness especially to the Holy Spirit: "For it is the function of the Church, led by the Holy Spirit who renews and purifies her ceaselessly, to make the Father and his Incarnate Son present and in a sense visible" (*GS* 21).

Contemplation Is Eminently Practical

All this shows how eminently practical Christian contemplation really is. Platonic contemplation and most oriental contemplation may aim at an escape from the hard realities of earthly life, but not so Christian contemplation, which deeply involves us in the paschal mystery of Christ who fully accepted the human condition and lived among us that we might find salvation in our everyday human living. In the light of the Holy Trinity, man solves his earthly problems as only a son of God led by the Holy Spirit can solve them.

If the Spirit's gift of knowledge enables one accurately to judge earthly realities in the divine light of faith, the gift of counsel commands practical action appropriate to the existential situation. Counsel must work in unison with the certitude of understanding and the practical insight of knowledge.

That the witness of a practical Christian life presupposes a contemplative process is brought out by Vatican II, declaring that it is possible to find God in every reality, every situation, every person, only if one meditates on the Word of God:

Only by the light of faith and by meditation on the word of God can one always and everywhere recognize God "in whom we live and move and have our being," (Acts 17:28), seek his will in every event, see Christ in all men whether they be close to us or strangers, and make correct judgments about the true meaning and value of temporal things, both in themselves and in their relation to man's final goal (*AA* 4).

In acquiring the Christian conscience which solves every problem in the light of the Gospel, sincere Christians do much contemplating in the light of Christ, without realizing how contemplative they really are! They ponder the word of God which they hear in preaching and in the liturgy. For example, one Quinquagesima Sunday, the housekeeper at the rectory where this author was in residence, heard at Mass the reading of St. Paul's great hymn to charity (1 Cor. 13). That day she received word of the death of a former neighbor of hers, a man who had died in total poverty, with no one to pay his funeral expenses. As she pondered this situation, the word of St. Paul which she had heard at Mass was also alive in her heart: "If I have not charity, I am nothing." Before the day was over, the Holy Spirit had led her to make the really generous sacrifice of paying for the man's funeral out of her own small savings. The fruitful word of God had fallen on good soil!

If the Word is kept in the heart in devoted pondering, then it will be kept in life. It will be lived; it will be expressed in the solution of life's everyday problems; Christian witness will be given. Contemplation of the word of God is eminently practical; it involves us in Christ's own love and action.

Contemplation of this practical kind is necessary for all Christians; there is no Christ-life without it. Every Christian, we have seen with St. Thomas, must participate some way in contemplation. This contemplation may be one's own personal contemplation, or it must be at least "borrowed contemplation," in the sense that one participates in the contemplation of the Christian community from which the preaching of the word springs. Or one participates in the contemplation of a preacher who arouses his hearers to a living faith. So, too, the child who learns to pray from parents who already pray, participates in the living prayer of the parents. The Christian family, however, participates in the contemplation of the whole Christian community.

Therefore, the Christian community needs to have a fullness of contemplation into which its new members can be caught up as they learn in community to pray.

Learning in Community to Pray

We learn to pray from others who pray. That is why prayer in common is of the very essence of the Christian community. No facet of the human personality can develop fully except in community, in interpersonal relationships. This is true also of man's life of prayer. Since prayer is a human response to God who calls, it has to be learned in the human way, from other human beings as well as from the indwelling Holy Spirit. The beginner learns to pray, and he is supported and caught up in his efforts by those who are already praying. Whenever the Christian community prays together, those more advanced in the ways of prayer draw others into their own orbit.

And the community prays all the better when their leader prays well. When the man who presides over the assembly and preaches is a praying man, a man of the word in the sense that he is ever listening to the word in lively faith, and preaches it, then all pray well. The purpose of his preaching is to catch up his listeners into his own contemplation of the word. For the purpose of all preaching is to bring forth a response to the word in living faith. Unless the preacher himself is alive to the word in continuing contemplation, he will not succeed in making his listeners alive to the word.

This is true of any Christian who influences the faith and prayer of others. The fruits of his contemplation which he gives to others are not just statements about God. Rather, the fruits are the living faith and love which he inflames in the hearts of those who hear and see him, who catch fire from his fire. He catches others into his own living contemplation to make them respond to God in prayer, in work and in their daily human relationships.

Those who experience the Christian reality more profoundly become leaders in the praying community, not necessarily in the sense that they lead the public prayers of the group, but in the sense that their more intense or profound prayer certainly influences the rest of the community. When a congregation is praying together, if quite a number of its members are really deeply at prayer, the rest of its members cannot help but pray better. They learn to pray from the influence of the better pray-ers; they are drawn into the prayer of the group.

It seems that even Peter, the first Pope, learned from the contemplative experiences of the youngest of the apostles, "the disciple whom Jesus loved." It was John who first recognized the risen Jesus the morning of the miraculous catch of fishes, and at once enlightened Peter (Jn. 21:7). John, too, it seems, was the first to understand the meaning of the empty tomb and the folded burial clothing of Jesus that morning of the Resurrection when he came with Peter to the tomb (Jn. 20:8).

Beginners in the Christian life, we said, learn the meaning of the prereflective, inarticulate cry of the Spirit within them when they see lives which are a true "Abba!" lives which authentically interpret the indwelling Word and Spirit.

But the Christian community authentically interprets this "Abba" in the form of daily living, only because they listen to the Word together in the liturgy or in the Scriptures as interpreted by the Church.

Contemplative listening to the word is as necessary as seeing the word in the witness which is a neighbor's Christian life. The two are mutually complementary. Listening to the word guides us in living the word, while the authentic witness of those who live the word helps us to understand both the Gospel and the interior word of one's personal graces in which God speaks to the individual.

It is the ones who are best living the word of God in their daily lives who will be best praying in response to the word of God in the Christian assembly. In the prayers of the assembly, families and individuals will be caught up into the contemplation of the whole group, and then will go out and keep the word in their living of it.

And to the assembly the fruits of contemplation will be brought. If the assembled Christians have lived and prayed the word all week long, then they will more easily and deeply pray in community and in turn inflame their fellow-worshippers.

The sincerity and impact of one's praying-witness in the assembly, drawing others into his own Christian experience, will be in proportion to his own experience of the paschal mystery, which is sonship in the Son, a sonship experienced in the very living of it as well as in the praying of it.

The man of prayer, the man who contemplates the mystery of Christ himself becomes deeply involved in that mystery; and his prayer and all his living become an eloquent "Father!" All who see and hear him also learn to be children of the Father in heaven.

Prayer in the Words of Others

In overreaction to the fact that the prayer of some people is mechanical recitation by rote of fixed formulas of prayer, there is a current tendency to reject the use of all "prefabricated" prayer formulas, even the divinely inspired psalms and canticles of the Bible. Everything must be new and spontaneous, we are told. It must spring from the heart, from the times, from the situation.

If we always refuse to pray in the words of others, however, we are depriving ourselves of a wonderful help from the Christian community. Just as we learn everything else from our fellowmen, so from them we learn to pray. We can truly pray with the words of others, because very frequently we find that these words express beautifully what the Holy Spirit has already put into our hearts by an interior grace which we were unable to articulate by ourselves. The words of others can help us to understand what is happening in our own hearts, and they can give us a medium for expressing and deepening what the Spirit inspires in us.

After some experience in prayer, of course, with increasing frequency there will be times when we can pray better in our own words or without words. But we will never be completely free of dependence upon the spiritual experience of our fellowmen, and the prayers of others will often renew our fading fervor.

There is another reason for sometimes praying in the words of others. When we pray as a community, or even alone but in the conscious effort to achieve solidarity with mankind in our prayer, the words of others such as the psalms often inspire us to pray for others who are in desperate situations which we have not yet experienced ourselves. Personally, we may never have experienced the deep anguish expressed in some of the psalms, but we can pray them fervently on behalf of others whom we know are in sore distress. That is one of the great beauties and special graces of the psalms, especially when they are prayed in the liturgy, the prayer of the whole Church. They have a way of broadening our prayer to embrace the multitude of our fellowmen. They bring us out of our narrow self-concern.

Or again, as St. Paul tells us, we know not what to pray for as we ought. There are things we should pray for but which we would never dream of because of our lack of experience of them.

The Holy Spirit has to inspire us to pray for these things beyond human understanding. Often he teaches us to do so by the words of our fellowmen who *have* experienced these transcendent things. By these words the Spirit helps us to understand them and to desire them. It is fitting that we use the words of others whose experience will broaden our own.

"Prefabricated" prayers can have a wonderful educative power, forming our hearts in the true ways of prayer. We should not foolishly deprive ourselves of these helps, especially the psalms, merely because it is the current fashion to be ever "creative" and "spontaneous" in whatever we do.

18

Contemplation and Our Daily Work

Father Edward Schillebeeckx tells the story of a Dutch boy who refused to pray before meals. When his father chided him for this, he replied, "Why should I say to God, 'Give us this day our daily bread,' when it is not God, but you, who gives it to me? The bread our family eats is given to us by the farmer who grows the wheat, the miller who grinds it to flour, the baker who makes it into bread, the distributor and the grocer who sell it to us, and by you who work hard each day to earn the money to buy it for us."

The boy's attitude reflects an attitude of contemporary man who refuses to expect from God what he can do for himself. Now that man has "come of age" and has mastered the world by his science and technology, he no longer needs a God to turn to in helplessness, as his ancestors had done for centuries.

In his inexperienced immaturity, the boy had not yet learned what St. Paul meant in saying to the Athenians, "God is not far from each one of us, for 'in him we live and move and have our being'" (Acts 17:27–28). Therefore, he did not appreciate the fact that God works in our work. He grants not only the spiritual increase when Paul plants and Apollo waters (1 Cor. 3:6), but also the natural increase when any man plants seed and cultivates the soil, or splits the atom and propels a rocket into outer space, and walks upon the moon.

God works in our work. To this we bear witness when we ask him to give the increase through our labors, "Give us this day our daily bread."

By praying thus, with understanding in the Holy Spirit, we learn to experience the presence and loving action of God in whatever happens in his universe. Although God is in all things giving them their existence and their action, he is not content to be in his world merely in that way. He wishes to dwell in the welcoming hearts of his people. To recognize with gratitude that he works not only in all nature, but also in our work, is to receive him into his world in this new way. Lovingly to acknowledge his presence with us and in our action is to receive him in faith and in love. And in that faith and love he dwells, or rather, he dwells in us, embraced in our faith and love.

The contemporary Christian, "come of age," does not ask for a miraculous accomplishment of those things which God expects him to do for himself; but this does not mean that he does not pray for the fruits of his labors. Trust in Divine Providence, we have seen, is not a shirking of responsibility, expecting God to do for us what we should do for ourselves. Nor, on the other hand, is the fulfilling of our responsibility a rejection of Divine Providence, for God provides for us through our own work. "He makes us his cooperators," says Dionysius, "and there is nothing more Godlike than this."[1] Thus, to express trust in Divine Providence by praying for our daily bread is not to deny human dignity; it is not abjectly to claim a helplessness which does not really exist.

Working in Communion with God

To recognize and welcome the fact that God works with us is to work and live in communion with him. The deeper our realization that he and we are working together, the deeper our communion with him in our work. "My Father is working still, and I am

1. *Coel. Hier.,* III.

working" (Jn. 5:17). "We know that in everything God works for good with those who love him" (Rom. 8:28).

A man and his son grow in profound fellowship when they work together. This I have learned by experience. One day when I was a boy, I was working with my father. He asked me to hold something taut for him while he hammered it into place. As he stooped over his work, a chill of fear went through me when I noticed that his dark hair had a broad stripe of gray in it which had not been there the day before. Since I had heard it said that gray hair comes from troubles and worries, I concluded at once that something terrible must have happened to my father since yesterday to make him turn gray overnight. And suddenly, thinking he was in trouble, I realized for the first time how deeply I loved him. (It turned out that the streak of gray was some ashes which had brushed into his hair when he was cleaning out the furnace!)

My father had never said to me in words that he loved me, nor had he ever, as far as I can recall, given me signs of affection which were affection for affection's sake. His way of loving was by *doing* for his family, living for us. And whenever he and I worked together, repairing screens or planting the lawn, it was always more or less silently. He spoke only to tell me what he wanted me to do. And yet, a very deep communion grew up between us as we worked. At the end of a task done together, there was often an unspoken yet deeply shared pride in our work as we surveyed together what we had accomplished.

So, too, God says to his sons: "Son, go and work in the vineyard today" (Matt. 21:28). The son who goes willingly and in the consciousness that God goes with him grows in deep communion with his heavenly Father.

God's Providence and Our Failures

Even when, by not doing our part, we fall short of what God's providence could have accomplished through us, his fatherly love is ever there, ready to work again through us, in a different way, for our good, if only we turn to him and repent our failings. Our failure to fulfill our responsibilities under his providence may have totally changed the course of our life, yet out of the changed situation this providence can set us on a new and successful course. He is ever there, ready to take up again where we have failed, to turn our failure into positive good through our repentant efforts to try again.

Therefore, without hesitation we pray, "Our Father . . . forgive us our trespasses . . . deliver us from the evil we have brought upon ourselves by our sins, from the entangling webs we have woven about our feet." In faith's understanding of our Father, we dare ask him to free us from the harm we have done ourselves, and to lead us to himself by another path when we have hindered his providence by our sins or stupid mistakes.

To pray, "Our Father, give us this day our daily bread," meaning, "Prosper the work of our hands for us, prosper the work of our hands!" (Ps. 89:17,c), is not only a witness to the truth that God works in our work. It also testifies to our personal deficiencies, our shortcomings in wisdom, our limitations in power, our weakness of will.

To pray regularly in this way, testifying to God's presence in our work, is to learn to find God everywhere. It is a humble willingness to have him there, and a joy that he is there sustaining us by his fatherly wisdom and loving power. It is a realization in filial fear that we can fall from him by sin, a firm hope that even if we sin he will be there in his compassionate providence ready to mend through our repentance and renewed labors any harm we may have done. "As a father has compassion on his children, so the Lord has compassion on those who fear him, for he knows how we are formed; he remembers that we are dust" (Ps. 102:13–14,c).

In prayer, our love for him thus meets his love for us. He is the living and merciful Father, ever actively concerned about his children, working to bring them into communion with himself.

Self-righteousness and Self-sufficiency

When Jesus told the parable of the two sons who were asked by their father to work in his vineyard, his intention was to contrast the self-righteous men who fails to enter the kingdom with the repentant sinners who do enter:

A man had two sons; and he went to the first and said, "Son, go and work in the vineyard today." And he answered, "I will not"; but afterward he repented and went. And he went to the second and said the same; and he answered, "I go, sir," but did not go. Which of the two did the will of his father?" They said, "The first." Jesus said to them, "Truly, I say to you, the tax collectors and the harlots go into the kingdom of God before you . . ." (Matt. 21:28–31).

The son who said, "I go, sir," but did not go, represents the same class of people whom Jesus condemned in saying, "Not everyone who says to me, 'Lord, Lord,' shall enter the kingdom of heaven, but he who does the will of my Father who is in heaven" (Matt. 7:21). Jesus had in mind the Pharisees of all times: those of us who are self-righteous, deceiving ourselves into thinking we are very holy, whereas our righteousness is very shallow. "Unless your righteousness exceeds that of the scribes and Pharisees you will never enter the kingdom of heaven" (Matt. 5:20).

The righteousness of the Pharisees was superficial, consisting of a meticulous attention to externals, things which they could do by their own power, while missing the whole point of the kingdom as a gift of God and communion with him. St. Paul calls this Pharisaic righteousness "a righteousness of my own" in contrast with "the righteousness that depends on faith" (Phil. 3:9–10). The Pharisee thought he needed nothing for holiness beyond what he could do by himself, and thereby acted as though he really did not need God for anything; though he continued to pray, "Lord, Lord," and to declare that he was a servant of God: "I go, sir!"

Contemporary man in a different way acts as if all depended upon himself. He sometimes even claims outright that he does not need a God and concentrates on what he can do by his own power, his power as master of the world, a power stupendously increased by his science and technology. But since he concentrates only on what he can do by his own power, and though he uses his power to the full, he builds a superficial and empty world, a world empty of God. Like the Pharisee, but for a different reason, he misses the whole point of the kingdom; he misses God's presence and self-giving.

Jesus, the Workman

He could learn much from Jesus, the workman, if only he would accept Jesus as Son of God.

On one of his visits to his native town, it was asked of Jesus, "Is not this the carpenter, the son of Mary?" (Mk. 6:3). Clearly, Jesus had worked with Joseph, the carpenter, and had learned his trade from him. And since Jesus "was about thirty years of age when he began his ministry" (Lk. 3:23), he must have worked as a carpenter for a dozen or more years in the hidden life at Nazareth.

Any carpenter could have done the work that Jesus did at Nazareth. Why then did Jesus, Son of God, waste his time doing what an ordinary man could have done?

He did not waste his time. He did an ordinary man's work precisely because he himself was truly a man, and a man's work has a real value of its own, whether done by an ordinary man or by the Son of God. But by doing a man's work, the Son of God reveals that there is much more to man's life than his work, his profession, his mastery over all nature and outer space. In his work man is to live as a son of God in communion with his heavenly Father. Jesus saw all his work as his Father's business, not just his later work as preacher of the Gospel, but also his earlier work as carpenter at Nazareth. Even before he took up carpentry, he had said, "Did you not know that I must be about my Father's business?" (Lk. 2:49,c). He carried out his whole life's work in deep communion with his Father in heaven. "My Father is working still, and I am working" (Jn. 5:17).

As a young man, then, Jesus worked for his living; he toiled for what he ate and drank and for what he put on. And yet he could say to all of us: "Do not be anxious about your life, what you shall eat or what you shall drink, nor about your body, what you shall put on. . . . Seek first the kingdom of your heavenly Father and his righteousness, and all these things shall be yours as well" (Matt. 6:25,33). The all-important thing is communion with the Father. One who works with the Father and realizes that the Father works with him, will have all these other things through his work; "your heavenly Father knows that you need them all" (6:32).

Work's Intrinsic Value

To say that there is more to a man's life than his work is not to say that the work is not important. In the drudgery and monotony and seeming fruitlessness of our labors we used to assure ourselves that none of this toil is in vain, for Jesus, too, had toiled, giving value to whatever we do in union with him. We seemed to speak as if the value of the work came only from the fact that the Son of God had been a worker, and as if otherwise it would have had no value. But lately we have learned to put it the other way around: the work of man is valuable in itself; and, therefore, because he was a man Jesus did the work of man. He showed every man how to sanctify his work and free it from the evils of sin. And he taught us to abide in him as we do our work, so that whatever we do may have a divine and eternal, as well as a human and temporal, value, inasmuch as it is the expression and deepening of our love and communion with the Father. God worked with man in the person of his Son working on earth with men to convince all men that he works with them and they with him.

Man's work is valuable in itself because in his work he develops his personality and grows to maturity even while developing God's creation as God's coworker. His work is valuable because by it he serves his fellowmen and deepens his interpersonal relationships with them, and thus perfects his humanity. Jesus, too, in doing his human work grew in a human way, developing his humanity, serving his fellowmen in love by working for those who came to him in need of his carpenter's skills. How else could he have been truly man, if not by growing to maturity in a human way, rendering such services of love to his fellowmen, growing personally in doing them, readying himself for his fuller ministry of salvation? Any man's work is valuable because it is his way of living as son of God in love's relationships with his fellowmen, using the riches of the earth in serving his own needs and theirs. When he works in communion with God, realizing that God works in his work, then he finds it easier to live and work in brotherhood with his fellow-workers.

Contemplative Insight in Our Work

As a boy, working with my earthly father, I had no difficulty in being conscious of his presence, because he was fully obvious to my senses. I could see his tall body moving about as we raked the lawn; I could hear his breathing alongside me as we pushed the heavy lawn-roller together; I could understand his occasional instructions; I was in total sympathy with his pride in his home and garden. So my communion with him could steadily deepen as we worked with one mind and heart.

But because God is transcendent even though he is immanent in every activity, he eludes our senses and our understanding and easily slips from our direct consciousness. Therefore we must frequently pray, "Give us this day our daily bread," to remind ourselves that he is present with us and works in our work, and that all the fruits of our labors, as well as our power and will to work, are the gifts of his love.

If we take care to foster faith's contemplative insight into all these truths, we will go into the vineyard each day willingly, and we will deepen our communion with God while we work. To work in the way men ought to work, to work in the way Jesus worked, always being about the Father's business, requires that we be contemplative at least in a minimum degree, focusing the attention of our faith's insight upon this true meaning of our tasks in the world. "Give us this day our daily bread by working in our work, giving us the fruit of our labors."

To pray thus is as much a thanksgiving as a petition. We recognize that not only the fruits of our work and the materials with which we work, but also our very ability and will to work are a gift and privilege from our Father in heaven.

Joy in What God Is

Prayer of petition is ridiculed nowadays as being some kind of magic by which we attempt to force a God to be at our service, doing for us what we cannot do for ourselves, or even the things we should be doing for ourselves.

That is not the way a Christian prays. Just as a child soon learns to love his good parents more than their good gifts to him, and all the more so when it is clear that their gifts flow from true love for him, so the Christian who says, "Our Father, give us this day our daily bread," soon learns to love the good God far more than his gifts. More and more his prayer witnesses to God's personal value as Father and Friend, lovable for what he is as person more than for what he does for us.

Some contemporary writers are insisting that God's revelation concerns only *what God is for us,* not what he is in himself. He reveals himself only in his action on our behalf, and we should be concerned about this, not about the qualities of his inner life. However, just as the child learns from his father's gifts to him and especially from what his father does for him that the father himself is good and lovable and should be loved more than his gifts or his actions, so from the contemplation of God's creative and salvific action man comes to know God's own inner goodness and his very nature as love, his personality as Father and Friend. Because God so loved the world that he gave his only Son, because he revealed himself in this giving, St. John came to the conclusion that God *is* love, and not merely *does* love.

And thus the Christian learns to rejoice not just in what God is for us, but even more in what God is in himself, just as a wife rightly rejoices more in the lovable person of her husband than in what he has done for her in love. She is happy because he is happy; she rejoices because he is what he is.

Yes, we rejoice in what God does for us. We rejoice that in some way he has revealed himself in his action on our behalf, but we rejoice even more that he is what he is. We rejoice because God is God. Joy that he is what he is, of course, is inseparable from joy that he has revealed to us what he is, or who he is. For, if he had not revealed himself, we could not rejoice in the wonders of his person. Our joy is the joy of communion with him in love and mutual self-giving.

Yes, he reveals what he is for us by his action on our behalf, but the supreme action on our behalf, the supreme thing he does for us is to reveal his very self in the very giving of himself to us to be possessed, so that in him personally we may have our joy, and not merely in his other gifts to us. In possessing him, in experiencing what he really is, we rejoice that God is joyous in the possession of his own lovable perfections which "make" him what he is. Only love can know what it means to rejoice that the beloved is what he is.

We shall continue, then, to pray, "Give us this day our daily bread," for in receiving the gifts of our good Father we shall learn to love him more than his gifts, more than what he does for us. We shall love him because he is lovable. We shall rejoice in his joy.

Mastery of the World and Leisure
for Contemplation

The day will come, Feuerbach and Marx tried to tell us (and the atheistic humanists of today agree with them) when man will be able to do everything for himself by his science and technology. Therefore, he will no longer need a God. Religion will disappear; prayer will be unnecessary.

It may be true that when man can do more for himself than ever before, he will need to put less effort into prayer of petition for things. But for that very reason he should also be in a better position than ever for the fullness of contemplative prayer. Undistracted by worry over life's necessities, he should be freer for the sheer happiness of being in the presence of the Father he loves. Instead of allowing prayer to disappear from his life, he should be able to engage in a deeper sort of prayer than petition for the necessities of this earthly life, the prayer in which he experiences and enjoys God himself and rejoices that he is what he is.

Unfortunately, it does not seem to work out that way. Why has man's increasing mastery over the world turned him to forgetfulness of God, or even to the denial of his existence? Is it because in his newfound power he thinks that he himself is God? Does he think that he is self-sufficient?

As much as ever before, man will always need to ask for his daily bread, lest he forget to love the Father who has given him the use of all creation and the fruits of their use. Through this petition which is also a thanksgiving, he must ever acknowledge the source of all he is and has, lest he forget that there is Someone more lovable than all he is and has.

Proverbs hits the nail right on the head:

> ... give me neither poverty nor riches;
>   Feed me with the food that is needful for me,
> Lest I be full and deny thee,

and say, "Who is the Lord?"
lest I be poor, and steal,
and profane the name of my God (Prov. 30:8–9).

Since our memories are so short, since in our self-sufficiency and mastery of the world we so easily forget God, the merciful God has to remind us of himself in the hard way—through the blessed gift of hardships and suffering. If he takes away some of his gifts to us so that we experience our helplessness again, we may once again become aware of him and his goodness. The way to communion with God will always be the way of the cross of Jesus.

19

The Apostolate
of Contemplation

God can be contemplated only to the extent that he chooses to reveal and communicate himself to men. This he does fully only in his Son: "In many and various ways God spoke of old to our fathers by the prophets; but in these last days he has spoken to us by a Son, whom he appointed the heir of all things, through whom also he created the world" (Heb. 1:1–2). Therefore, the Christian contemplates above all Christ, the Incarnate Word, especially in his paschal mystery.

However, the mystery of Christ finds its full meaning only in fulfilling the needs of men, since it was "for us men and for our salvation" that he came down from heaven. Therefore, in the light of Christ we must contemplate also the life of our times. This life does not have its full meaning except in the glory of the risen Lord, just as the mystery of salvation does not have its full meaning except in confronting the needs of men. We have not rightly contemplated the mystery of Christ till we have seen the salvation it contains for the men of our times and have become involved in the mystery of bringing it into contemporary life. Like the men of every era, we in our times are part of the paschal mystery which must be accomplished in the people of today as in the peoples of every other time and place. The life of our times must enter into the very texture of our contemplation.

In Jesus, who has been exalted as Lord of Glory because of his paschal obedience, we can find all the answers to the search for meaning which so plagues modern man:

In the face of the modern development of the world, the number constantly swells of the people who raise the most basic questions or recognize them with a new sharpness: What is man? What is the meaning of sorrow, of evil, of death, which continue to exist despite so much progress? For what purpose are those victories won at so high a price? What can man offer to society, what can he expect from it? What follows this earthly life? (*GS* 10).

Indeed, only in the mystery of the Incarnate Word is the mystery of man clarified. . . . In revealing the mystery of the Father and his love, Christ the Lord, the New Adam, fully reveals man to man himself, and makes his sublime calling clear (*GS* 22).

The Contemplative Role of the Church

Therefore, we must contemplate Christ precisely in his relationship to the world of today. We must not look upon the paschal mystery merely as something accomplished in the past. We must not stand back and gaze upon it as a beautiful tableau which is already completed. Rather, we must contemplate the mystery of salvation here and now at work among us. We must learn exactly how Christ is the answer to the needs of modern man, and how he gives authentic meaning to contemporary life. Moved by faith, the people of God "strive to discern the true signs of the presence and purpose of God in the events, the needs and the hopes which they share with the other men of our times. For faith illumines all things with a new light and manifests God's design for the integral vocation of man" (*GS* 11).

Repeatedly Vatican II speaks of this role of the Church in modern man's search for meaning. Christians not only have the obligation "to work with all men in the building of a more human world," but the mystery of the Christian faith stimulates them "to uncover the full meaning of this activity so that human culture may obtain its eminent place in the integral vocation of man" (*GS*

57). By casting over the whole earth "the reflected light of the divine life which she communicates to men, the Church . . . imbues the everyday activity of man with a deeper meaning and importance" (*GS* 40). By revealing the mystery of God who is the ultimate end of man, "she opens up to man at the same time the meaning of his own existence, the innermost truth about men" (*GS* 41).

"In revealing the mystery of the Father and his love, Christ fully reveals man to man himself": he shows that man's integral vocation is to be "a son in the Son," in communion with the Father (*GS* 22).

If all this has been already revealed, why do we say that it is the contemplative task of the Church to *search* with contemporary man for the meaning of life?

Because the general revelation of the mystery of Christ must be made specific for our times. How does a son of God live in our rapidly changing world? How does he act in the scientific age? How does he adapt his life in the Spirit so that it will thrive in the midst of the modern world? What is the meaning of cultural progress in deepening our divine sonship? How does man solve the special problems engendered by modern progress, problems which tend to obscure the authentic meaning of life?

For though Christ has revealed the mystery of God's love in which he adopts us as sons, God, and man's life with God, are still a mystery. This mystery must be contemplated anew by each man and by each community of men so that man's fellowship with the Father and with Christ his Son may be embodied anew in the life and culture of every time and place.

Moreover, the mystery of our call to divine sonship is always inseparable from the mystery of suffering, and the mystery of iniquity. And our faith in the Fatherhood of God is ever being put to the test. In our day perhaps more acutely than ever the Son of God is challenged by the taunt: "Where is your God?" (Ps. 42:10). "He styles himself a child of the Lord. . . . He boasts that God is his Father. Let us see whether his words be true. . . . Let us condemn him to a shameful death; for according to his own words, God will take care of him" (Wis. 2:13–20). What is the meaning of modern progress which seems to bring only troubles in its train: the destructiveness of modern warfare, the deepening misery of the masses which seems to accompany the increasing wealth of mankind, etc.? Is God telling us something in all of this?

Contemplation today is as much a search for meaning as it was in the days of the Old Testament prophets. Frequently the prophets received the word of God in response to their questioning of God concerning the problems of their times. Habakkuk, for example, is especially insistent in quizzing God for an explanation of his treating his chosen people in a way which seems contrary to his promises.

We, too, must search for the meaning of the troubles and the hopes of our times. The pondering of human problems in the presence of God eventually wins the necessary insight for their solution. The search for meaning is a contemplative process which seeks to discern, in the light of the Spirit, the signs of God's presence and purpose in the situation at hand. St. Dominic, in his concern over the disorders of his times which were causing the loss of Christians and the destruction of Christian society, would cry out in anguish in his prayer vigils, "What is to become of the sinners?" At the same time, in his daily action he would meet the problem in the best way he could. Gradually the divine answer to the problem, insight into God's purpose in the situation, matured in Dominic's mind and action, culminating in his founding of the Order of Preachers.

It has always been so with the great saints. The Christian contemplative does not seek to hide himself in God from the reality of the world's troubles in the way that the proverbial ostrich hides his head in the sand. The inner peace of the true contemplative is not an escape from reality. It is a discovery of a more profound reality, "the peace of God which surpasses all understanding" (Phil. 4:7), just as Jesus found peace and serenity in his agony by contemplating and embracing the salvific will of the Father.

Even apart from the problem of suffering and evil in the modern world, there is the sapiential task of directing human progress into the right channels. This is one of the truly acute problems of the times. Man, we have seen, does not have an innate wisdom like the instinct of animals. He must persistently seek the meaning of his situation and his activities.

His basic wisdom, however, is Christ Jesus, "who has become for us God-given wisdom" (1 Cor. 1:30,c), Christ, who alone fully reveals man to man.

The contemplative or sapiential task in practical daily life, then, is to trace the pattern of Christ into the life of our times. Human life today is changing with dizzying rapidity. The contemplative mission of the Church is to "scrutinize the signs of the times and interpret them in the light of the Gospel" (*GS* 4). This task can be accomplished only in the light of the Holy Spirit. "It is through the gift of the Holy Spirit that man comes in faith to the contemplation and appreciation of the mystery of the divine plan" (*GS* 15). "God who spoke of old ceaselessly converses with the bride of his beloved Son, and the Holy Spirit through whom the living voice of the Gospel resounds in the Church and through her in the world leads into all the truth those who believe, and makes the word of God dwell in them abundantly" (*DV* 8).

Therefore, the Christian must be ever listening to God in openness to the Spirit. Modern life and progress must be directed in the light of the word of God. Faith seeking understanding of the word of God, we said, is a contemplative process. Faith is not merely the acceptance of divine revelation as true in itself. Faith is fruitless unless in the light of this revelation it seeks understanding of the totality of life and directs all of life by this light. Faith tries to understand not just the totality of each man's personal life, but the total life and culture of all mankind.

The word of God in the Scriptures, in tradition, in the living magisterium of the Church, is no finished blueprint showing to the last detail what man must do. God's word fully respects man's autonomy and freedom; it does not revoke or contradict the creative dominion over the world which God has given to man. But it does direct the use of that dominion according to the ultimate purposes of God.

Therefore, the word of God passes judgment on how man uses his freedom and dominion. Consequently, man must contemplate not just the word of God, but, in the light of that word, the totality of his personal life and the life and culture of his times so that he may direct this life in a positive way according to that word.

Precisely because the word of God is not a detailed blueprint, but gives full freedom to man's creative action in developing the world and in building human culture, contemplation must be an ever-continuing process, a continuing search for divine meaning, a search made by the people of God in cooperation with their contemporaries. The word of God must be brought to bear upon the totality of human life as a critical judgment upon it to see whether or not that life measures true to God's invitations to man to live as his sons. The prophetic role of Christians is to make this judgment upon contemporary life in the light of the word of God, and by their lives and by their speech and action influence their fellowmen to correct and direct their personal lives and the life of the times according to that word. Obviously, this prophetic role is a contemplative function, for it can be carried out only in faith seeking and finding understanding.

For throwing light on the totality of life, Christian contemplation is eminently practical. It is no mere gazing on past history, on Christ's earthly life, death and resurrection; it is a bringing of that mystery into our life today, a directing of our life toward the eschatological hope, to the building up of the Body of Christ in love (Eph. 4:16). The Mystical Body, "the whole Christ," will have grown "to mature manhood, to the measure of the stature of the fullness of Christ" (Eph. 4:13), when mankind and all of human life has been rebuilt in the power of the Holy Spirit according to the pattern of Christ, the image of the Maker. The contemplative task is to guide mankind in putting on "the new self which will progress toward true knowledge the more it is renewed in the image of its Creator" (Col. 3:10,j), the knowledge of "the love of Christ which surpasses knowledge" (Eph. 3:19), the experience of that love in God's self-revelation through his gift of self, "that you may be filled with all the fullness of God."

Contemplation: Openness to All Reality

It is clear, then, that Christian contemplation is an openness to all reality, for the Christian must be involved in the task of "uniting all things in Christ, things in heaven and things on earth" (Eph. 1:10), "that God may be all in all" (1 Cor. 15:28).

For, we said, the mystery of Christ is meaningful only when it is seen as the mystery of the salvation of all men in the totality of their world. And the world and man's life are meaningful only in the light of Christ, the Lord of Glory, the authentic man exalted to lordship over all things because of his filial obedience to the Father. Jesus is Lord over the totality of the cosmos. "He is the image of the invisible God . . . all things were created through him and for him. . . . For in him all the fullness of God was pleased to dwell and through him to reconcile to himself all things, whether on earth or in heaven, making peace by the blood of his cross" (Col. 1:15–20).

But, says Hebrews, "as it is, we do not yet see everything in subjection to him" (Heb. 2:8). Though by divine right as Son of God all things are his, and though his exaltation to the right hand of the Father because of his filial obedience shows that as man he has earned the right to be Lord over all, his rights have not yet been acknowledged by all men. His reign in their hearts and, therefore, in the cosmos has not yet been effectively established in full.

Therefore, the contemplative search for the meaning of all things and especially of human life is the search to discover how to bring Christ into all things, how to bring everything under his headship so that God may be all in all. Christian contemplation is thus an openness to all reality. It is not so much a searching to *find* God in all things. It is a seeking to *bring* him into everything in the way he wills to be there, for he wills to be there in a fuller way than merely as Creator upholding all things and governing them. The key to this fuller presence of God in his creation is his presence in the hearts and lives of men. The task of restoring all things in Christ is fundamentally the task of bringing all men into the mystery of Christ's sonship. The mystery of Christ, Son of God, must be made incarnate in all men, so that all may live and act as sons of God in every life situation, in the life and culture of the times, and in directing the whole course of their lives and cultural development according to the design of God.

Contemplation: Openness to the Reality of the Father and His Love

Like Jesus, the contemplative in every situation of life will look to the Father to detect his will, and he will discern his presence and purpose in all the events of life. After contemplating and understanding the divine plan in faith through the gift of the Holy Spirit (*GS* 15), he will direct his involvement in life accordingly.

The root and determinant of the nature of Christ's own involvement in human life and in each situation he encountered was always his relationship with his Father, his total consecration to him in love, his openness to the purposes of his love. The search for meaning is as simple as that. How does a son of God act in such and such a situation? What is the overall plan of God for his sons?

The purpose of God is to make all men his children in Christ. "He destined us in love to be his sons through Jesus Christ, according to the purpose of his will, to the praise of his glorious grace which he freely bestowed on us in the Beloved" (Eph. 1:5–6). He proposes to grant these sons a share in Christ's own mission to bring all men to the Father, a share in bringing his saving action into all of human life (Eph. 1:10,11).

The contemplation of the signs of the times and the events and needs and hopes which we share with our fellowmen to discern in them God's presence and purpose is, therefore, a seeking to discover what action we must take in order to continue Christ's own saving action; what steps we must take to advance the kingdom of God in the human kingdom. It is a seeking to lay hold of God's saving power to put it to work in our own creative action in building the world according to his will, a more human world which will be a worthy dwelling place for the sons of God, a world which will be more receptive to the grace of God's word calling all men to this divine sonship.

Since the overall purpose of God is the adoption of men as his sons in Christ, Christian contemplation in seeking the meaning of life is above all openness to the reality of God-with-us, "the mystery of the Father and his love" revealed and present in the Son of God (*GS* 22). Jesus, we said, contemplated all reality in that light. He saw all men as destined to be sons with him and to see the face of the Father in heaven, and he saw all else as the gift of the Father to his children.

Contemplation: Openness to our Fellowmen

Our grace of sonship, our self-understanding as sons of God, is not lived in a vacuum. It is lived in the Church and in the world in the brotherhood of men. Jesus, we have seen, had to find the meaning of his incarnate Sonship in terms of his mission in the world. He had to look repeatedly to discover his Father's will for him as manifested in the situation of the moment, in the needs of his contemporaries, in the Scriptures, and so on. So, too, our contemplative search is ever asking: What does it mean for man to be a son of God? Always each man has to be a son of God *in his humanity,* which means in his human society, in the fellowship of men, in his own times.

In the contemplative light of faith we must ever see ourselves as children of God in whom the compassionate love and mercy of the Father are revealed to all men. "You are the light of the World. . . . Let your light so shine before men, that they may see your good works and give glory to your Father who is in heaven" (Matt.

5:15,16). Jesus makes it clear, in subsequent verses of the Sermon on the Mount, what type of "good works" manifest our Father in heaven: all the works of righteousness which he outlines, but especially the works of love and compassion:

> But I say to you, Love your enemies and pray for those who persecute you, so that you may be sons of your Father who is in heaven; for he makes his sun rise on the evil and on the good, and sends rain on the just and on the unjust. For if you love those who love you, what reward have you? Do not even the Gentiles do the same? You, therefore, must be perfect, as your heavenly Father is perfect (Matt. 5: 43–48).

Our continuing openness to our fellowmen, our living awareness of them in faith as actual or potential children of God, our deep reverence for them as God's image and glory, are elements in the so-called "horizontal prayer." We can call this relationship with our fellowmen "prayer" to the extent that it is really a response in faith to God's self-revelation. He manifests himself to our faith in the person of our fellowman, and the "horizontal prayer" is our loving response to him in the gift of self to neighbor, in the Christian manner called for by the situation.

The ability to see each fellowman in vivid faith as beloved by God, and reacting to him as God would act toward him, is what we have called active contemplation or contemplative action, since both contemplation and action are elements of it. Even the direct contemplation of God, of course, is active, in the sense that it results in a deep reaction to God, deeply involving us in God's own interior life. Infused contemplation is itself a participation in God's own inner light and love, bringing us into this light and love which is his very life.

The Apostolate of Christian Contemplation

When we see and deeply experience the Father and his love for us; when we are ever vividly alive to our fellowmen and their needs, then we will see everything else in the right light. We will see all creation and everything in it as the Father's gift to his children to be used only for the benefit of his children. Then alone does man's God-given dominion over the cosmos have its true meaning and purpose. Man has true dominion over the cosmos only when as son of God he uses it in the service of the brotherhood of mankind. Only then are all things restored in Christ; only then is "everything in subjection to him" (Heb. 2:8). When Christ reigns in the hearts of men; when they are sons of God in him and use all things according to his will in making the world more human, then his reign effectively extends to the whole cosmos.

To see all reality in this way presupposes that we see God as the Father of all and all men as his children. It is the apostolate of Christian contemplation to bring all mankind into this "light of the world." Truly, the prophetic role of the Christian in the world is a contemplative task. The witness he gives by meeting every situation and solving every problem in the light of faith, requires that he be deeply immersed in the light, Christ, who wills to enlighten every man. In total openness to the Father, such a Christian always acts as a son of God in whatever he does in his relationships with his fellowmen and in his use of God's creation. Thus "he makes God the Father and his Son present and in a sense visible. This he achieves chiefly by the witness of a living and mature faith, namely, one trained to see difficulties clearly and to master them" (*GS* 21).

Truly, Christian contemplation and Christian action are but two different elements in the awareness of the presence of God and response to him. When I accurately discern God's presence and purpose in "the signs of the times" and surrender myself to his saving action in total availability, carrying out the appropriate action in which he continues his work through me, my contemplation is bearing its fruits. Then my faith and understanding and gift of knowledge are not sterile because in the Spirit of counsel I carry out my mission as son of God in the world of men.

Contemplation and mission are both rooted in Baptism. What we have just been saying makes it clear that the fruitfulness of Baptism in the fulfillment of mission presupposes the fullness of contemplation.

20
Building a World Open to God's Self-revelation

It is true that Christian contemplation requires openness to all reality. It is true also that Christians have always contemplated God as revealed in his saving action, as did the people of Israel before them. It is true that to discern God's presence and purpose in the signs of the times is to see his saving action continuing in the world today. It is true, moreover, that we see God as somehow manifest in our neighbor and that we somehow experience him in our relationships with our fellowmen in Christian love. All of these are elements in Christian contemplation.

But that is not all there is to it. No one of these elements, nor all of them together can substitute for the direct contemplation or experience of God himself.

God's creative action in the world and his saving action in his people are, indeed, signs of his presence. But signs always point to a deeper reality. We are invited by the signs to open ourselves to receive the direct gift of the reality in the graces of infused contemplation, the quasi experience of the very being of the Divine Persons. The lover of God cannot be content to see God only in the *signs* of his presence.

The lover of God is like a man returning home from work toward evening and finding signs of his wife's loving presence wherever he looks. As he walks up the path to the front door, he notices that she has weeded the flower garden, and the neatness of the yard is like her smile of welcome home. She has polished the brass plate on the door engraved with his name, so that it seems to beam forth her pride in him. As he opens the door, the delightful aroma of her cooking rushes to greet his nostrils, and he is embraced by the warmth and cheer of the homey atmosphere she has created in the house. The living room is swept and dusted; his pipes and tobacco are laid out on the little table beside his chair. Everything speaks to him of the love and devotion of the woman he loves.

But he is not content just to contemplate the signs of her love. It is not enough for him to know that she was there all day and that she is still somewhere in the house preparing something else to please him. Nor is he content to contemplate her likeness in the faces and actions of their children who crowd around him. The many signs of her love only make him the more avid to see her face-to-face and to embrace her very person, and to give himself to her in a return of love.

But he awaits her good pleasure. With faith in her love for him, he patiently watches for her to appear. For love is never demanding. It ever respects the person of the beloved and never forces itself upon her. It knows how to wait until she gives her love. Love given in answer to a demand is not really love. True love is given freely and spontaneously.

So, too, we cannot be content to contemplate only the signs of God's love, though these are present wherever we look. And we cannot be satisfied just to see God in our fellowmen, his children who are his image and likeness. We ardently desire to see him in his own person.

But we await his good pleasure. Though we cannot experience his love and presence every time we would like to, our faith in his love for us remains unshaken, and we are willing to wait for him. For only when he sees fit does the divine Lover reveal himself in his gifts of infused contemplation that we might deeply experience his love and presence. Only when he sees that our hearts are adequately prepared for such an experience; only when he knows that we are strong enough to bear the all-consuming fire of his love; only when we are open to him in loving surrender and thus capable of receiving his self-giving does he reveal himself.

Yes, God is somehow revealed in his action in the world. But his work in his creation is only a witness pointing to a possible deeper knowledge of him. He made men "that they should seek God, in the hope that they might feel after him and find him. . . . He did not leave himself without witness, for he did good and gave you rains and fruitful seasons, satisfying your hearts with food and gladness" (Acts 17:27; 14:17).

Likewise, God was somehow manifest in his salvation action in the history of Israel. Each salvation event was the sign that he was with his people, the sign that the "hidden God" (Isa. 45:15) was really there in his powerful but unseen presence. His very name, Yahweh, means, "He who is there to save." But those who loved him were never content merely with these signs of his presence. "Do let me see your glory!" cried Moses in his eagerness to see God face-to-face.

All the signs of God point to God himself, and all his saving action leads toward his supreme action of self-revelation and self-giving in the hearts of those who love him.

Even the revelation of God in Jesus his Son, even his presence in the salvation action of the death and resurrection of Jesus, are but the preparation for his interior spiritual manifestation of himself to those who keep his commandments: "In that day you will know that I am in my Father, and you in me and I in you. . . . He who loves me will be loved by my Father, and I will love and manifest myself to him. . . . We will come to him and make our home with him" (Jn. 14:20,21,23).

Only when one experiences God's presence in one's very person is his salvation action experienced as action for one's personal salvation. Only this personal experience of God gives meaning to all else that God does in his creative and saving action in the world and in his Church.

Obviously, we have been using the word "contemplation" analogically, in saying that we contemplate God in all reality in his action in his creation, in his redemptive action in the death and resurrection of his Son, in his presence in our fellowmen, in his action in the signs of the times, and in his intimate personal self-revelation in the gifts of infused contemplation. The word "contemplation" does not mean exactly the same thing in each of these applications of the word. In Christian usage, the word has come to mean especially *infused* contemplation in which God himself is experienced directly.

We are justified, however, in applying the word to all the other ways of seeing God to the extent that they are elements in a complex process. Christian contemplation must include all these elements, though not necessarily simultaneously. For the other elements are a preparation for a direct personal experience of God in the interior grace of infused contemplation. Moreover, these interior graces can be fully appreciated and interpreted only in the context of the other signs of God's presence, action and purpose. All these signs are meaningless without the interior grace of faith and its ever-deepening insight through the gifts of wisdom, understanding and knowledge. We must not stop at the lesser elements in the contemplative process under the delusion that we can fully find God in them. For example, though a man can somehow experience God in his Christian love for his wife, if that experience is authentic it will impel him to find a more direct and profound experience of God in explicit prayer. We shall return to this idea in a later chapter.

The very etymology of the word "contemplation" with its derivation from pagan sources, and the increasing depth of meaning it acquired through the Christian experience illustrates our point. The word comes from *com* plus *templum,* a space marked out for the observation of auguries, probably akin to *tempus,* time. In its earliest meaning, the word meant "to study an augury" to discover the fitting time or manner of action. Thus, contemplation was ever a search for the meaning of life.

The Christian, of course, in his search for meaning, finds all the answers in God and Christ, the Alpha and the Omega. All the auguries, all the signs of God's presence and purpose point to God himself as the ultimate meaning of everything. Only in God's personal self-revelation to him does the human person find his fulfillment, and Christian experience knows that this self-revelation is given in what is known as infused contemplation. In its original meaning, then, contemplation was the study of the signs of the divine will in auguries. The Christian, however, is led from the scrutiny of the signs of God to the direct contemplation of God himself.

And if "temple" originally meant the space marked out for the observation of auguries, it came to mean a place for the worship of God. For Christians, however, the temple is the people of God and the individual persons who are that people; for God dwells in them: "You are . . . built upon the foundation of the apostles and prophets, Christ himself being the cornerstone, in whom the whole structure is joined together and grows into a holy temple in the Lord; in whom you also are built into it for a dwelling place of God in the Spirit" (Eph. 2:21–22).

All of God's creating and saving action has but one purpose: to build his people as the temple of his personal presence. We must not be content to observe him in his action of preparing his temple. We must *be* his temple, welcoming his self-revelation in our hearts. That is why we said that contemplation is not so much a searching to find God in all things, but a seeking to bring him into the world in the way he wills to be there. And he wills to be in the hearts of all men, in their knowledge and love as in a living temple.

Thus, too, all of God's saving action in and through his Church has this one same purpose: to make his people the living temple of his presence. This is the purpose of the liturgy from which all other activity of the Church springs and to which all other activity leads (*SC* 10). All the Church's action "is ordered to contemplation and is subordinate to it. . . . The liturgy is daily building up those within the Church into a holy temple in the Lord, a dwelling place of God in the Spirit" (*SC* 2).

More than that, the Church sees its task in the world as the building of a temple for God, the building of a world open to God's self-revelation. "Man was not made just to master the world," says Bernard Haring, "but to receive God into his world."[1] Hence Vatican II declares: "The Church calls for the effective liberty of believers, that they might build up even in this world the temple of God" (*GS* 21) wherein man can live his vocation to communion with God.

The mission of the laity in the world, too, declares the Council, is to make the world more human (*GS* 26, 57) and more receptive to the word of God (*LG* 36), the word by which men are begotten as children of God and called to communion with their Father. In making the world more human, they make it a more suitable environment for the growth of God's children to divine maturity (*GS* 21, 38).

The world order must not be self-sufficient and closed in upon itself. The human fellowship in Christian love is not merely *patterned* upon the unity of the three Divine Persons in the Holy Trinity. It is a union in the very life of that Trinity. The word of God is proclaimed, says St. John, "so that you may have fellowship with us; and our fellowship is with the Father and with his Son Jesus Christ" (1 Jn. 1:3).

All of human life must, therefore, be structured in openness to the Father in his Son. Christian openness to the world and to our fellowmen is not an abandoning of the contemplation of God for the sake of presence with fellowmen; it is rather a bringing of this contemplation to all mankind, drawing all our fellowmen into our own communion with the Father and his Son Jesus Christ.

Such is the Church's apostolate of contemplation: to build a whole world which is open to God and his personal self-revelation.

Thus, contemplation is even more deeply rooted in Baptism than is mission to one's fellowmen; for the very mission has as its goal the bringing of our fellowman, too, into the contemplation of God.

1. *Renewal Through Theology,* a series of tape-recorded lectures (Chicago: Argus Communications, 1966), lecture 1.

Rather, the goal is to call him to God that he might receive the ever fuller enlightenment from the divine presence. All preaching of the word, for example, has as its purpose the calling forth of the response in faith in which one is open to God to receive his light and love. And everyone's Bapitsm in which he professes his faith has its ultimate fullness in the contemplative possession of God in the light and love of glory.

21

Imaging God to Others in Family Life and in Celibacy

"Since Christ is the Light of the Nations, this Sacred Council . . . ardently desires that all men be illumined by his glory shining on the face of the Church" (*LG* 1). Contemplating the glory of God shining on the face of Christ (2 Cor. 4:6), the people of God are being transformed from one degree of glory to another into his own likeness, and so themselves become the image and glory of God. They become a presence of God to their fellowmen, a revelation of the Father. They fulfill the apostolate of contemplation, the contemplative mission to bring others to contemplate the Father.

"Show us the Father!" is the implicit cry of every human heart. In Christ and his Church, the face of God is turned toward them, responding to the cry which he himself built into every heart, speaking his Word of invitation to divine sonship, inviting them to turn to him in the Sonship of Jesus.

The Church is truly a real presence of Christ and God. "Fervent in action and at leisure for contemplation . . ." says Vatican II, the Church is daily being built "into a temple holy in the Lord, a dwelling place for God in the Spirit . . . and shines as a sign lifted up for the nations, under which the scattered children of God are gathered together into one" (*SC* 2). As temple of the living God, the People of God are truly a presence and manifestation of him to their fellowmen. "For it is the function of the Church, led by the Holy Spirit who renews and purifies her ceaselessly, to make God the Father and his incarnate Son present and in a sense visible" (*GS* 21).

The people of God as a whole must fulfill this mission, but can succeed in doing so only to the extent that the various individuals and groups who are the people are truly sons and image, each in keeping with his own specific vocation in the people. And always, no matter which secondary characteristic of Christ they live and show forth, all must first of all be like Christ in what is most basic in his personality. Each Christian must become like Jesus, not in any superficial way, but in that which is most profound in his existence.

No one can become his true personality except in relationship with others. No one can become truly an "I" except in relationship with others whom he can call "thou." By his very nature as social being, man can be fully himself only when he is a presence to others, only when he is in communion with them in an exchange of knowledge and love.

This is not at all surprising, for that is how it is within the Holy Trinity in whose image and likeness mankind is made. The three Divine Persons are personalities precisely because of their relationships with one another. Each of the three is distinctive, unique, only by reason of his distinctive relationship with the other Persons.

Christ's Deepest Personality

The Son is his true self only in his relationship of love with the Father. His name, "the Son," expresses what is most profound in his personality, and it expresses precisely what makes him the person he is. As Son, he has an entirely personal relationship with the Father. The whole dynamic quality of his personality is expressed in his cry of love, "Father," in response to the Father's cry, "You are my Son, today I have begotten you" (Ps. 2:7).

Contemplating the glory which is his as only Son of the Father, beholding him in his filial relationship with the Father, we "are being changed into his likeness from one degree of glory to another" (2 Cor. 3:18). All of us have to be sons, completely open to the Father, turned to him in filial obedience, in self-offering with Jesus.

To the extent that we are sons of God in reality, in Christ's relationship to the Father, to that extent we, too, will be the image and glory of God, showing him forth and making him present to our fellowmen.

Let us consider some specific ways in the Church of being son of God and image.

Parents, Image of God to Their Children

Our blessed Lord suggests that even in the natural order earthly fathers are images of the heavenly Father for their children: "What father among you, if his son asks for a fish, will instead of a fish give him a serpent; or if he asks for an egg, will give him a scorpion? If you then who are evil know how to give good gifts to your children, how much more will the heavenly Father give the Holy Spirit to those who ask him" (Lk. 11:11–13).

But, if in addition to being naturally good to their children, earthly fathers are themselves true sons of God in Christ participating in the divine life, how much more fully will they be images of God for their children and wives, drawing them to a deeper love of God? To the extent that they themselves are obedient to the will of God they will be image and presence of the obedient Christ, inspiring his sonship in their children.

If in earthly fathers we are to see the heavenly Father, in woman we are to see God as mother. The motherly qualities of God, reproduced in woman his image and likeness, are indicated by the prophet Isaiah: "Can a woman forget her sucking child, that she should have no compassion on the son of her womb? Even these may forget, yet I will not forget you" (Isa. 49:15). A child who has experienced the tender, patient, nourishing, unselfish love of a good mother will be able to understand the compassionate, gentle, undying love of God.

Saints, such as St. Catherine of Siena, in their personal relationships with the Holy Spirit experienced him precisely as the clemency of God, the compassionate gift of divine forgiveness, the God of "kindness and forbearance and patience" (Rom. 2:4) who knows how to bring out the best that is in weak man, not with wrath and arbitrary commands, but by motherly gentleness combined with paternal firmness. Catherine experienced the Father as upholding power, the Son as wisdom, the Holy Spirit as the clemency of love.[1]

Obedience to parents is obedience to the Lord. Parents who truly image the firmness and gentleness of God to their children will win their children's obedience to themselves and to God. "Children, obey your parents in the Lord, for this is right" (Eph. 6:1). Fathers, be firm but just and compassionate: "Fathers, do not provoke your children to anger (lest they become discouraged (Col. 3:21), but bring them up in the discipline and instruction of the Lord" (Eph. 5:4).

Husband and Wife, Image of God for One Another

St. Paul speaks specifically of husband as image of God for his wife: "The head of every man is Christ, the head of a woman is her husband. . . . Man is the image and glory of God; but woman is the glory of man" (1 Cor. 11:3,7). The husband has to be Christ toward his wife: "Husbands, love your wives as Christ loved the Church, and gave himself up for her" (Eph. 5:25). Acting like Christ, letting Christ so act in him, the husband is the image mediating Christ to his wife. And the wife, in her response, finds Christ through the mediation of her husband: "Wives, be subject to your husband as to the Lord" (Eph. 5:23).

If husbands in Christ are to love their wives as Christ loves the Church, so wives in Christ should respond to their husbands as the Church does to Christ. If Christ as son and image of God shows

1. See Paul Hinnebusch, *Religious Life: A Living Liturgy* (New York: Sheed and Ward, 1965), p. 43.

forth God's offer of sonship to all, husband as image of Christ for his wife and children shows forth this offer to them, inviting them to live as children of God. And wife, image of the Church, shows forth the Church's acceptance of this offer in loving obedience. Her loving submission to her husband is a fulfilling of her life as child of the heavenly Father.

Authentically Christian husband and wife, then, are images mediating Christ to one another and to their children. We can say, indeed, that by reason of the sacrament of Matrimony they are "in Christ like a sacrament or sign and instrument of intimate union with God, and of the unity of the whole human race" (*LG* 1). As the basic unit of human society, the family is a basic bond of the unity of the human race. When husband and wife are in intimate union with God in Christ and united in God with one another and with their children, they are sign and instrument of the unity of mankind, which is possible only in union with God. In them, the Church is "image and glory of God," and "like a sacrament or sign and instrument."

"Woman is the Glory of Man"

"Man is the image and glory of God" by reflecting God's glory which dwells in him; "woman is the glory of man" by reflecting man in his Christ-like subjection to God showing forth his submissive openness to God to receive the glory of his presence. For man is the glory of God only in possessing God. But he can possess God only when he is subject to him in the receptive openness of obedience. The wife by her submission to her husband images Christ's submission to the Father, and thus inspires this submission to God in her husband, so that in obedience he can receive the glory of God which is to shine in him to others.

In matrimony as sign of the mutual relationships of Christ and the Church, husband is sign in a special way of Christ, and wife is sign in a special way of the Church. Nevertheless, wife is certainly also image and presence of Christ for her husband, as he is the same for her.

St. Peter shows how even a woman married to a pagan can be word and image of God for her unbelieving husband, and this precisely by her submission to him as to the Lord (1 Pet. 3:1–6). Her quiet, obedient spirit in relationship to her husband is, indeed, an obedience to God; and, therefore, it is an image of Christ's own obedience to the Father, inviting her husband to the same obedience. All this is effective, of course, in proportion to her truly Christian motivation, her truly Christian openness to the Father in heaven by her faith in the word.

In the passage in question, St. Peter's point of reference is "obedience to the word" (v. 1); that is, Christian faith in the word of the Gospel, faith in Christ the Word. Husband will be won to this word by his wife's obedience to it as expressed in her reverence for her husband:

Likewise you wives, be submissive to your husbands, so that some, though they do not obey the word, may be won without a word by the behavior of their wives, when they see your reverent and chaste behavior. Let not yours be the outward adorning with braiding of hair, decoration of gold and wearing of robes, but let it be the hidden person of the heart with the imperishable jewel of a gentle and quiet spirit, which in God's sight is very precious. So once the holy women who hoped in God used to adorn themselves and were submissive to their husbands, as Sarah obeyed Abraham calling him lord. And you are now her children if you do right and let nothing terrify you (1 Pet. 3:1–6).

Why is "the hidden person of the heart," adorned with "a gentle and quiet spirit," so very precious in God's sight? Is it merely because it is God's will that a wife have such an attitude toward her husband? Or is it precious for the much more profound reason that such an attitude toward her husband, image of God, is an expression of the basic attitude which every human person ought to have toward God himself? Certainly such an attitude toward a husband "as to the Lord" (Eph. 5:23) is an openness to God in the same quiet and gentle spirit. Husband is truly an image and presence of God to such a one. By her gentle reverence, she is open to God's grace and is made holy in this relationship with God and husband.

Openness to Fellowmen

Since "a gentle and quiet spirit" adorning "the hidden person of the heart" should be man's basic attitude toward God, it should be also the basic attitude in relationship to all the children of God, images of our Father in heaven. This reverential openness to others, this respect for them as images of God, is the opposite of the proud, closed selfish spirit which repels every approach of God and man. "God opposes the proud, but gives grace to the humble" (1 Pet. 5:5). The proud resist the grace of God, their hearts are closed to it.

Openness to all our fellowmen in a gentle and quiet spirit, inspired by reverence for them as images of God, will open us to God's grace in all our human relationships. As Christ is image and word of the Father to us, so we will see every fellowman in every situation as an appeal from the Father in heaven for family love among us. When we live in this way, our whole life is a prayer, a contemplation of the image of the heavenly Father in his children, a communion with the Father as mediated to us in his image. He who reverences God in his image is open for God's direct manifestation of himself in the graces of profound contemplative prayer to which, of course, he must cultivate conscious attention.

Obviously, such a prayerful attitude toward our fellowmen can exist only if accompanied by the courageous mortification of the pride and selfishness which closes us to one another. This persistent killing of selfishness in the measure which each new situation with our fellowman requires is the indispensable condition for a deep life of prayer. This is the existential asceticism or mortification which should be the warp and woof of our whole Christian existence. This is the truly meaningful penance for our times, as for all times.

These are some of the ways, then, in which we make it possible for our fellowmen to find God in us. And these are ways in which our own still imperfect divine sonship is inspired toward further perfection when God is imaged forth to us by others.

Virginity and Celibacy: Bypassing the Image

The marriage ideal in which husband and wife mediate Christ to one another is so sublime that one may wonder why there is need for celibacy and consecrated virginity in the Church. If husband and wife are image and presence of Christ for one another and for their children, why should anyone abandon this precious way to God to seek him in the solitude of celibacy?

An answer was given succinctly many centuries ago by St. Leo the Great in the Preface he composed for the solemn consecration of virgins. The preface points out that virginity is a special charism of the Holy Spirit granted to certain persons. However, the Preface adds, this grace given to some members of Christ in no way diminishes the honor of marriage. God's nuptial blessing ever remains upon the union of man and woman. Nevertheless, by the special charism of consecrated chastity, certain persons bypass this union of man and woman, "desiring rather the divine mystery signified in that union; without imitating what takes place in marriage, they devote their entire love to the mystery signified by marriage," namely, the union of Christ and his bride, the Church. They are intent upon participating as intimately as possible in the Church's direct union with Christ. Instead of seeking union with Christ through the meditation of an earthly spouse, the celibate seeks union with him directly.

Let us consider these ideas of the Preface in terms of Christ, Son and image of the invisible God, and in terms of husband, image of Christ for his wife.

Christ is always Son, ever "toward the Father." "In the beginning was the Word, and the Word was with God." The word "with"
has the strong, dynamic meaning of "toward." The Word was
toward God, ever facing the Father, contemplating him in love, ever
going toward him in the embrace of love. The Son's deepest personality is the loving cry of his total being, "Father," in response to
the Father's love for him.

Even in his human existence, Jesus is first of all Son of the
Father. In his humanity, he is "image of the invisible God" (Col.
1:15); he manifests the Father to his fellowmen. As image and
glory of God he is mediator; or, better still, he is presence of
God. In him the Father is present and manifest to us; he is within
our reach. "No one comes to the Father but by me. If you had
known me, you would have known my Father also; henceforth you
know him and have seen him" (Jn. 15:6–7).

Therefore, Christians center their whole life on Jesus. The Church
is ever "toward Christ." God's people in giving themselves to Christ
give themselves as sons in the Son to the Father.

In this response to Jesus and in him, as sons of God in the Son,
Christians in turn are image and presence of God to their fellowmen, manifesting the presence of God and Christ. Because husband
is image of Christ for his wife, she can give herself to Christ in
giving herself to her husband. The husband, giving self to wife, can
thereby give himself to Christ. She is image of Christ for her husband, as he is for her, just as all Christians in differing ways are to
be signs of Christ for one another.

The virgin, however, and the celibate, concentrate their whole
effort upon direct union with Christ, bypassing the mediation of a
husband and wife. Does this imply that reaching Christ through
the mediation of a human being is less effective than reaching him
directly in his own person? Not at all. For several reasons, however, husbands and wives and all Christians need the special witness
of celibacy to help them better understand their own way of reaching Christ.

First, indirect union with Christ through a mediator is never enough. A mediator such as a husband is only a bridge leading to Christ in his own person. For a married woman to achieve union with God in Christ, it is not enough for her to achieve union with her husband. Over and above her indirect contacts with Christ through a husband whom she loves in Christ, she needs a great deal of direct contact with Christ. There is a profound place in her soul which no creature, no husband, no family can fill, but only God. In addition to her communion with her husband, which should be one element in her communion with God, she needs direct communion with God in interior prayer.

This explains, no doubt, why St. Paul seems to take it for granted that Christian husbands and wives will abstain at times from intimate sexual communion for the sake of direct communion with God in prayer. He writes, "Do not refuse one another (the conjugal rights) except perhaps by agreement for a season, that you may devote yourselves to prayer" (1 Cor. 6:5).

Celibates, called by special vocation to direct union with God without the mediation of a human spouse, by their way of life bear witness before all Christians that no Christian should stop at human mediators, even so intimate a one as husband or wife. He must go beyond and achieve also a direct union with God in frequent prayer.

Moreover, celibacy bears witness to an ultimate union with God in which there will be no more need for human mediators (though in heaven we will continue to love those who were our mediators): "The children of this world marry and are given in marriage. But those who shall be accounted worthy of that world and of the resurrection from the dead neither marry nor take wives. For neither shall they be able to die anymore, for they are equal to the angels and are sons of God, being sons of the resurrection" (Lk. 20:34–36). Sons of God like the Word, they will be directly "toward God," looking to him along with their fellowmen whom they will continue to love, now more deeply than ever.

There is further reason for the witness of consecrated virginity. The divine mystery signified by the union of husband and wife is the union of Christ and the Church. Spouses, however, run the risk of confusing the sign with what is signified, making idols of one another. Though love of a creature is meant to lead one to the love of God, when the love of creatures is closed in upon itself it can be an obstacle to the love of God. Lest husband and wife seek fulfillment only in one another, loving one another as idols and thus missing the deeper fulfillment which can be found only in a direct relationship with God, the celibate by his manner of life without spouse is a striking witness to this direct relationship.

The reader may be wondering why we are treating these matters in a book on the contemplation of God. We are doing so because, as St. Paul seems to take for granted, even the married have to be contemplative at times. He says they may wish to abstain for a season from sexual relationship to devote themselves to prayer. If they really are finding Christ in their union with one another, then they will experience the need of a more direct union with him in prayer. For one who finds Christ hungers ever more ardently for him.

We are treating these matters, furthermore, to illustrate some of the ways of carrying out the Christian vocation to lead one another to the contemplation of God. Celibacy and virginity, for example, are in the realm of witness. Through their deep prayerful union with Christ they are a striking image of the relationship of the people of God with Christ. By this witness they help the reflective Christian to contemplate the Christian mystery; they help him interpret his own interior grace which is a call to intimate personal union with Christ in prayer and contemplation. They are a perpetual reminder of the deeper reality which is signified by marriage, the union of the Church with Christ, a reality which the married miss if they are idols of one another, rather than images of Christ and his Church.

Finding God in Fellowman

It is very important that we understand rightly how we find God in our fellowman as image and mediator of God. We do not find God in neighbor in such a way that a direct seeking of God in prayer is superfluous, or that there is no difference, for example, between our union with God in Holy Communion and our union with God in serving neighbor or in loving wife.

Perhaps the difference will be clear if we understand that one person is not the image of Christ for another person in the same way that Christ is the image of the invisible God. There is a profound difference, which we must not overlook.

When a wife is subject in love to her husband "as to the Lord" (Eph. 5:22), when a husband serves his wife or a slave serves his master "as to the Lord" (Eph. 6:7), when a Christian cares for the hungry and the poor and thus cares for Christ, the husband or wife or master or poor man who is loved and served *represents* Christ—"you did it to me" (Matt. 25:40)—but is not Christ in his own person.

Christ, however, as image of the invisible God does not merely represent God. He *is* God in person. He is God present in full reality and not merely in image or symbol. He is image and represents God in the sense that God's invisible divinity is manifest to our limited powers of perception through his humanity. The natural range of our knowledge and love is the finite; his humanity enables us to focus our knowledge and love on his infinite divine person really present and revealed in his finite human nature.

Or, to put it in terms of mediation: husband as image of Christ is a mediator between Christ and his wife; and, as we said, indirect union with Christ through a mediator is not enough. But Christ as image of the invisible God is mediator in a different sense. His humanity is mediator in the sense of making his invisible divinity (immediately present to us in his humanity) easily perceptible to our human nature. Our nature has access to intelligible and spiritual realities only through sense-perceptible signs. For this reason, our access to the invisible God is through the image which is Christ. But the very reality of God is present in the image. Consequently, in Christ we achieve direct union with God, whereas in a husband, as image of Christ, God is not present in the same way.

In addition to any contact with Christ which a wife has through her husband, Christ's image, she needs also direct contact with Christ in his very person.

Lest Christians lose sight of this need of direct contact with Christ, virgins and celibates are called to seek him directly, rather than through an earthly spouse. The very existence of the celibate is a witness to all Christians that this direct approach must not be neglected in their lives. Christ must be sought directly in prayer and adoration as well as indirectly in neighbor.

The everyday experience of sincere Christian husbands and wives shows that it is not enough to seek God only in fellowman, his image. The Christian mother, for example, who tries to be an image of God for her children knows only too well how often she lets them down because of her human frailty. She knows how often she sets them a bad example because of her unjust anger, her precipitous injustice, her quarrellings with her husband, and so on. So she soon realizes her need of going directly to God in prayer for help.

Even when she is not guilty of any serious bad example she finds that all her efforts at showing God forth to her children do not get the full results she hopes for. Her children are not as good as she had expected, and again she realizes the need of going directly to God in prayer for help.

In other words, she has not found God fully enough in serving her family, and they have not found God fully enough in imitating her. All need, in addition, a direct union with God in prayer and the sacraments. The celibate life in which one is directly espoused to God bears witness to this truth.

Though consecrated celibacy is a striking sign of man's need of direct union with God, and though the celibate of necessity must cultivate a deep life of prayer in order to live a virginal life, it does not follow that the celibate achieves union with God exclusively in this direct way. The religious and the priest, too, find God in neighbor, in serving him and in being served by him. Community life is a necessary mediation; God's love is mediated to the religious in the community. At the same time, however, celibacy, so effective in bringing one into direct union with God, makes the celibate more effective as a mediator of God to others.

The thoughtful Christians knows how to contemplate God in husband or wife, in parents or in children, in fellow religious or in the poor and needy. This sort of contemplation is a necessary disposition for infused contemplation, for only he who loves neighbor will see God.

22

"Love Is from God"

God became man to show men how to live like God. That means he had to show us how to love like God, for God is love.

We can love like God only by participating in God's own love, only by loving with God's love. Christian love is so called because it is Christ's own love in us. It is God's own love communicated to us in Christ.

Christian love is not mere human love. It is divine love in a human heart, expressing itself in a way which is simultaneously human and divine. "God is my witness," says St. Paul, "how I long for you all in the heart of Christ Jesus" (Phil. 1:8,c). He means that he is loving them with Christ's own divine love.

True Christian love, then, has its source and model in Christ. The way he loved God and neighbor is the only standard for judging whether our love is truly Christian and not a counterfeit.

The proof of our Lord's love for the Father was his obedience to the Father. "I do as the Father has commanded me, so that the world may know that I love the Father" (Jn. 14:31). The specific deed he carried out in that obedient love was laying down his life in sacrifice. Not just laying down his life, but laying it down for love of us. "I lay down my life for my sheep. . . . Such is the command I have received from my Father" (Jn. 10:16–18).

So, too, the proof of our love for God is our love for neighbor. "This commandment we have from him, that he who loves God should love his brother also" (1 Jn. 4:21). Love of neighbor is the embodiment of love for God. "If anyone says, 'I love God,' and hates his brother, he is a liar; for he who does not love his brother whom he has seen, cannot love God whom he has not seen" (1 Jn. 4:19–20). Brother is a sign of God in whom we can, as it were, touch God himself. In God's plan, genuine love of God necessarily includes love of neighbor. It is but one love. Love of neighbor makes it easier for us to love God in a way in keeping with our human nature, contacting God, as it were, in a tangible way, contemplating him in our brother.

And yet in this love we are faced with two dangers, at opposite extremes.

Neighbor is a sign of God, and in loving the sign we should also be loving God, the reality manifest in the sign. But it is possible to stop at the sign and never reach the reality. It is possible to fail to contemplate God in the neighbor we love. There is a way of loving neighbor which is not love of God, a way of loving neighbor in which we stop at the sign and never get to God, the reality signified in the sign. A woman in loving her husband, for example, can make of him an idol replacing God. Not all love of fellowman is love of God.

The other danger is the attempt to use neighbor as a mere stepping stone to God, a mere means for reaching him.

In the first case we do not love God; in the second case we do not love neighbor. Authentic love of God and neighbor, however, are inseparable.

The Test of Love of Neighbor

St. John tells us how to test whether our love of neighbor is really a Christian love, really a love in which we are reaching God, and not just stopping at neighbor in some sort of selfish love. He says, "By this we know that we love the children of God *when we love God* and obey his commandments" (1 Jn. 5:2). When we love God, our love of neighbor is true, for authentic love of neighbor expresses love of God. But true love of God loves neighbor according to God's commandments which regulate the love of neighbor, showing how to love neighbor in a truly unselfish, divine way. Not any kind of love of fellowman is love of God. How often we rationalize a selfish love of neighbor, a wrong kind of friendship by deceiving ourselves into thinking that this selfish love of another is bringing us closer to God. If our love of neighbor were more deeply rooted in true love of God, it would lead us back to God. It would not be counterfeit; it would not stop at neighbor.

Love of neighbor is the expression and deepening of our love of the Father. It is one and the same love with which we love God our Father and man our brother. Love's impulse toward the Father remains in love's impulse toward brother. The impulse toward God in the Holy Spirit is the vital power of the impulse toward neighbor. We love the Father in his children, just as our Lord's love for us in laying down his life for us was the proof and expression of his love for the Father.

Neighbor is Not a Means to God

But if one danger in loving neighbor is the possibility that we will stop at neighbor and love him in a selfish way, another danger is the attempt to use neighbor only as a means to God, a stepping stone to God, without truly loving neighbor himself.

The remedy for both extremes is really the same: it is to love neighbor with a really divine love which is in our hearts from God: "Beloved, let us love one another, for love is of God, and he who loves is born of God and knows God" (1 Jn. 4:7). We should love neighbor with a love springing from genuine love of the Father, a love which holds neighbor in high esteem and reverence because of his true worth as one who is either a child of God by grace or is destined to become one. One has to recognize God as Father in a true experience of God himself if he is to be able to recognize neighbor as child of God.

For Christian love—the charity communicated to us from the

heart of Christ, the love which is a participation in his own love of
the Father in the Holy Spirit—rises to the infinitely lovable God
in response to the divine love pouring itself into our hearts in the
gift of the Holy Spirit. Because our charity in the Holy Spirit has
penetrated into the heart of the Creator and is a participation in his
own love by which he loves all his creatures, charity can then love
all creatures in the way the Creator himself loves them. On the
one hand, true charity does not stop at creatures. On the other hand,
it does not use creatures merely as unloved means to God. In
charity we truly love creatures. By loving them truly, we express
and deepen our love of the Father.

Charity—God's love in us—loves all creatures in the way the
Creator loves them. God's creative and redemptive love is the whole
explanation of all things. Things exist only because God's creative
love has brought them into being.

> For you love all things that are
>   and loathe nothing that you have made;
>   for what you hated, you would not have fashioned.
> And how could a thing remain, unless you willed it;
>   or be preserved, had it not been called forth by you?
> But you spare all things, because they are yours,
>   O Lord and lover of life (Wis. 11:24–26,c).

God's love desires that things be, and that is why they are. Each
thing is a distinct product of his love. He loves each thing in its
own existent reality, even though it may still be imperfect and
undeveloped or defective and in need of redemption. For God's love
wills not only that each thing be, but that it should come to the
fullness of being which he intends for it. His creative and redemptive love is thus drawing all things to their fulfillment. His is a
forever merciful love which first brings things out of their nothing-
ness and continues to love them even with their deficiencies. It is a
compassionate love which is successively bestowing upon them, in
ever greater fullness, the perfection his love and call wills them to
have.

And so, too, charity in us, which is from God's heart and has brought us into God's heart, enables us to love all that he loves with his own creative and redemptive love. Charity gives us a truly divine sympathy for all that God has made, a compassionate love which loves things as they are with a benevolent, beneficent love which longs to bestow upon them the full perfection which God's love desires them to have. Our charity, like God's, loves creatures in their own existent reality. Like God's love, our charity desires them to be, and to be in all their perfection. It desires that they be their true selves.

Love of neighbor is not some sort of vague, global love of mankind in the abstract. Rather, it goes out to each individual as he is in the state in which we find him, whether we find him saint or sinner, whether we find him worthy of love or not. For charity is a creative and redemptive love which seeks to make the beloved worthy by bringing him to his true fulfillment in God.

Charity is ever a redeeming love, and so it can reverence and esteem even a sinner. This redeeming love accepts the human condition of our fellowmen. It recognizes that they are still undergoing the process of being redeemed, and it can hold men in esteem no matter how degraded they may be, for redeeming love can bring them to divine sonship. Only a divine love can love in this way. Charity never disparages, never despises fellowman, no matter what it finds in him, for it reverences the God-given potentialities of this being and his call to divine sonship. Though charity never despises, it does lovingly rebuke and correct when necessary.

God's charity and ours desires that each and every man made in the image and likeness of God should reach his true fulfillment by receiving into himself the divine life of the children of God. That is what charity desires above all for neighbor and labors to give him. Only one who is himself a child of God, who has gone to the Father in love because God's own love has been poured into his heart, can truly love neighbor in this way and desire that he, too, rise to the Father in love.

The more deeply we are rooted in love, the more powerful we

are in loving neighbor with God's own creative, redemptive, life-giving love. We must prayerfully abide in God. We must contemplate his redemptive love manifest in Christ crucified, if we would love neighbor with this truly Christian love, which is the expression and deepening of our love of the Father. "Beloved, let us love one another; for love is of God, and he who loves is born of God and knows God" (1 Jn. 4:7).

IV
St. John's Course
in Contemplation

Introduction

Christian contemplation, we have seen, is a participation in Christ's own light and love, a sharing in his personal experience of his Father's love for him. It is a development of baptismal grace, a perfecting of the initial enlightenment received when we were born again of water and the Holy Spirit.

No doubt it was chiefly the Gospel of St. John which gave rise to the ancient Christian understanding of Baptism as "the Enlightening." John's ninth chapter is the story of the man born blind who is given sight by Jesus. "The man called Jesus made clay and anointed my eyes and said to me, 'Go to Siloam and wash;' so I went and washed and received my sight" (Jn. 9:11).

This gift of sight to the blind man is a sign, and John pointedly gives the clue to the meaning of the sign: the name of the pool of Siloam means *Sent* (Jn. 9:7). Repeatedly in his Gospel (about forty times), John refers to Jesus as the one whom God has sent. To be plunged into the pool of Baptism is to be plunged into Jesus who has been sent as the light of the world. The sign, the blind man receiving his sight, is presented in the context of our Lord's discourse concerning himself as the light: "I am the light of the world; he who follows me will not walk in darkness, but will have the light of life" (Jn. 8:12).

Baptism is a grace of continuing openness to the Light for ever-increasing enlightenment. It is a power of lasting receptivity to Jesus in faith, hope and love. It is not enough to come to the Light once; one must follow the Light throughout life; one must repeatedly come to him.

In John's Gospel, "to come to Jesus" is a synonym for "to believe in Jesus." One comes to Jesus, however, to receive life and light from him. There is an active element in faith and a receptive element—the active commitment of self to the person of Jesus in a continuing reliance upon him and his word, and the ever more profound enlightenment one receives from him as one contemplates him and listens to his word.[1]

"If 'to come to' is synonymous with the active element in the concept of believing, 'to know' is partially synonymous with the receptive element in believing."[2] The *knowing* of the Father and of Jesus is no mere intellectual knowledge; it is an experiencing of God in love. The knowing is a gift from God, a grace of deep interior enlightenment from the God dwelling in us. It is a receiving of God's self-communication, the experiencing of his presence in one's heart. "You *know* him, for he dwells with you, and will be in you" (Jn. 14:17). "This is eternal life, that they may *know* thee, the only true God, and Jesus Christ whom thou hast sent" (Jn. 17:3).

To know, in John's vocabulary, means to experience in love. Knowing is a mutual exchange in love: "I am the good shepherd; I know my own and my own know me, as the Father knows me and I know the Father; and I lay down my life for the sheep" (Jn. 10:14–15). "As the Father has loved me, so have I loved you; abide in my love" (Jn. 15:9). The "knowing" is perfected in love's giving. The Shepherd knows and loves his sheep to the extent of giving his life for them. We know him in responding to this love by the gift of our whole being to him in a repeatedly renewed and

1. Raymond E. Brown, ed. *The Gospel According to John. The Anchor Bible,* 29 (New York, Doubleday & Co., Inc., 1966), pp. 512–513.
2. *Ibid.,* p. 514.

deepened commitment in faith. He responds by giving us a deeper experience of his love.

To know, then, is to experience. A good example of deep spiritual knowledge gained by experience is found in Peter's words: "Lord, to whom shall we go? You have the words of eternal life; and we have believed, and have come to *know*, that you are the Holy One of God" (Jn. 6:68–69).

Believing is thus perfected in knowing. One actively comes to Jesus; one commits oneself totally to him in faith to receive ever more fully the divine enlightenment and to experience ever more profoundly the divine love: "I have made known to them thy name, and I will make it known, that the love with which thou hast loved me may be in them, and I in them" (Jn. 17:26).

One must come to Jesus, then, to *receive* ever more profoundly the revelation of the Father, the experience of his love. Faith is perfected only by the reception from Jesus of this contemplative light and love. Faith by its very nature is an openness to receive these gifts of the Holy Spirit. It is up to us to keep ourselves open, repeatedly coming to Jesus, incessantly looking at him. "Come and see!" is a persistent theme in the Gospel of St. John.[3] They who come see his glory ever more profoundly and penetrate the mystery of Jesus ever more deeply because they receive the light and because the Spirit leads them ever more fully into the Truth. "We have seen the Lord!" (20:18,25) is the joyous refrain at the end of John's Gospel sung by those who at its beginning accepted the invitation, "Come and see!"

In other words, infused contemplation, the enlightening, the "knowing", or experiencing of God's love, is the work of "the Lord who is Spirit" (2 Cor. 3:18). Our part is to acquire and maintain the contemplative attitude, ever beholding the Son of God in openness to his light and surrendering to the action of his Spirit. "We all, with unveiled face, beholding the glory of the Lord, are

3. Cf., 1:39, 46; 2:11; 5:40; 6:40; 6:45–47; 12:32 with 12:21; 12:44–46; 14:21; 17:24, etc.

being changed into his likeness from one degree of glory to another; for this comes from the Lord who is the Spirit" (2 Cor. 3:18).

All this is taught to us by St. John through his persistent theme: "Behold the Lamb of God!"

23

"Behold the Lamb of God"

We should be able to read the Gospels in such a way that as we read we encounter Christ as a living Presence, a person to whom we respond in love and adoration. The entire Gospel according to St. John is a series of lessons on how to do this.

This is *lectio divina,* reading the Scriptures in a prayerful way, in a contemplative disposition, in receptiveness to Christ the light. In such reading our attention is focused on the person of Jesus, and we meet him as truly Son of God. And in meeting him personally, we encounter the invisible God revealed and made present to us in this Incarnate Word: "He who has seen me has seen the Father" (Jn. 14:9).

"Fixing His Eyes on Jesus"

By the very way he tells his story, John the Evangelist is teaching us to read the Gospel in this contemplative manner. John records how the other John, the Baptist, was standing one day with two of his disciples. "Fixing his eyes on Jesus, who was walking by, he said, 'Look! There is the Lamb of God!'" (Jn. 1:36, Kleist-Lilly).

John the Baptist wants us also to fix our eyes, our whole attention, steadfastly upon Jesus. "Behold the Lamb of God!" The word "behold" derives from the Anglo-Saxon for "hold." "Behold" means more than look at. It means "hold on to," look at with concentration.

John the Baptist, "fixing his eyes on Jesus," setting the example by this penetrating look, wants us to penetrate to the very Person of Jesus in no superficial way. "Behold the Lamb of God" is an invitation to contemplate the Person pointed out, to look attentively upon him, to come really to know him and to recognize and acknowledge him for what he is. It is not merely an admission in an indifferent sort of way, "Yes, he is the Son of God." It is an affirmation of love of that truth. It is an acknowledgment of that Person in love and joy. It means that I accept him in love and adoration and give myself totally to him.

All that belongs to the process of contemplation. St. John, the contemplative, gives example after example of this process in his Gospel which is a course in contemplation. Each incident in the life of Jesus recorded by John cries out: "Behold Jesus! Look at this Person with loving attention till you can embrace him with all your heart and soul, saying with Thomas, 'My Lord and my God!' " (Jn. 20:28). Contemplation brings us into intimate personal relationship with Christ in whom God is a living Presence for us.

To the Person through Word, Sign, Event

To help us focus our love's attention upon Jesus in each scene which he presents John offers adequate material for our contemplation: words and signs and events in which the divine Person of Jesus is revealed and made present. We are not to stop at the signs; we are not to get lost in the words; we are not to be distracted by other persons, such as John the Baptist, who is only the lamp. We are to go straight to Jesus who is the Light.

All the words of the Scriptures—Old Testament and New— point to the Person of Jesus: "You search the Scriptures, because in them you think that you have life everlasting, and it is they that bear witness to *me*. Yet you are not willing to *come to me* that you may have life. . . . If you believed Moses, you would believe me also, for he wrote of *me*" (Jn. 5:39–46).

Do not stop, then, at the mere words, whether of Moses or of the Gospel; and do not stop at exegesis, at the ideas which you find in the words. Do not stop at biblical theology. No! Go straight through the words and ideas and the theology to the very Person of him who is the Word. Any words or ideas about Jesus should not be abstracted from his Person, distracting from his Person. They should lead only to his Person. With the help of words and ideas and theology we must contemplate the Person himself: "Behold the Lamb!" (Jn. 1:29). "Behold the man!" (19:6). "Behold your king!" (19:15). "Look upon him whom you have pierced" (cf. 19:37). And do not reject him, as the crowds did. Do not give him a homage of mockery, as the soldiers did. Believe in him, accept his word, adore his person.

And do not stop at the signs worked by Jesus, nor at the symbols and types presented in the Old Testament. For all these, too, point to the person of the Son of God (Jn. 2:22; 12:16). When Jesus complains, "Unless you see signs and wonders, you do not believe" (4:48), he is saying: Do not stop at the outward signs I work, but penetrate to their deeper meaning. They point to me, as the One sent by the Father, and they show what I mean to you. Look at me; in seeing me as the Son, you will see also the Father who sent me.

And in beholding me, do not stop at the outward appearances— "Is not this Jesus, the son of Joseph, whose father and mother we know?" (6:42); behold, and you will see "the bread that has come down from heaven" (6:41). "Whoever beholds *the Son* and believes in him, shall have everlasting life" (6:40).

Nor again should love of any human person distract us from this divine person. Modern man is being told he must find God in his fellowman. Only in our brothers can we encounter God, they say. This is true up to a point. We encounter God in our fellowmen only when we see fellowman as sign and witness pointing to God, as

John the Baptist was. If we stop at man, the sign, we will not reach the reality signified. The sign must fade away so that only the reality continues to shine. John "was not himself the light, but was to bear witness to the light. . . . He was the lamp, burning and shining, and you desired to rejoice for a while in his light. . . . He has borne witness to the truth . . . 'I am not the Christ, but have been sent before him. . . . He must increase, but I must decrease' " (1:18; 5:35,33; 3:28–30). The witness exists only to point to the person of Jesus. Every word, every sign, every person must focus our attention on his person.

When we penetrate beneath the surface appearances of him who seems to be but the son of Joseph and behold the Son, and believe in him, we have life everlasting!

Who He Is

In each incident of his Gospel, then, St. John is saying, "Behold this person!" as he presents material for our contemplation, words and signs and events which bring out to us various aspects of the infinite riches of this divine person. As we contemplate the one revealed in these details, we penetrate more deeply into Who He Is and what he is for us.

First, Who He Is. In ever so many scenes of the Gospel, we are led to acknowledge that Christ's true name is "I Am." Thus, his great debate with the Jews about who he is and where he is from reaches a climax in his declaration, "Before Abraham came to be, I am" (8:58). The Jews reject him, taking up stones to cast at him. But we who behold him in the way the two Johns would have us behold him accept him as God in loving adoration.

In the ninth chapter, we behold Jesus involved in the intense drama ensuing from his cure of the man born blind. The action reaches its climax when Jesus, rejected by his adversaries, spiritually blind, asks the man to whom he has given sight, "Do you believe in the Son of Man?" The man answered, "And who is he, sir, that

I may believe in him?" Jesus said to him, "You have seen him, and *it is he* who speaks to you" (9:35–37).

It is he echoes the Name Yahweh, *He who is.*

The man said, "Lord, I believe." And he worshipped him. We who behold this scene do likewise.

To the Samaritan woman also Jesus hints that his name is "I Am." "The woman said to him, 'I know that Messiah, that is, Christ is coming, and when he comes he will tell us everything.' 'I who am speaking to you,' said Jesus, '*I am he*'" (4:25–26,j). At these words, again we adore God present to us in Jesus.

In the great storm on the lake, that night after feeding the five thousand, Jesus comes walking on the sea, and says simply, "*It is I, do not be afraid*" (6:20), using the same words which Yahweh, the God of Israel, had used so often in revealing his saving presence: "It is I, who said to the deep: Be dry!" (Is. 44:27). "It is I, I the Lord; there is no savior but me . . . I am God, yes, from eternity, I am he" (Is. 43:11–13). "I am the first and I am the last" (Is. 44:6). "Fear not, for I have redeemed you; I have called you by name: you are mine. When you pass through the water, I will be with you" (Is. 43:1–2).

In this scene—Jesus walking on the water—St. John would have us know not only who Jesus is, but that he is with us to save. In beholding him, in contemplating him, we meet a person present to us here and now for our salvation. He is the eternal One, the Omnipresent, the everliving Christ, present everywhere by his creative and salvific power, revealed to us, present to us in the faith in which we respond to these signs and wonders which point to him.

What He Is for Us

So that we may contemplate and penetrate ever more deeply into the spiritual nature of the salvation present to us in Jesus, St. John points out the Lord to us in a variety of scenes in which Jesus declares not merely "I Am," but says: I am nourishment and life for you. John shows us the Lord feeding five thousand with five loaves and saying, "I am the bread of life"; giving sight to the man born blind, and saying, "I am the light of the world"; raising the dead Lazarus and declaring, "I am the resurrection and the life"; dining with his disciples, giving them the Eucharist, and saying, "I am the true vine; abide in me."

And John usually shows us also the effect that these actions and words have upon those who see and hear Jesus. Some take up stones to cast at him (8:59). Some go away, for the saying of Jesus is too hard (6:62,67). Peter, and the ones who behold Jesus in the right way, say, "Lord, to whom shall we go? You have the words of eternal life; and we have believed and have come to know, that you are the Holy One of God" (6:68–69).

All the words and signs and witness point to the Person of Jesus. And in beholding him contemplatively, prayerfully, following up all that is indicated in the words and signs and witness, we meet him as God truly with us. His presence is revealed, his life-giving power is manifest. In beholding, we penetrate the deepest mystery of his person and acknowledge him as the Son in whom we meet God. We adore him; we embrace him; we hold him fast; for in him is our life.

We who begin by beholding him as pointed out by others, end by holding him in his own person, like Mary Magdalen who on the morning of his Resurrection, fell at his feet and held him fast (20:17). We cannot let him go; we must not let him go, for he alone is our life. He said, "I am the vine; remain in me. He who does not remain in me withers and dies and is cut off and is burned in the fire."

Bearing Witness: Fruit of Contemplation

If he says to Mary, "Do not hold me," he means it in a physical sense. You no longer need hold on to my natural presence, for you have penetrated beyond the outward appearances. You have grasped me as a divine Person, the eternal Son, and by faith and love, you hold me permanently in your heart.

So go and tell others; bear witness! "Go to my brethren and say to them, I am ascending to my Father and your Father, to my God and your God" (20:17). Bring these others to my divine Person, that I may bring them to my Father.

Only those who behold him and adore him can be sent to tell others. Only from adoration like Mary's does he send his apostles forth. "The disciples were glad when they saw the *Lord*." Only then, when they saw him as Lord God, did Jesus say, "As the Father has sent me, even so do I send you" (20:20–21). Only they who have first found *Him Who Is* can tell others where to find him. "I have seen the Lord!" said Mary (20:18). A witness is one who has seen the Lord. "We have seen the Lord," said the disciples to Thomas (20:25). "We speak of what we know, and we bear witness to what we have seen" (3:11).

When the disciples first beheld the Lamb of God, pointed out by John the Baptist, they went to tell others. "We have found the Messiah," said Andrew to Peter (1:41; cf. 1:45). "Come and see!" said Philip to Nathanael (1:46). And the witnesses themselves returned to Jesus to behold him more. After beholding Jesus in each of that series of signs and words and actions, which St. John presents again for us, the disciples' original word of witness "We have found the Messiah" is transformed into "We have seen the Lord!" Their superficial seeing him as Messiah, Son of David, is deepened into their seeing him as Lord God, Son of the Father.

As Andrew on that first occasion had said to Peter, and as Philip had said to Nathanael, "Come and see!" so all the disciples, when they said to Thomas, "We have seen the Lord," must have added, "Come and see!" For Thomas was with them when Jesus revealed himself again. And Thomas beheld the wounds of Jesus and adored, saying, "My Lord and my God!"

Our witnessing to Christ, then, is capable of a progressive deepening, when we return from telling others about Jesus and behold him again ourselves. In repeated contemplation of the same signs and words and events, we grasp Jesus more profoundly. We enter into a more intimate personal relationship with him, and our consequent new witness to him has a deeper ring of sincerity, a more persuasive tone of conviction.

24

The Lamb's Self-revelation

St. John's Concept of Faith

When the risen Jesus tells Thomas to behold the wounds in his hands and in his side and says, "Do not be faithless, but believing" (Jn. 20:27), Thomas responds at once in loving adoration: "My Lord and my God!" Adoration like that of Thomas is inseparable from true believing in Jesus. For to believe is to penetrate to the very person of the *Son of God,* to recognize and acknowledge him as such, and to respond in a fully personal way in the giving of one's own person to him in an act of adoration: "*My* Lord, *my* God, I am yours!"

This adoration, this believing, is the commitment of one's own person to the person of the Son of God. Throughout John's Gospel, faith is presented as just such a gift of self. For St. John, believing is always dynamic, an active commitment, a coming to Jesus. Never in his Gospel does John use the noun "faith." He prefers to use the verb, "to believe *in.*" The *in* implies movement toward the person in whom one believes.[1]

Therefore, "to come to Jesus" is a synonym for "to believe in Jesus": I am the bread of life; he who comes to me shall not hunger, and he who believes in me shall never thirst (6:35).

This commitment of one's person to the person of Jesus is the

1. Brown, *op. cit.,* pp. 512–513.

gift of self to God, for in Christ one meets God himself: "Believe in God, believe also in me. . . . He who has seen me has seen the Father" (14:1,9). In Jesus we contemplate and adore God himself, committing self to him.

Receiving His Self-revelation

The active commitment of self to Christ in coming to him by believing in him necessarily engages one in a continuing action of keeping his word, fulfilling his commandments. For, if in believing one commits self to this person, it is because one accepts him for who and what he really is: the Son of God who brings the life-giving word of God: "My teaching is not mine, but his who sent me" (7:16). Believing is going to Christ to receive God's word: "Lord, to whom shall we go? You have the words of eternal life" (6:68). For though Christ himself is the Word and Person to whom we give ourselves, nevertheless we do go to the Person through his words.

Only to those whose commitment in believing is continued and completed in keeping his word and doing his will does he trust himself or reveal himself. For, if contemplation is a beholding of God revealed in Christ, this contemplation is possible only to those to whom he trusts himself and manifests himself.

But to whom does he trust himself? There was something incomplete about the faith of many, and so he could not reveal himself to them. He could not give himself to them: "Many believed in his name when they saw the signs that he did; but Jesus did not trust himself to them because he knew all men . . ." (2:23). It seems that these people stopped at the signs and did not penetrate to who the Person really was. They did not surrender themselves to him to receive and keep his word; consequently, they did not receive his more profound self-revelation.

But to those who trust themselves to his person and do keep his word, he does trust himself. That is, he reveals his person ever more fully: "He who has my commandments and keeps them, he it is who loves me; and he who loves me will be loved by my Father, and I will love him and manifest myself to him" (14:21).

This is an interior manifestation. For when Judas (not the Iscariot) asks for an explanation, Jesus adds, "If a man loves me, he will keep my word, and my Father will love him, and we will come to him and make our home with him" (14:23).

Our active commitment of self to him in believing, perfected in the accomplishment of his commandments, is thus presupposed to the ever more perfect contemplation of him in this interior manifestation. He reveals himself interiorly to those in whom he dwells, but he dwells in those who keep his word.

His commandment is above all the love of neighbor. "And this is his commandment, that we should *believe* in the name of his Son Jesus Christ and *love one another,* just as he has commanded us. All who keep his commandments abide in him and he in them" (1 Jn. 3:23–24). Believing in Jesus and loving one another are thus inseparable. The gift of self to Jesus in faith is perfected, expressed, in this charity for one another. Only those who love one another can receive the deeper revelation which he grants to those who keep his word.

Such are the ones, he says, who will "behold my glory" (17:24); namely, they who are one, in love. I pray "for those who believe in me through their word, that they all may be one; even as thou, Father, art in me, and I in thee, that they also may be one in us, so that the world may believe that thou hast sent me" (17:20–21). Christian unity in God manifest in Christian love is the proof that the Father has sent Jesus. This unity in love is a revelation of Jesus, a witness that Jesus is in our midst. It is an invitation to all to come and behold him.

Receptive Believing

Our contemplative beholding of Jesus, our penetration to who this person is, we said, always terminates in adoration, in love's active commitment of self to him. If our commitment is not deepened in

each new beholding of this person, then we have not truly contemplated; we have not received our Lord's self-revelation; we
have not been adequately receptive.

For if contemplation terminates in love's action of adoration and
self-giving, it begins in love's receptivity. Faith is receptive before
it is active, and its active commitment of self brings a more perfect
receptivity. Faith is receptive before it actively goes to Jesus in the
gift of self, for, says Jesus, "No one can come to me unless the
Father who sent me draws him. . . . Every one who has heard and
learned from the Father comes to me" (6:44–45). One must be
open to God; one must listen to him. This receptivity, this listening, is the indispensable, basic contemplative attitude.

When one has listened, when one has been open to God and has
received the light, in the light he beholds the Son and comes to
him in the gift of self. The listening to the Father and the coming
to the Son may be simultaneous in time, but the active going to
the Son is the effect of what has been received from God. The
commitment of self to the Son is itself an openness to his word and
Spirit. When his word is kept, the Word himself more fully manifests himself to the one who is thus receptive.

This process is evident in the Nathanael incidents in John's Gospel. Philip finds Nathanael and bears witness to Jesus: "We have
found him of whom Moses in the law and also the prophets wrote,
Jesus of Nazareth, the son of Joseph" (1:45). By these words,
Philip shows that he himself has not yet penetrated very deeply
into the person of Jesus. He is still too much on the level of outward appearances. For him, Jesus is still "son of Joseph." But at
least Philip has seen something in Jesus, and urges Nathanael,
"Come and see!" (1:46).

Jesus looks into the heart of Nathanael, and this penetration of
his intimate person by Jesus brings Nathanael the grace to behold
Jesus, to believe in him and commit himself to him: "Rabbi, you
are the Son of God! You are the King of Israel!" (1:49). But
Nathanael's vision, too, is still limited; he sees Jesus only as

Messiah, not as eternal Son. For "Son of God" on his lips still carries only its Old Testament meaning, David's son whom God treats as if he were his own son (Ps. 2:7). We, of course, hearing Nathanael's words, contemplating this scene, interpret the title on a deeper level than Nathanael did, and adore the eternal Son.

Nathanael has seen much, but he has not seen all that is to be seen in the person of Jesus: "Because I said to you, I saw you under the fig tree, do you believe? You shall see greater things than these" (1:50). After the resurrection of Jesus, Nathanael was among those who went fishing with Peter (21:2). And they saw the Lord! At the miraculous catch, John, beholding the stranger on the beach in a new light, said to Peter, "It is the Lord!" (21:7). ... "Now none of the disciples dared ask him, 'Who are you?' They knew it was the Lord" (21:12). Nathanael had seen the greater things! He and the other disciples could now go forth and tell the world, "We have seen the Lord!"

Each time we contemplate this scene anew with Nathanael, we behold the Lord and adore; we deepen our commitment to Jesus.

Jesus Beholding Us

The Lord's beholding the heart of Nathanael was the beginning of Nathanael's beholding of the Lord. We can penetrate the full mystery of the person of Jesus only in response to his penetration of our person, his fixing his gaze on us, his reading of our heart. Seeing into our heart and finding it receptive—he found Nathanael guileless, simple of heart—he reveals himself; he trusts himself to us. Only in his self-revelation, this interior, purifying light which he gives to our receptive hearts, can we behold him for what he is.

This truth is brought out not only in the Nathanael sequence, but in various other incidents in John. Jesus did not trust himself to many "because he knew all men and needed no one to bear witness of man" (2:24–25).

He knew the heart of Peter. "Andrew found his brother Simon

... and brought him to Jesus. Jesus looked at him ..." (1:41–42). That one look penetrated Peter's innermost self and saw that Simon was receptive to his call; and he called this sheep by name: "You shall be called Peter" (1:42).

In St. Matthew's version of this incident, Simon first acknowledges Jesus as the Messiah: "You are the Christ!" And Jesus responds: "And you are the Rock!" (Matt. 16:16,18). St. John's account, however, brings out better that the initiative came from Jesus. The call to the heart of Peter, the penetration of Christ's grace into his heart, enables Peter eventually to recognize Jesus as the Christ and finally as Lord. John and Matthew agree that the initiative came from God: "Flesh and blood has not revealed this to you, but my Father who is in heaven" (Matt. 16:17). "No one can come to me unless the Father who sent me draws him" (Jn. 6:44). Contemplation is always the gift of God. "If you knew the gift of God ..." (Jn. 6:10).

The allegory of the Good Shepherd also shows that we recognize Christ and come to him only in response to the personal, intimate call of grace. "The sheep hear his voice, and he calls his own sheep by name. . . . I am the good shepherd; I know my own and my own know me" (10:3,14). Because he knows them, because he reads their hearts and calls them, they know him. Mary Magdalen thought that the risen Jesus was the gardener. She did not recognize him till he addressed her by name, "Mary!" "She knew him then and said to him in Hebrew, 'Rabboni!' " (20:16,j). With this new call, this new enlightenment by divine grace, she knew him in a way she had not known him before.

The basic contemplative attitude, then, is receptivity to his call, responsiveness to his initiatives, listening for his word, opening self to the purposes of his love, coming to him for his self-revelation, trusting self to him that he might trust himself to us. Beholding Jesus begins in this receptivity and ends in adoration and commitment. And commitment, self-surrender, brings more profound receptivity and openness to greater divine light.

Facing up to Self

The contemplation of Jesus, then—the fixing of the eyes of the heart upon his person till we have penetrated his mystery and see and adore God—is a response to Jesus who first penetrates the heart of those he meets; who sees their true person in a way in which they do not even see themselves, and who calls them to be the self they ought to be.

If his penetration of our heart finds it simple and innocent like Nathanael's, he manifests himself sooner. If he finds our heart in the state of the Samaritan woman's, he must first make us face our own person before we can face the mystery of his person. "If you knew who it is who is speaking to you," he says to the Samaritan woman (4:10). If you knew. . . . Her heart is not yet capable of recognizing him, but he sees her heart and is beginning his purifying work in it. She must examine her conscience in the light he gives.

He must show her what she is now before he can show her the true self she can still become. "If you knew the gift of God . . ." (4:10). You cannot know it till you remove that camouflage of sin and self-deception which hides your true self from you.

The greatest obstacle to the contemplation of God is self-deception, unwillingness to face one's true self. "Every one who does evil hates the light and does not come to the light, lest his deeds should be exposed" (3:20). But one who admits his sinfulness and comes in humility to the light is purified by the light.

After Jesus delicately brings the woman to acknowledge her own state, she is able to recognize him as the Christ, and bear witness to him before others: "Come, see a man who told me all that I ever did. Can this be the Christ?" (4:29). By putting her profession of faith in question form, "Can this be the Christ?" she wants all of us to say, "Yes!" She wants to draw a willing response from our hearts, for believing can be forced upon no one.

Several times in John's Gospel the Evangelist records similar questions: "Are you greater than our father Jacob, who gave us the well?" (4:12). "Are you greater than our father Abraham, who died?" (9:53). The Evangelist ardently desires to draw from our hearts a firm "Yes!" to these questions. He wants us to say, in the fullness of believing, "Jesus, you are the living One, greater than Abraham who died; you give the living waters!" Your pierced side is the well of Jacob from which gushes the water of the Holy Spirit.

If such a response presupposes a grace from God, a look into our hearts and a call from Christ, the response is none the less free and voluntary.

Nor can a witness by himself call forth the full response from another's heart. The witness can only say, "Come and see!" He can only bring the prospective believer to the person of Christ. Each one must personally behold Christ and hear his word, and experience his power over hearts: "Many more believed because of his word. They said to the woman, 'It is no longer because of your words that we believe, for we have heard for ourselves, and we know that this is indeed the Savior of the world' " (4:42). The witness must decrease, Jesus must increase.

Behold the Lamb of God!

If each of the incidents of John's Gospel calls upon us to behold Jesus under one aspect or another—as light or life, vine or bread —and to respond in adoration of his person, the Gospel as a whole directs us above all to behold the Paschal Lamb.

The first "behold" in the Gospel is "Behold the Lamb of God who takes away the sins of the world" (1:29). That is also the last "behold" of the Gospel, for in chapter nineteen, the story of the crucifixion, and in chapter twenty, the story of the resurrection, we are told to behold the lamb pierced with a lance.

. . . when they came to Jesus and saw that he was already dead, they did not break his legs. But one of the soldiers pierced his side with a spear, and at once there came out blood and water. He who saw it has borne witness—his testimony is true, and he knows that he tells the truth—that you also may believe. For these things took place that the scripture might be fulfilled, "Not a bone of him shall be broken." And again another scripture says, "They shall look on him whom they have pierced" (19:33–37).

Behold the one you have pierced by your sins. See his unbroken bones, revealing him as the true Paschal Lamb.

The Gospel ends with Thomas looking at the glorious wounds of the pierced One and professing his faith in adoration: "My Lord and my God!"

I Am He

John, then, would have us behold above all the crucified Lamb. "When you have lifted up the Son of Man, then you will know that *I am he* . . ." (8:28). I am he, Yahweh present to save:

> You are my witnesses, says the Lord,
> and my servant whom I have chosen,
> that you may know and believe me
> and understand that *I am he*. . . .
> I, I am the Lord
> and besides me there is no savior (Is. 43:10–11).

Behold the Lamb in the Eucharist!

St. John would like us to behold the crucified and risen Lamb in the eucharistic mystery. He would like us to contemplate the person of the risen Lord giving us his flesh and blood in the Eucharistic Sacrifice that we may have life everlasting.

Such is the significance of the twenty-first chapter of John's Gospel. After the miraculous catch of fish, the risen Lord invites the fishermen: "Come and have breakfast" (21:12).

It is clear from the way in which he tells the story that the Evangelist means to connect this event with the miracle in which Jesus has fed five thousand with five loaves and two fish and with the Eucharistic discourse which followed that miracle. Both events took place on the shores of the same lake, the Sea of Tiberias (6:1–3; 21:1). John calls it the place "where they ate the bread after the Lord had given thanks" (6:23). This phrase bears witness to the Eucharistic significance of both these events.

The Lord's invitation, "Come and breakfast," is an allusion to the words of Wisdom in *Proverbs* as she says, "Come, eat my bread and drink of the wine I have mixed" (Prov. 9:5). Jesus had echoed the same invitation in his discourse on the bread of life after feeding the five thousand: "He who comes to me shall not hunger, and he who believes in me shall never thirst" (6:35).

The action of Jesus on both occasions is described in practically the same words. In feeding the five thousand, says John, "Jesus took the loaves, and when he had given thanks, he distributed them to those who were seated; so also the fish" (6:11). And as host at the glorious breakfast, says John, "Jesus came and took the bread and gave it to them, and so with the fish" (21:13). These words clearly echo the eucharistic formula of the Last Supper: "And he took bread, and when he had given thanks he broke it and gave it to them, saying, 'This is my body'" (Lk. 22:19).

Obviously, there is eucharistic significance in both these events on the shore of the Sea of Tiberias, just as there is in our Lord's meal with the disciples of Emmaus. At Emmaus, "when he was at table with them, he took the bread and blessed and broke it and gave it to them. And their eyes were opened and they recognized him" (Lk. 24:31).

The Evangelists Luke and John would like us, too, to recognize the Lord in the eucharistic breaking of the bread. None of the disciples who accepted the invitation, "Come and have breakfast," dared ask "Who are you?" for "they knew it was the Lord" (Jn. 21:12).

So, too, the Church has always known that it is the Lord who feeds us in the Eucharist. In the Eucharist she would have us contemplate the same person who once was pointed out by John the Baptist. As she holds up the Host for us to see before Holy Communion, she repeats his words, "Behold the Lamb of God, who takes away the sins of the world."

Likewise, though no rubric prescribes it, most of the faithful when they see the Host after the Consecration say the words of Thomas in their hearts, "My Lord and my God!"

Our contemplation of the Lamb and the adoration which is its inseparable consequences brings us ever more intimately into the living reality of *He Who Is,* present with us as Savior and giver of life.

V
The Our Father and the Eucharistic Sacrifice

Introduction

The chief action of Christian contemplation is participation in the eucharistic mysteries because the Christian contemplates, above all, Christ in his paschal mystery. Through this contemplation his whole life is deeply involved in that mystery.

Contemplation is necessary for eucharistic participation. Unless by faith and understanding we penetrate the divine meaning of the words and gestures of the liturgy, we stand around the altar in vain. The more profound is our contemplation of the eucharistic mysteries in faith, love and commitment, the deeper is our participation in them.

In what follows, we shall try to bring out the relationship of the Lord's Prayer and the eucharistic sacrifice. We must take to heart Christ's intentions and self-giving expressed in this prayer. And we must make them our own by the grace of the eucharistic offering.

25

The Lord's Sacrifice Is
the Lord's Prayer

The priestly prayer of Jesus in the seventeenth chapter of St. John is an excellent commentary on the Our Father, and it also reveals the profound meaning of the Lord's sacrifice. Contemplating Jesus as presented in this chapter, listening to the words of his prayer, we learn the intimate relationship between his life, his prayer, his sacrifice on the cross, his eucharistic sacrifice, and our participation in all of this.

In this priestly prayer, Jesus expresses clearly the intentions for which he offers the sacrifice of the cross. Indeed, in the prayer he is already making the offering. It is the prayer of oblation in "the hour" of his paschal sacrifice. "Father, the hour has come," he says (17:1) as he proceeds to present the intentions of his sacrifice. He thereby manifests also the Father's purpose of love which he accepts and accomplishes by his immolation.

This prayer is thus an integral part of the sacrifice of the cross. The prayer is the oblation; the events of Calvary are the immolation. Just as word and liturgical action unite as one sign in the sacraments, so the words of oblation at the Last Supper unite with the action and the immolation on the cross to form one paschal mystery. The oblation expresses the inner meaning of the sacrifice, whereas the immolation on the cross is the accomplishment of the sacrifice in its external reality, embodying the interior love and obedience and the intentions in which it is offered. The prayer expressing the intentions and the sacrificial death thus coalesce as one reality. The sacrifice *is* the prayer in its full expression. The sacrifice of the cross is the Lord's prayer to the Father for the realization of all his intentions; and these intentions, we shall see, are the same ones he expressed in the Our Father. The Lord's sacrifice *is* the Lord's Prayer.

A Eucharistic Prayer

The intentions of Jesus in the sacrifice of the cross remain the same in every Mass; for in saying, "Do this in remembrance of me" (1 Cor. 11:24), Jesus was empowering his Church to offer the sacrifice of the cross through the eucharistic signs. The prayer in John 17, pronounced on the occasion of the institution of the eucharistic sacrifice, is truly our Lord's eucharistic prayer, expressing his intentions in every Mass. *The Mass* is the Lord's Prayer.

The Prayer as expressed in John 17 has three parts. First, Jesus prays for himself (17:1–5); secondly, for the unity of his apostles (6–19); and thirdly, for the unity of the whole Church to be gathered together and united in God through the preaching of the apostles (20–23). Finally, he prays for the reunion of "his own" in glory with himself (24), and for the indwelling of the Holy Trinity in them even now on earth (26). These are the realities the Christian must grasp in his eucharistic contemplation.

All these intentions are really only one intention. For the Lord's prayer for himself is really a prayer that God will accept his sacrifice and grant its fruits (1–5). His prayer for his apostles is a prayer that they will be faithful in bringing the fruits of this sacrifice to mankind (6–19). And his prayer for the Church is a prayer specifying these fruits, namely, the communion of men with God, unity with God and with one another in God (20–25). In the beginning of the prayer he asks for his own glory so that he may communicate this glory to all whom the Father has given him (22,24).

The prayer may be described as priestly, apostolic and ecclesial.

It is *priestly,* bceause in it Jesus expresses the intentions of his sacrifice, asking that his sacrifice be accepted and his petitions be granted. The most immediate fruit he asks is his own glorification, manifesting that his sacrifice has been accepted and empowering him to give all the other fruits. In every Mass, we give thanks that the Father has heard this petition for the Son's glorification.

The prayer (and the eucharistic prayer in every Mass) is *apostolic,* for the prayer and sacrifice of Jesus gives fruitfulness to the apostolate of his Church; it gives power to the word of the Gospel. "The liturgy is the summit toward which the activity of the Church is directed and at the same time the fountain from which all her power flows" (*SC* 10). The intermediate petition, then, is for the unity and fruitfulness of his apostles and their successors, the hierarchy of the Church (6–19).

The prayer (and every Mass) is *ecclesial,* for faith in that fruitful word of the apostles gathers believers into unity in God and with one another. This is the ultimate petition and fruit of his sacrifice toward which the others are ordered: "That they may all be one; even as thou, Father, art in me, and I in thee" (17:21).

"The Liturgy of the Word" at the Last Supper

Chapters thirteen to seventeen of John's Gospel are somewhat like a Mass. The Mass is made up of two parts, the liturgy of the word and the eucharistic liturgy which integrate into one single act of worship (*SC* 56). What we hear from God in the liturgy of the word must go back to God as prayer and sacrifice—our response to the word—in the eucharistic liturgy.

So, too, at the Last Supper our Lord's words of instruction to his apostles in John 13–16 are reexpressed in chapter seventeen in his prayer to the Father: "When Jesus had spoken these words, he lifted up his eyes to heaven and prayed" (Jn. 17:1).

Our Lord's prayer in John 17 is the model of our response in prayer and sacrifice to his words in the preceding chapters and to all his words.

Indeed, our Lord's own prayer and sacrifice is his personal response to the word of the Father. "For this reason the Father loves me, because I lay down my life. . . . This charge I have received from my Father" (Jn. 10:17–18) And our response must be united with his.

A Prayer of Thanksgiving

By expressing the intentions of our Lord's sacrifice, the prayer in John 17 truly expresses what that sacrifice *accomplishes;* for the Father always hears Jesus. Before raising Lazarus, Jesus says, "Father, I thank you for hearing my prayer. I knew indeed that you always hear me, but I speak for the sake of all these who stand round me, so that they may believe it was you who sent me" (Jn. 11:41,42,j). Since the raising of Lazarus is a prefiguring of our resurrection in the Lord's resurrection, these words of thanksgiving in advance for the raising of Lazarus apply even more to Christ's own resurrection for which he asks in John 17:1, and to his gift of life to us, John 17:2.

Therefore just as Christ's petition for the raising of Lazarus is already a thanksgiving, "a Eucharist," so, too, his petitions and ours at the Last Supper and in the Mass are already a thanksgiving, since all that we ask is already ours in the Risen Christ.

In this light we should interpret all that Jesus taught about prayer in the "liturgy of the word" at the Last Supper. To "ask in his name" (16:26) is to ask believing in all that Jesus is (for his name signifies who and what he is), the Messiah sent by the Father to give us life, the Son who has gone to the Father in his paschal sacrifice that he might bestow this life in giving the Holy Spirit (16:26–28). To ask in his name is to ask in his sacrifice, with thanksgiving, convinced that whatever we ask is as good as ours, since his prayer is always heard.

"In that day"—the time of my glorification, the new era which begins with my going to the Father in death and resurrection—"you will ask in my name and I do not say that I shall pray to the

Father for you" (for Christ's prayer for us has already been heard
in his glorification which manifests the acceptance of his sacrifice).
"For the Father himself loves you, because you have loved me and
have believed that I came from the Father. I came from the Father
and have come into the world; again I am leaving the world and
going to the Father" (16:26–28).

To ask in his name, then, is to pray in his prayer, his sacrifice.
It is to ask with faith in his sacrifice, believing that he really came
from the Father and has gone to the Father by way of the cross,
and from the Father he sends the Holy Spirit as the fruit of his
sacrifice.

The Lord's prayer, his sacrifice, thus gives fruitfulness to all
prayers said in his name, all prayers prayed in union with him in
his paschal mystery.

The same point has been made in the allegory of the vine and
its branches. "I am the vine, you are the branches. . . . If you
abide in me, and my words abide in you, ask whatever you will,
and it shall be done for you" (15:5,7). To ask in his name and
to abide in the vine are equivalent expressions. He is the vine in
the eucharistic mystery in which he communicates to us the fruits
of his sacrificial prayer. He gives these fruits of eternal life to us
in "the fruit of the vine" (Mk. 14:25), his precious blood given to
us in the eucharistic wine.

Praying in union with his eucharistic sacrifice is thus a response
to the Last Supper "liturgy of the word" in which he taught the
meaning of "asking in his name."

Asking for the Fruits of the Apostolate

Though Jesus is always heard, and, therefore, our petitions in
the eucharistic sacrifice are already a thanksgiving, it is necessary
just the same for us to ask explicitly, and through these petitions
participate in his sacrifice which is his prayer. Commenting on the
words, "When Jesus had spoken these words, he lifted up his eyes
to heaven and prayed" (Jn. 17:1), Thomas Aquinas, true friar

preacher, says: "Thus he gave us an example, that we should help by prayer those whom we instruct by word. For the divine word has its effect in the hearts of the hearers especially when it is strengthened by prayer in which the divine aid is implored."

In the allegory of the Vine, Jesus himself had taught that all apostles must pray in union with his own eucharistic prayer for the fruits of their apostolate. When he says, "If you abide in me . . . ask whatever you will" (15:7), he is speaking specifically about asking for the fruits of their apostolic labors, for he adds at once: "By this is my Father glorified, that you bear much fruit, and so prove to be my disciples" (15:9). He continues, a few verses later, "You did not choose me, but I chose you and appointed that you should go and bear fruit and that your fruit should abide; so that whatever you ask the Father in my name, he may give it to you" (15:16).

That all apostolic fruitfulness flows from prayer in union with Christ's eucharistic sacrifice is implicit also in Vatican II's teaching that the liturgy is the fountain from which all the Church's power flows (*SC* 10).

This does not mean that only preachers and missionaries and other apostles are to pray for the fruits of their apostolate. The whole Church prays for these fruits in the eucharistic sacrifice. Moreover, certain members of the Church have a special vocation to pray and offer their lives as a sacrificial prayer with Jesus for this fruitfulness of the Church. "For it is God who sends workers into the harvest when he is asked to do so, who opens the minds of non-Christians to hear the gospel, and who makes the word of salvation fruitful in their hearts" (*AG* 40).[1]

Likewise, in his Last Supper prayer, Jesus says that he consecrates himself as a sacrifice that his disciples may be consecrated as apostles: "For them do I consecrate myself, that they also may be

1. Vatican II is speaking of the role of the contemplative religious life in the missionary activity of the Church; all Christians, however, must share in some way in this role of prayer and sacrifice for the fruitfulness of the Church.

consecrated in truth" (17:19). In other words, their apostolic power (and their steadfast fidelity in their mission) is the fruit of his sacrifice. His sacrifice, continued in the eucharistic liturgy, is the living prayer of their apostolate.

Christ's Prayer Echoed in Our Eucharistic Prayers

In the Mass the Church consciously reproduces our blessed Lord's own prayer and sacrifice. It is to be expected, then, that John 17, one of the scriptural expressions of our Lord's intentions in his sacrifice, will be echoed in a variety of ways in the words and gestures of the eucharistic prayer of the Mass.

For example, in the old Roman Canon, the priest says, while repeating the gestures of Jesus, "The day before he suffered, he took bread in his sacred hands, and *looking up to heaven* to you, his almighty Father." In John 17, our Lord's raising of his eyes to the Father as he begins his prayer indicates at once the eucharistic character of the prayer: "When Jesus had spoken these words, he *lifted up his eyes to heaven* and said, 'Father!' " (17:1).

This is the third time that John tells us that Jesus lifted his eyes, and each time it is a gesture of thanksgiving. Whenever John indicates this gesture of Jesus, he intends to give eucharistic significance to the event he is narrating.

For example, he begins the account of the miracle of the feeding of the five thousand with five loaves, saying, "*Lifting up his eyes* and seeing that a multitude was coming to him . . . Jesus then took the loaves, *and when he had given thanks* . . ." (6:5,11). Later on, he refers to the place of the miracle as "the place where they ate the bread after the Lord had *given thanks*" (6:23).

So, too, John gives eucharistic significance to the raising of Lazarus: "And Jesus *lifted up his eyes* and said, 'Father, I *thank thee* that thou hast heard me' " (11:41). John thus ties in the raising of Lazarus with the Eucharist. The raising of Lazarus is a sign foreshadowing our participation in the resurrection of Jesus. This participation is accomplished through eucharistic participation: "He who eats my flesh and drinks my blood has eternal life, and I will raise him up at the last day" (6:54). The Eucharist is a thanksgiving for the spiritual resurrection, the eternal life which we already have. It is an expectation of our bodily resurrection at the Lord's second coming: "For as often as you eat this bread and drink the cup, you proclaim the Lord's death until he comes" (1 Cor. 11:26).

Therefore, we pray in eucharistic prayer III, "Ready to greet him when he comes again . . . we hope to enjoy forever the vision of your glory." This hope is certain, for it is grounded in the eucharistic petition of Jesus: "Father, I desire that they also whom thou hast given me, may be with me where I am, to behold my glory which thou hast given me in thy love for me before the foundation of the world" (17:24).

Therefore, "it is right and just that we always and everywhere give thanks" in offering this sacrifice, thanking the Father for the very things we petition, for these things are granted to us in Christ whose prayer is always heard.

Similarly, the great petition of John 17 is for unity. This, too, is our petition in all the eucharistic prayers, for example, "May all of us who share in the body and blood of Christ be brought together in unity by the Holy Spirit" (II).

Jesus prayed likewise for the unity of his apostles (17:11) and for all those who believe in their word (17:20). Therefore, in each of the eucharistic prayers we pray for the hierarchy, the successors of the Apostles: "For our pope, our bishop, and for all who hold and teach the Catholic faith that comes to us from the apostles."

We have given these few examples, and shall give more later, as a key to the contemplation of the eucharistic mystery. As a prayerful response to John 13–16, John 17 expresses many of the divine realities which the Christian must deeply penetrate in his contemplative participation in the eucharistic sacrifice.

26
Dynamic Involvement in the Lord's Prayer

"When Jesus had spoken these words, he lifted up his eyes *to heaven* and said, *'Father!'* " (Jn. 17:1). Here we see Jesus practicing what he had preached in the Sermon on the Mount: "Pray then like this: 'Our Father, who art in heaven'" (Matt. 6.9).

Christ's eucharistic prayer in John 17 corresponds closely to the Our Father. When we realize that this prayer expresses the intentions of our Lord's sacrifice, and that these are practically the same as the intentions of the Our Father, we will see that the Our Father finds its fullest meaning only when it is prayed as a eucharistic prayer, as a participation in our Lord's sacrifice. Whether we pray it at Mass or at other times, if we pray it with deep contemplative understanding, it will involve *our whole lives* ever more intimately in the paschal mystery.

From St. John we learn that our Lord's *sacrifice* is the Lord's prayer. From St. Luke we learn that his *life* is the Lord's prayer. The Our Father expresses the intentions of Jesus in all that he did. We shall develop these two ideas in all that follows.

"Lord, Teach Us to Pray"

The disciples, seeing Jesus at prayer, were moved with the desire to pray, and said, "Lord, teach us to pray!" (Lk. 11:1). In response,

Jesus gave them the Lord's Prayer which is the model of all Christian prayer and the expression of its true spirit.

Impressed with the fact that our Lord's example had inspired the *desire* to pray, St. Luke realized that this same example also teaches effectively *how* to pray. Therefore, throughout his Gospel Luke takes every opportunity to show us Jesus at prayer, and especially before each significant step in his earthly career. Thus, St. Luke's Gospel, too, is a course in contemplation. Jesus taught *in words* the petitions of the Our Father. But did he also teach each one of these petitions by his example as well?

"*Father!*"

All the Evangelists show us Jesus again and again addressing God as Father. St. Luke records two such occasions mentioned by none of the others: "Father, forgive them; for they know not what they do" (Lk. 23:34); and, "Father, into thy hands I commit my spirit!" (Lk. 23:46).

Is not the latter the supremely perfect prayer: the joyous surrender of one's whole being to the Father in love, the perfect expression of love of God?

And the former, "Father, forgive them," is the supreme expression of love of neighbor, offering self in sacrifice for them, bearing witness to the Father's own compassionate mercy toward all his children. In praying thus, Jesus is practicing what he preached in his parable of the prodigal son. He is absolutely convinced of the Father's compassion which he had described so movingly in that story (Lk. 15).

He shows himself the complete opposite of the elder brother in the parable who was angry that the prodigal son had been forgiven. Jesus, true elder brother of all the children of God, says to Dismas, his brother, "Truly, I say to you, today you will be with me in Paradise" (Lk. 23:43). Jesus has not the least hesitation about receiving sinners into his Father's house. He is fully convinced that his sacrifice will be accepted, giving him power over all flesh to give eternal life to all whom the Father has given him (Jn. 17:2). He has experienced the Father's love for him as Son as a love which embraces also all his brothers who come to him for forgiveness. He would have all his sinful brothers come home like the prodigal, saying, "Our Father, who art in heaven, we have sinned. . . . Forgive us our trespasses. . . ."

The Gospel in a Word

In two words, "Our Father!", is contained the whole Gospel and the perfect response to it. The Good News proclaimed by Jesus is that God wills to be our Father: "Father, I have manifested thy name to the men whom thou gavest me out of the world"—thy name Father! (Jn. 17:6); "Go to my brothers and say to them, I am ascending to my Father and your Father" (Jn. 20:17).

The whole life and being of Jesus cries out "Father!" and his cry is at once the revelation of the Father and mankind's loving response to this revelation. The perfect description of his sacrifice —"Father, I am coming to thee!" (Jn. 17:11)—is also the summary of our Lord's entire life on earth.

Containing the complete Gospel of Jesus, the word "Father" sums up the message of each day's liturgy of the word in the Mass. So, too, our response in the liturgy of the Eucharist is summed up in the prayer, "Our Father, who art in heaven." It is most appropriate to pray the Our Father immediately after the eucharistic prayer as we begin the Communion. For the eucharistic prayer is our Lord's own prayer and sacrificial action made visible and present in the prayer and action of the priest. Immediately after this priestly prayer and action, we express our full participation in them by saying, together with the priest, "Our Father . . ." thus indicating in prayer the profound meaning of our communion in the sacrifice through our receiving of our Lord's Body and Blood.

The Holy Spirit, Our Daily Bread

In St. Luke's Gospel, immediately after teaching the words of the Our Father, Jesus presents two parables which teach perseverance in prayer. In these stories we learn that God is more than a friend (Lk. 11:5–6). He is our Father (11:13). If earthly fathers know how to give good things to their children, "how much more will the heavenly Father give the Holy Spirit to those who ask him" (11:13).

Only in St. Luke's version does Jesus say, "The heavenly Father will give the Holy Spirit to those who ask him." In St. Matthew's version he says that the Father will give "good things" (Matt. 7:11). St. Luke, it seems, is making explicit what was only implicit in our Lord's original words; namely, that the gift par excellence from the Father is the Holy Spirit of adoption, in whom alone we can call him Father.

"The heavenly Father will give the Holy Spirit to those who ask him." We must ask for the Holy Spirit, for we can effectively act upon the words of Jesus telling us to call God "Our Father" only if the Holy Spirit teaches us interiorly, "bearing witness with our spirit that we are children of God" (Rom. 8:16). Therefore, our Lord's full response to the request, "Lord, teach us to pray," is the sending of the Holy Spirit into our hearts. He who would learn how to pray must desire the Holy Spirit and be attentive to his inspirations.

In some ancient manuscripts of St. Luke's Gospel instead of the petition "Give us this day our daily bread" (Lk. 11:3), we read, "Let the Holy Spirit come upon us and purify us." No doubt in reading Luke 11:11–13—"What father among you, if his son asks for bread, will give him a stone?" and "The Father will give the Holy Spirit to those who ask him"—some homilist had realized that the bread of life we ask of our heavenly Father is the Holy Spirit. More precisely, he may have realized that the Holy Spirit is given to us in the eucharistic bread, the body of Christ. For the

Spirit is the fruit of the paschal sacrifice. Because Jesus has gone to the Father in his sacrifice, he is empowered to send us the Holy Spirit in whom we, too, can go to the Father.

When, therefore, we pray before the Communion of the Mass, "Our Father . . . give us this day our daily bread," we are asking for the fruits of the eucharistic banquet, a new outpouring of the Holy Spirit of love, in whom we will be able to experience God as our Father more deeply than ever; and in whom we will be united more intimately to our brothers in love.

"Hallowed Be Thy Name!"

St. Luke, we said, shows us Jesus not only telling us to pray the Our Father, but praying it himself on various occasions of his life on earth.

When did he say, "Hallowed by thy name"? That day when he thrilled with joy in the Holy Spirit and said, "I praise thee, Father, Lord of heaven and earth that thou . . . didst reveal these things to little ones" (Lk. 10:21). God's name is hallowed or glorified when his excellence shines forth and man responds by praising it. God has revealed his glory as Father. Jesus acknowledges that glory and joyously praises it. The Father's supreme excellence is his Fatherhood of the eternal Son. Jesus rejoices that this has been revealed to the little ones in their very grace of adoption as sons. In accepting the revelation of the Father and the Son, they, too, become sons of the Father. By this sonship more than by anything else, is the Father glorified; by this above all is his name hallowed. "By this my Father is glorified that you bear much fruit" (Jn. 15:8), bringing many sons to the Father, through the preaching of your word.

St. Luke shows us the psychological situation giving rise to our Lord's thrill of joy that the Father had seen fit to reveal himself. "The seventy returned *with joy,* saying, 'Lord, even the demons are subject to us in your name!'" (Lk. 10:17). But Jesus gives them a more wonderful reason for rejoicing than the fact that they have apostolic powers: "Do not rejoice in this, that the spirits are subject to you; but rejoice that your names are written in heaven" (10:20). Rejoice because you are recorded in the family register of the heavenly Father!

As he speaks, his reflection upon these wonderful things fills Jesus himself with joy and gratitude: "In that same hour he rejoiced in the Holy Spirit and said, 'I thank thee, Father . . . that thou hast revealed these things to the little ones!' " (10:21). The mere thought that their names are written in heaven and that all these brothers of his will one day see the face of the Father with him in heaven, overwhelms Jesus with joy in the Holy Spirit, and he hallows the Father's name in thanksgiving!

When we pray, then, "Father, hallowed be thy name!" we should mean: "Father, may you reveal yourself to a multitude of men who will glorify you with Jesus forever!"

"Glorify Thy Son That Thy Son May Glorify Thee!"

This petition of Jesus in John 17:1 corresponds to "Hallowed be thy name!" "Father, glorify thy Son that thy Son may glorify thee. . . . Glorify thou me in thy own presence with the glory which I had with thee before the world was made" (17:1,5).

In asking to be taken into the Father's presence and glory, we said, Jesus is really asking the Father to accept his sacrifice. For the purpose in offering sacrifice is communion with God, presence with him.

Our Lord's Resurrection, in which his whole being is transfigured with divine glory, in which he is manifest to us as true Son of God filled with the Father's glory, is the sign that his sacrifice has been accepted. His sacrifice has been effective and his petitions have been granted, above all, his petition for eternal life for his brethren. "Glorify thy Son that the Son may glorify thee, since thou hast given him power over all flesh, to give eternal life to all whom thou hast given him" (17:1–2). The Father is hallowed by the gift of divine life to us.

The Kingdom: Knowing the Father and the Son

This petition is also the equivalent of "Thy kingdom come!" Except
in one place (Jn. 3:3,5), St. John always refers to the Kingdom of
God as "life" or "eternal life." "This is eternal life"; this is the
kingdom of God, "that they may know thee, the only true God,
and Jesus Christ whom thou hast sent" (17:3). "Know" means to
be in a vital and intimate relationship with the Father and Jesus,
and such a relationship comes through believing in Jesus and hearing his words. This relationship, this communion with God, is the
fruit of our Lord's sacrifice. It is the answer to his petition, "Thy
kingdom come!"

To pray "thy kingdom come" in preparation for Holy Communion at Mass is to ask for the full fruits of our participation in
our Lord's sacrifice: intimate communion with the Father in
Jesus in communion with all his children that thus the Father may
be glorified, and his name be hallowed.

However, this knowing the Father and Jesus Christ in this life
through faith, this experiencing of them in intimate communion,
is only the initial fruit of our Lord's sacrifice. Jesus prays that he
may bring us into the *fullness* of his own glory: "Father, I desire
that they also whom thou hast given me *may be with me where
I am,* to behold my glory . . ." (17:24).

In the "liturgy of the word" before this eucharistic prayer, Jesus
had instructed his disciples, saying, "I go to prepare a place for
you and . . . I will come again and will take you to myself *that
where I am you also may be*" (14:23). What he had first said to
his disciples in word he expresses to the Father in the form of a
petition in his sacrifice. He asks to be glorified with the Father in
his own presence (17:5). He asks that his sacrifice be accepted
so that he may prepare in the Father's presence a place for his
disciples. "The glory thou hast given to me I have given to them.
. . . I desire that they . . . may be with me where I am" (17:22,24).

Such is the full meaning of the petition, "Thy kingdom come!"

"Thy Kingdom Come" in Luke

For St. Luke, too, the hallowing of the Father's name is brought about by the coming of the kingdom. The kingdom, for Luke as for John, consists in knowing the Father and the Son, receiving in faith the experiential knowledge of God given by Jesus in love through the Holy Spirit. "No one knows who the Son is except the Father, or who the Father is except the Son and any one to whom the Son chooses to reveal him" (Lk. 10:22).

A close parallelism between two sayings of Jesus in Luke brings out the identity of the kingdom with the knowing of the Father and Son. "Fear not, little flock, for it is your Father's good pleasure to give you the kingdom" (12:32). It is to the little ones that the kingdom is given (12:32). It is to the little ones that the Father reveals the Son and the Son reveals the Father (10:21). It is the "Father's good pleasure" (12:32) to give the kingdom to the little flock. It is the Father's "gracious will" (10:21) to reveal the mystery of the Son to the little ones. "It is the pleasure of the Son to reveal the Father" to them (10:22,s).

"Then turning to the disciples he said privately, 'Blessed are the eyes which see what you see! For I tell you that many prophets and kings desired to see what you see, and did not see it, and to hear what you hear, and did not hear it'" (Lk. 10:23). Luke places these words immediately after our Lord's words about the revelation of the Father and the Son to bring out that the kingdom desired by the kings and prophets was really this revelation.

All these sayings are a commentary on the beatitude, "Blessed are you poor, for yours is the kingdom of God" (Lk. 6:20). To the poor, the little ones, the humble and lowly, the Father and the Son are revealed. Theirs is the kingdom, the knowledge of the Father and the Son: "Blessed are the eyes which see what you see!" (Lk. 10:23). "Blessed are the pure in heart, for they shall see God" (Matt. 5:8).

In the very knowing of the Father and the Son by the little ones,

God is glorified. His name, his presence, is hallowed in our hearts, and our lips give joyous expression of praise and thanks: "I thank thee, Father, Lord of heaven and earth that thou . . . hast revealed these things to little ones" (10:21).

St. Luke is the Evangelist of the divine graciousness and man's recognition of this graciousness in joyous glorification of the Father: "Yes, Father, for such was thy gracious will" (10:21). The knowing of God through his self-revelation to the little ones, is sheerly the gift of his good pleasure, his graciousness to those whom he favors: Glory to God in the heights of heaven And on earth peace to men whom he favors" (Lk. 2:14).

St. Luke, the Evangelist of prayer and thanksgiving, loves to show man's joyous response to the divine grace.

The concert of praise inaugurated by the angels at the cradle of the divine Infant sounds again and again through all the pages of the gospel. Luke is happy to note all the manifestations of gratitude and joy aroused by the benefits of the Lord. The sound of singing hearts is heard throughout his work of optimism, which opens with the *Gloria in excelsis Deo* and comes to a fitting conclusion in the scene of the apostles blessing God in the temple (24:53).[1]

"The shepherds returned, glorifying and praising God for all they had heard and seen" (2:20). The paralytic whose sins were forgiven took up his bed and "went home glorifying God. And amazement seized them all, and they glorified God" (5:25–26). When the son of the widow was raised from the dead, "Fear seized them all and they glorified God" (7:16). "And immediately he received his sight and followed him, glorifying God; and all the people, when they saw it, gave praise to God" (18:43). Other examples are found in 2:38; 10:17; 13:17; 19:37; 24:41,52; and above all, of course, in the Magnificat and the Benedictus (1:46–55; 68–79). In these canticles, the Church daily hallows the Name of God with Mary: "Holy is his Name" (1:49).

1. E. Osty, *L'Evangile selon Saint Luc. La Sainte Bible de l'Ecole Biblique de Jerusalem* (Paris: Les Editions Du Cerf, 1961), p. 25.

St. Luke, then, is certainly concerned that we take seriously the Lord's command to pray thus: "Father, hallowed be thy name!" (11:2). It is not enough just to say those words. Following all the examples Luke has indicated, we should ever be joyously glorifying God for the wonders of grace he has accomplished in us. The joy will be deepest, the glorifying will be sincerest in those who know the Father and the Son, those who lovingly experience his interior self-revelation.

When we pray, therefore, "hallowed by thy name, thy kingdom come," we should mean it this way: "Father, reveal the mystery of your Fatherhood in the hearts of all men. Let them experience your love in the grace of filial adoption in the Holy Spirit, that the joy of Jesus may be in them, that they may respond in the joyous glorifying of your name!"

In Word and Deed Jesus Prays "Thy Kingdom Come!"

Throughout St. Luke's Gospel we see Jesus praying for the coming of the Kingdom. For Luke shows us Jesus praying at each crucial step in his work of establishing the Kingdom of God. Everything that Jesus gives to his disciples and to his Church he receives from the Father in answer to his petitions. Before he taught his apostles to ask for whatever they hoped to give in their apostolate, he himself practiced what he preached, praying for the fruits of his work.

Luke records that Jesus *was praying* (3:21) as he began his messianic work at his Baptism when "the Holy Spirit descended upon him in bodily form as a dove" 3:22). If Jesus taught his disciples to ask the Father above all for the Holy Spirit (11:13), was he not himself asking for the Holy Spirit for his people when "he was praying" at his Baptism in the Jordan? For the Spirit descending as a dove from heaven and remaining upon him manifested him as the one who gives the Holy Spirit (Jn. 1:32–33).

Even when great crowds press upon him to receive the benefits

of his apostolate, this greatest of Apostles nevertheless goes aside
to pray for these benefits. "Great multitudes gathered to hear and to
be healed of their infirmities. But he withdrew to the wilderness
and prayed" (Lk. 5:15–16). Even the most urgent af apostolates
must be rooted in prayer.

Those about whom we are concerned in love are not a distrac-
tion in prayer; rather, their neediness impels us to the Father to
petition what they need. Every true apostle prays, and Jesus himself did.

Again, in St. Luke's account, Jesus "was praying alone," though
the disciples were with him, "when he turned to them to elicit
from them their profession of faith in his mission: "But who do
you say that I am?" (Lk. 9:18–20). If our Lord's question springs
from prayer, does not this suggest that he was praying for his
disciples that they would give the right response to his question,
praying that they would understand, in faith, who he really was?
And Peter answered, "The Christ of God!" (9:21).

It is even clearer in Luke 22:32 that Peter's faith is the fruit of
our Lord's petition for it: "Simon, Simon, Satan demanded to have
you, that he might sift you like wheat, but I have prayed for you
that your faith may not fail; and when you have turned again,
strengthen your brethren."

The same is true in John 17 where Jesus asks for firmness of
faith for his disciples: "Consecrate them in the truth" (Jn. 17:17).

Luke points out also that Jesus before starting his journey up to
Jerusalem where he knew he would suffer and die, "ascended the
mountain to pray, and *while he prayed*" the Transfiguration took
place (9:28–29). No doubt he prayed not only for his personal
courage in facing his sufferings, but also for his disciples that they
would not be scandalized by these sufferings. He had good reason
to worry about them, for had not Peter rejected the idea of a
suffering Messiah just after confessing that Jesus was the Messiah!
Had he not rebuked Jesus when he foretold his sufferings! (Matt.
16:21). The prayer of Jesus must have been, "Lead them not into
temptation." Let them not fail in the agonizing test of their faith

which they will undergo in seeing the sufferings of the Messiah. Jesus was always praying for us, always worried about us!

Jesus prays in the garden, and in answer receives strength from heaven to face his cross (Lk. 22:41).

Jesus prays for the coming of the Kingdom, then, by praying before each phase of his work in establishing it. "Thy kingdom come!" If he tells his disciples to pray without cease (18:1–5), he is asking them to do no more than he himself has done. In his ceaseless prayer he is in perpetual union with the Father as he goes about the Father's business of establishing the kingdom. He ever looks to the Father to discern his will. He "joins contemplation with apostolic love" (*PC* 5).

Like Jesus, we pray, "thy kingdom come," and then prove the sincerity of the petition by laboring to establish the kingdom in the hearts of our fellowmen.

27

Thy Will Be Done

As with the other petitions of the Our Father, Jesus set the example in praying this one, too. "Father, if thou art willing, remove this cup from me; nevertheless not my will, but thine, be done" (Lk. 22:42).

The will of the Father referred to in this prayer of Jesus and also in the Our Father, is not merely God's will for this situation or that. It is the whole salvific will of God, his total plan of salvation.

This is especially clear in St. Mark's account of our Lord's agony and prayer. The Father's will which Jesus embraces is called "the hour" and "the cup." "And going a little farther, he fell on the ground and prayed that, if it were possible, *the hour* might pass from him. And he said, 'Abba, Father, all things are possible to thee; remove *this cup* from me; yet not what I will, but what thou wilt'" (Mk. 14:35–36).

"The Cup"

The Jewish custom of the father of the family filling the cups of all at table gave rise to the common metaphor of "the cup" signifying the lot in life which God has destined for each one. The Father in heaven has prepared our cups. "My cup overflows" (Ps. 23:5). "The Lord is my chosen portion and my cup; thou holdest my lot"

(Ps. 16:5). And of the wicked it is said, "A scorching wind shall be the portion of their cup" (Ps. 11:6).

In Mark 10:38, in the discussion with James and John, our Lord's cup is presented in parallelism with his Baptism, so that cup and Baptism are equivalent expressions: "Are you able to drink the cup that I drink, or to be baptized with the Baptism with which I am baptized?" To baptize means to plunge into water. Waters, however, were a symbol of suffering and sorrows (cf. Ps. 68:1–5). Thus, the cup of Jesus, his lot in life, is suffering.

The cup, the Baptism, of Jesus is not any sort of suffering and death, but precisely Messianic suffering. This is not a case of a mere private individual facing hardships and death. For the point at issue in this discussion with James and John and with the other ten who were angry with the two (Mk. 10:35–45), is precisely the nature of our Lord's messianic role. He is not an earthly Messiah, but one sent to save the world through sufferings. He is the Suffering Servant; the cup and the baptism signify his sufferings for the accomplishment of the salvific plan of Yahweh: "If he gives his life as an offering for sin . . . *the will of the Lord* shall be accomplished through him. . . . Through his suffering, my servant shall justify many, and their guilt he shall bear" (Isa. 53:10–11,c).

Clearly, Jesus is claiming to be this Suffering Servant, for he ends the discussion, saying, "The Son of man also came not to be served but to serve, and to give his life as a ransom for many" (Mk. 10:45). The will of the Lord which is accomplished when Jesus drinks the cup is the plan of salvation. "Thy will be done," as said by Jesus in his agony, and by all his people as they pray the Our Father with him, is a prayer for the implementation of God's will to save mankind.

"The Hour"

"The Hour," we said, is another expression for "the cup," bringing out a different aspect of the meaning of our Lord's passion and death. "Cup" and "Baptism" put the emphasis on the full human reality of our Lord's sufferings, the bitterness of the gall he must drink. "Hour," however, puts the emphasis on the eternal will or decree of God, and his saving action through Jesus in implementing his decree.

In the Scriptures, expressions such as "hour," "the day," "the times" had a religious meaning, indicating God's activity in history. "Hour" signifies a turning point in history, a decisive stage in God's salvation plan.

Speaking, for example, of the second coming, Jesus says, "Of that day or that hour no one knows, not even the angels in heaven, nor the Son, but only the Father" (Mk. 13:32). The plan of God is decreed in heaven by the Father; it is not the role of the Son on earth to make the plan, but, as servant, to carry it out on earth.

Our Lord in his human way, dreading the sufferings which would be his in the hour, "prayed that if it were possible the hour might pass from him." But it was not possible; the hour is divinely decreed, and what is decreed in heaven must be accomplished on earth. And, therefore, Jesus arises from his prayer, saying, "It is enough; *the hour has come*"; it cannot pass me by; "the Son of man is betrayed into the hands of sinners. Rise, let us be going; see, my betrayer is at hand" (Mk. 14:41–42).

The hour is accomplished on earth, however, not through the working of some blind, inexorable fate, but through the free acceptance and implementation of the plan by the Son and Servant. "*If he gives* his life as an offering for sin . . . the will of the Lord shall be accomplished through him" (Isa. 53:10). The Son makes the gift of self; he accepts the plan: "Not my will, but thine, be done!" Then he says, "The hour has come; rise, let us be going!" I must be about my Father's business. The will of the Lord will be accomplished through my willing implementation of it. The providence of God works through man's fulfillment of responsibility.

Thus, not only the eternal decree is involved, but the acceptance and execution of the decree by the human will of Jesus, the Servant of Yahweh. "Thy will be done on earth as it is in heaven"—what

was decreed in heaven is accomplished on earth, when the will of
the Son of Man willingly carries out the will of the Father, the
will to save mankind. In this meeting of wills, the new covenant
is established (Heb. 10:9–10); God's kingdom is inaugurated.

The Son of Man in Daniel, with whom Jesus identifies himself,
is an eschatological figure, and the term, "the hour" evokes his
coming. At his coming, the Son of Man receives the Kingdom
(Dan. 7:14). When, therefore, Jesus says, "The hour has come!"
it means the eschatological kingdom is here! The kingdom is
present in the person of Christ; the reign of God is inaugurated in
"the hour" of the paschal mystery. The kingdom begins when
Jesus says, "Thy will be done!" God reigns where his will is done.

Thus, in the Our Father, "thy will be done" (Matt. 6:10) is
practically a synonym for "thy kingdom come," and is not found
in St. Luke's version, which is probably the earlier form of the
Lord's Prayer. Matthew's addition, "thy will be done," is an interpretation making explicit what is implicit in "thy kingdom come."

In the accomplishment of this salvific will of the Father, the
Kingdom is inaugurated and the Father's Name is hallowed. "I
have glorified thee on earth, I have accomplished the work thou
hast given me to do . . ." (Jn. 17:4).

"Thy Will Be Done"

In the prayer of Jesus at the Last Supper, "the hour" is presented
in terms of the paschal sacrifice of Jesus and in relationship to the
eucharistic sacrifice. "Father, *the hour* has come! Glorify thy Son
that thy Son may glorify thee" (Jn. 17:1). The entire Last Supper
scene in John is presented in the context of the feast of the Passover: "Now before the feast of the Passover, when Jesus knew that
his hour had come to depart out of this world to the Father . . ."
(13:1). Jesus passes out of this world to the Father, just as in the
original passover Israel had passed from the slavery of Egypt to
the Promised Land.

There are two aspects of the one paschal mystery, the one

sacrifice: the earthly and the heavenly phases. "I glorified thee on earth, having accomplished the work which thou gavest me to do" (17:4) refers to the earthly phase. "Glorify thy Son that the Son may glorify thee" is a prayer for the heavenly phase; "Glorify thou me in thy own presence with the glory which I had with thee before the world was made" (17:5). On earth Jesus offers himself in sacrifice; he goes to the Father by way of his death. From his glory in the presence of the Father, with "power over all flesh to give eternal life" (17:2), the Son of God carries on the heavenly phase, sending the fruit of his sacrifice, the Holy Spirit, who brings us to the Father.

The Last Supper, the Passion and Death of Jesus, his Resurrection and Ascension to the Father's right hand, and the sending of the Holy Spirit, are all one same paschal mystery, which is now being accomplished in us on earth through the heavenly activity of Jesus. This activity is manifest to us especially in the eucharistic sacrifice.

"Thy will be done on earth as it is in heaven" is a prayer that Christ's heavenly power work effectively in us, that his paschal mystery continue and complete its work in us, especially through our participation in the Eucharistic Sacrifice in which we solemnly pray the Lord's prayer for this intention. "Thy will be done" is a prayer that, through Christ, God will accomplish his saving will in us.

But this can be only through the response of our will, like the response of Jesus in his agony. It can only be through our drinking of the cup with him, through our acceptance of the salvific will of God in every life-situation. For the will of God is all-embracing; nothing escapes his love's purpose to reconcile all things to himself in his Son, "making peace by the blood of his cross" (Col. 1:20). "We know that in everything God works for good with those who love him" (Rom. 8:28). "Thy will be done," therefore, means: May the paschal obedience of Christ be accomplished in us—by God's fatherly love and grace and the cooperation of our love and obedience—that we may be glorified with Jesus in the Father's presence.

A Will for Unity

"The will of the Lord" (Isa. 53:10) for whose accomplishment we pray in the Our Father, is descibed more specifically by St. Paul in the magnificent prologue to Ephesians: "The mystery of his purpose . . . to bring everything together under Christ as head" (1:10,j). It is a will for unity, for the reconciliation of all mankind with God and with one another in Christ.

For this the Lord prayed in his Our Father, his eucharistic prayer at the Last Supper and on the Cross: "That they may all be one" (Jn. 17:21).

Before expressing this in his eucharistic prayer, Jesus had first taught it in his "liturgy of the word." He had proclaimed that the mark of his true disciples is their unity in love for one another: "By this all men will know that you are my disciples, if you have love for one another" (Jn. 13:35). Under the allegory of the vine, he had taught that he himself in the eucharistic mystery is the source of this unity. In the allegory of the Good Shepherd, he had taught that his sacrifice is the only source of the unity of his apostles and of the whole flock. The Good Shepherd lays down his life so that "there shall be one flock, one shepherd" (10:16); "to gather into one the children of God who are scattered abroad" (11:52).

To emphasize that his sacrifice is the only source of unity for scattered mankind, one of the last words he spoke before beginning his eucharistic prayer was his prediction that even his closest followers, his apostles, his specially chosen ones, would be scattered: "Do you now believe? The hour is coming, indeed it has come, when you will be scattered, every man to his home, and will leave me alone" (Jn. 16:32). Jesus prays and dies alone.

But his sacrifice will reunite them and he expresses this purpose and efficacy of his sacrifice in his eucharistic prayer: "Holy Father, keep them in thy name, which thou hast given me, that they may be one, even as we are one. . . . I do not pray for these only, but also for those who believe in me through their word, that they may all be one; even as thou, Father, art in me, and I in thee, that they also may be in us, so that the world may believe that thou hast sent me" (17:11, 20–21).

Their love and unity is the proof that God is in their midst in the person of Jesus his Son. It is the sign that God's own love is in them, and that the Son is in them: "that the love with which thou hast loved me may be in them, and I in them" (17:26).

For all this we pray when we say, "Thy kingdom come, thy will be done!"

"Forgive Us Our Trespasses..."

In praying for unity, Jesus was praying also for the removal of the obstacles to unity, praying for the forgiveness of sins against God and neighbor. Implicit, therefore, in his prayer for unity was the petition, "forgive us our trespasses as we forgive those who trespass against us!" "Father, forgive them, for they know not what they do," he prayed at his crucifixion, thus practicing what he had preached. Only they who forgive can say in full truth, "Our Father!"

The Will of God, Our Daily Bread

Nowhere do the Evangelists show us Jesus asking for his daily food. Does this mean that he himself did not practice this particular petition of the Our Father which he preached to us?

The Gospels do show us Jesus *giving thanks* for the bread with which he miraculously fed five thousand (Jn. 6:11,23), and for the eucharistic bread with which he feeds all of us (Lk. 22:17,19).

Does Jesus give thanks for bread without even petitioning for it? Does he hint to us that our prayer for bread, for life's necessities,

should be practically a thanksgiving in advance, so certain are we
in faith that this bread will be given us, if we seek first the kingdom (Matt. 6:23), and if our true food is the will of the Father:
"Thy kingdom come, thy will be done!"

When the disciples were surprised that the hungry and weary
Jesus was not eating, they urged him, saying "Rabbi, eat!" (Jn.
4:31). Jesus replied, "I have food to eat of which you do not
know. . . . My food is to do the will of him who sent me, and to
accomplish his work" (Jn. 4:32,34). The Samaritan woman's new
thirst for the waters welling up to life eternal made her forget
her physical thirst: "the woman left her water jar and went away
into the city and said to the people, 'Come see a man who told
me all that I ever did!' " (Jn. 4:28–29). So, too, the hunger of
Jesus for the salvation of this woman and her fellow-citizens made
him forget his physical hunger. Seeing the woman run off to bring
the townsfolk back to him, Jesus forgot to eat no doubt because
he was praying for the accomplishment of the Father's salvific will
in their regard. Seeing the fields of wheat stretching out before him,
with his contemplative insight he saw a great harvest of men ripe
for eternal life: "I tell you, lift up your eyes and see the fields are
already white for harvest" (4:35).

The fields of wheat make us think of the eucharistic wheat in
which Jesus gives us the grace and strength to do the will of the
Father and accomplish his work of salvation in ourselves and in
others. "Give us this day our eucharistic bread!"

Hebrews tells us that when Jesus accepted and implemented the
salvific will of the Father in this meeting of wills the new covenant
was established: "Lo, I have come to do thy will; he abolishes the
first in order to establish the second; and by that will we have been
sanctified through the offering of the body of Jesus Christ once for
all" (Heb. 10:9–10). In the sacrifice of Jesus, the new and eternal
covenant is ratified in his blood (Heb. 9:15–20).

If Jesus says that doing the will of the Father and accomplishing
his work is his food, no doubt he wishes to relate this work to the
eucharistic food in which we participate in his obedient will and,

therefore, in the new covenant. The meeting of our wills, in Christ, with the will of the Father brings us into the new covenant. Our eating of the eucharistic bread is the celebration and the strengthening of this covenant for it strengthens us to accept and implement the salvific will of the Father in our daily life, as we do our work in the consciousness that God works in our work, for the redemption of our world.

"Give us this day our daily Bread" is a further unfolding of the petition, "Thy will be done," even as "thy will be done" unfolds "hallowed be thy name through the coming of thy kingdom." May the eucharistic bread give us power to do your will and accomplish your work of salvation. If we thus seek first your kingdom and its justice, we need not be solicitous about what we shall eat or what we shall put on, for all else will be given to us (Matt. 6:25–33) through our fruitful labors.

Once again we see how the Our Father finds its fullest meaning in relationship with our Lord's paschal sacrifice and our eucharistic participation in it.

The Sacrifice "Once for All"

If Jesus labored throughout his life for the establishment of the Kingdom of God; if he prayed for the coming of the Kingdom as he began each new stage of this work, then "thy kingdom come" must have been a petition very dear to his heart. It must have sprung spontaneously to his lips when his disciples said, "Lord, teach us to pray."

Even more fundamental, of course, was his love of the Father and concern for his glory: "Father, hallowed be thy name!" Ever conscious of the Father and of the mission the Father had given him, Jesus was eager to glorify the Father through the fulfillment of this mission, the establishment of the reign of the Father in the hearts of his children. The eagerness of his lifelong consecration to the Father's glory is clearly manifest in his prayer, "Father, I have glorified thee on earth; I have *accomplished* the work thou hast given me to do" (17:4).

How could he say he had accomplished this work when he had not yet finished it and when he had not yet laid down his life for his sheep?

His words ring true, for they really mean: "Father, I have so totally accepted my mission in my heart; I have so made your will my own that it is as good as accomplished! I am irrevocably consecrated to you, Father, and to the work you have given me. The sacrifice on the cross will be the outward sign of the sacrifice already offered in my heart."

For his prayer, "I have accomplished the work thou hast given me to do," is to be understood in connection with the words he spoke as he died. "It is finished," he said; and he bowed his head and gave up his spirit (Jn. 19:30).

By saying, "*I have accomplished* the work thou hast given me to do, rather than, "*I shall* finish it," Jesus brings out the timeless element, the eternal dimension, the "once for all" character of his sacrifice and its enduring power and efficacy in all times and places. "He entered once for all into the Holy Place . . . ; through the eternal Spirit he offered himself without blemish to God" (Heb. 9:12,14).

"The eternal Spirit" is a reference to the immortality of the divine person of Jesus.[1] The Epistle to the Hebrews had already brought out this point in a variety of ways. It was enough for Jesus to offer himself once. His sacrifice did not have to be repeated year after year like that of the levitical priests on the day of atonement. The high priests of old, "ordinary mortal men," died in succession, one after the other. But of Jesus "it is testified that he lives" (7:8). "He always lives to make intercession for us" (7:25).

1. See C. Spicq, *L'Épitre aux Hébreaux* in *La Sainte Bible de l'École Biblique de Jerusalem* (Paris: Les Editions Du Cerf, 1957), notes on Heb. 9:14 and 7:8.

He is a priest "not by virtue of a law about physical descent, but by the power of an indestructible life" (7:16).

In virtue of his imperishable power, his eternal life, his personality subsisting beyond death, the "Son who has been made perfect forever" (7:28) has obtained "an eternal redemption" for us (9:12) because he has "offered for all time a single sacrifice for sins" (10:12).

Because his sacrifice is timeless, it is ever timely, effective in all times and places.

These truths are thus expressed by Father Edward Schillebeeckx:

> The incarnation of God is the personal entry of the Eternal into the boundaries of time, Eternity itself in temporal form. And this happens in such a way that the historical actions of the man Jesus are personal actions of the eternal Son of God. . . . Since the sacrifice of the Cross and all the mysteries of the life of Jesus are personal acts of God, they are eternally actual and enduring. God the Son himself is therefore present in these human acts in a manner that transcends time. . . . Being radically the act of the personal God, Jesus' human act of redemption, in spite of its true historicity, cannot be merely something of the historical past.[2]

Therefore, Jesus in his action of offering his sacrifice at the Last Supper and on the Cross, can be and *is* fully present in our time and place in the Mass through the eucharistic signs manifesting his sacrifice and making it effective in us.

As we participate in the eucharistic liturgy, through our contemplation of this presence of Jesus offering himself for us, we are dynamically drawn into the paschal mystery. The Father's will for our salvation and the Son's acceptance and implementation of this will on earth are effectively at work, through the eucharistic liturgy, in those who participate with living faith and love.

This is indicated in these words of Jesus, spoken in a eucharistic context at "the place where . . . the Lord had given thanks" (Jn. 6:23:

2. Edward Schillebeeckx, *Christ, the Sacrament of the Encounter with God* (New York: Sheed and Ward, 1963), pp. 55, 57.

All that the Father gives me will come to me; and him who comes to me I will not cast out. For I have come down from heaven, not to do my own will, but the will of him who sent me; and this is the will of him who sent me, that I should lose nothing of all that he has given me, but raise it up at the last day. For this is the will of my Father, that everyone who beholds the Son and believes in him should have eternal life; and I will raise him at the last day (Jn. 6:37–40).

In our eucharistic participation with full contemplative insight we should behold the Son carrying out the Father's will, losing no one whom the Father gives him. Jesus, who did the Father's will on earth, continues to do it in heaven, giving eternal life to those who believe in him as the Father wills he should. And the Father's will is done on earth by those who believe in Jesus: "This is the work of God, that you believe in him whom he has sent" (Jn. 6:29).

Thy will be done!

28
Lead Us Not into Temptation

Jesus,"Tempted As We Are"

"I have accomplished the work thou hast given me to do!" These words of Jesus at the Last Supper, we said, express his total consecration to his mission. In his heart he has already offered his sacrifice. It is as good as accomplished!

And yet when the hour comes for him to drink the cup, when he comes face to face with his sufferings, he seems to draw back. "They came to a place called Gethsemane, and he said to his disciples, 'Sit down here while I pray.' And he took Peter, James and John along with him, and he began to feel distress and dread, and he said to them, 'My heart is almost breaking. You must stay here and keep watch'" (Mk. 14:32–34, Goodspeed).

His dismay and dread result from the shock of suddenly realizing for the first time in a fully human way what it really means to be the suffering Messiah. Though he had long realized that he would have to suffer and die at the hands of his enemies, the full emotional reaction of his whole being comes only when he is actually face to face with the threatening evils.

How very like all of us he was! An explorer who undertakes a very dangerous and laborious journey into the wilderness can make up his mind before he starts that he will achieve his goal no matter how great a cost he will have to pay. When the danger is still at a distance, he can coolly estimate it mentally and be determined to face it. But his thinking about it in advance can never fully appreciate what it will really be like. It is only when one comes at last into the midst of the dangers and grasps the real situation with all these senses and emotions of his body that he reacts to it with his whole being. So it was with Jesus.

The emotional process of our Lord's reactions at the tomb of Lazarus helps us understand what must have happened in the Garden of Olives. Four days before he had already known intellectually that Lazarus was dead and that his sisters Mary and Martha were deeply sorrowed. Yet he did not burst into tears till he came face to face with the living reality of their tears.

Mary went to Jesus, and as soon as she saw him she threw herself at his feet, saying, 'Lord, if you had been here, my brother would not have died.' At the sight of her tears, and those of the Jews who followed her, Jesus said in great distress, with a sigh that came straight from the heart, 'Where have you put him?' They said, 'Lord, come and see. Jesus wept" (Jn. 11:32–34,j). . . . . Then Jesus, deeply moved again, came to the tomb (11:38).

What he knew intellectually before his arrival at Bethany, he now *experiences* in the concrete reality. He lives to the full the human tragedy of the death of his friend and the sorrow of the dead man's sisters. As true man, he reacts in a completely human way. He is profoundly moved. He weeps.

Similarly, Jesus knew intellectually far in advance that he would have to suffer. But the powerful emotional reaction came only when he was actually faced with the threatening evils. It was then that he began to know by experience, not just mentally, what his sufferings would be; and he reacted with sorrow and dread. "He began to be greatly distressed and troubled, and he said to them, 'My soul is very sorrowful, even to death' " (Mk. 14:33–34).

His whole human nature draws back in dread from the cup which he must drink. In Jesus himself is verified what he declares to his disciples, "The spirit indeed is willing, but the flesh is weak"

(Mk. 14:38). How eager and willing he was to drink his chalice when he said on an earlier occasion, "I came to cast fire upon the earth; and would that it were already kindled! I have a baptism to be baptized with; and how I am constrained until it is accomplished!" (Lk. 12:49–50).

His willing spirit is firmly consecrated to his mission, but how his poor human nature, weak precisely because it is human, draws back in distress and dread when the baptism in suffering is suddenly upon him! He asks his disciples to watch with him. He seems to need the strength of their presence.

Though his human nature draws back in fear, in his prayer to his Father he struggles to give full and faithful expression to the interior consecration of his heart to his mission. Not for an instant is he unfaithful to his consecration; not for a moment does his will waver. But he must bring the rest of his being into obedience to his loving heart. He dreads sufferings and death, but he dreads still more the evil of disobedience to the Father. "He learned obedience through what he suffered" (Heb. 5:8).

His love for his Father triumphs. His zeal for the Father's glory holds firm. His dedication to his mission is unwavering. "Now is my soul troubled! And what shall I say? 'Father, save me from this hour'? No, for this purpose I have come to this hour. Father, glorify thy name!" (Jn. 12:27–28).

When he has mastered his fear and distress, he says to his disciples, "The hour has come . . . Rise, let us be going!" Let us face it with courage. (Mk. 14:41–42).

Jesus spoke with conviction stemming from his personal experience of human fear and suffering when he said to his disciples, "Watch and pray that you may not enter into temptation; the spirit indeed is willing, but the flesh is weak" (Mk. 14:38). "In the days of his flesh" (Heb. 5:7), when he "was beset with weakness" (5:2), Jesus was put to the test. He "offered up prayers and supplications, with loud cries and tears, to him who was able to save him from death, and he was heard for his reverent fear" (Heb. 5:7).

As his own love for his Father brings him through victorious, so in prayer his disciples must strengthen their love for the Father if they are not to be defeated in temptation: "Lead us not into temptation." Truly, Jesus is "one who in every respect has been tempted as we are, yet without sinning" (Heb. 4:15).

Lead Us Not Into Temptation

The words of Jesus in his prayer at the Last Supper, "I do not pray that thou shouldst take them out of the world, but that thou shouldst keep them from the evil one" (Jn. 17:15), clarify the last petition of the Our Father, "Lead us not into temptation, but deliver us from evil" (Matt. 6:13).

In both these passages, the same Greek word can be translated either as "evil" or as "the Evil One." The Jerusalem Bible translates the last two lines of the Our Father thus: "Do not put us to the test, but save us from the Evil One" (Matt. 6:13,j). It seems, then, that "deliver us from evil" in Matthew 6:13 is the same petition as "keep them from the Evil One" in Our Lord's prayer at the Last Supper (Jn. 17:15).

The preceding clause, "I do not pray that thou shouldst take them out of the world," thus corresponds to the petition, "lead us not into temptation" or "do not put us to the test."

The Eschatological Temptation

The petition seems to be concerned with the eschatological test. And what do we mean by that?

"Eschatological" refers to "the last days" (Heb. 1:2), the final era of salvation history. In the Old Testament God is frequently described as putting his people to the test to see who are really his. He tests to see who will choose him in obedience or reject him in disobedience (Exod. 16:4). In the eschatological test one chooses the Kingdom of God brought by the Messiah or rejects it: "He who is not with me is against me" (Matt. 12:30).

In St. John's Gospel, the eschatological choice is presented in terms of light and darkness, Christ and Satan. It is a choice between the fallen world under the domination of Satan, prince of this world, and the Kingdom of God, "the things that are to come" (Jn. 16:13), to be brought about by Christ's death and resurrection.

John's Gospel puts much emphasis on eschatology already being accomplished. "The last days," "the things to come," the era the Jews were looking forward to, are already here in the person of Jesus Christ. To choose or reject him is to make the eschatological choice.

There is still the possibility of reversing one's choice of Christ when one falls into severe trials. In the "liturgy of the word" at the Last Supper, Jesus tells his disciples that they will be severely persecuted by the world (Jn. 15:18–16:33) and will be tempted to abandon him: "I have said all this to you to keep you from falling away" (16:1). Then in the eucharistic prayer he prays for them that they will be protected from the Evil One. For, if they were to fall away from Jesus, they would fall under the domination of the Evil One.

Even through any occasion in which one must choose between accepting Christ or rejecting him is an eschatological test, the biblical term "the test" or "the temptation" is applied in a special way to a more severe testing in great tribulation, a testing in which one's perseverance in Christ is at stake.

Above all, the great tribulations at the end of the world would seem to merit the name "the eschatological test," for then Satan will make his supreme efforts "to lead astray, if possible, even the elect" (Matt. 24:24). The eschatological temptation is a temptation to apostasy from Christ and God, a temptation to rebellion in the likeness of Satan, a lapse from the kingdom of Christ into the kingdom of Satan. This is the great apostasy or rebellion spoken of by St. Paul as immediately preceding the revelation and destruction of the anti-Christ (2 Thess. 2:3). Our Lord seems to be referring to the same widespread apostasy from the faith when he asks,

"When the Son of man comes, will he find faith on the earth?" (Lk. 18:8).

The petition, "Lead us not into temptation" or "Do not put us to the test" finds its full meaning against that background. We pray, "Save us from a test in which we would fall away from you and succumb to Satan." "Lead us not into temptation but deliver us from the evil one" is really but one petition—a petition to be rescued from the temptation to succumb to the devil and fall from God.

The petition seems to say, "Do not put us to the test; but, if you judge it necessary to do so, knowing our weakness, we ask that in the test you save us from the Evil One."

The Necessity of the Test

God does wish that we be put to the test. It is in the very nature of human freedom that we choose God or reject him. Freedom is the power to love; but love is not love unless it is a free gift of self springing from one's choice of the beloved. There are, however, many rivals for our love. Satan will certainly try to win us by appealing to us through our love for riches, pleasure, or the will for power. God will permit Satan to tempt us as he tempted even Jesus.

When, therefore, Jesus prays, "Father, I am not asking you to take them out of the world, but that you keep them from the Evil One," it amounts to saying, "I am not asking that there be no temptations in their lives, but that in these testings you protect them from Satan."

In fact, the Apostles, and the whole Church after them, will have to participate in Christ's own eschatological battle and victory over the Evil One and "the world" he rules. This is the main theme of that long section of our Lord's "Liturgy of the word" at the Last Supper (Jn. 15:18–16:33): "If the world hates you, know that it has hated me before you. . . . Truly, truly, I say to you, you will weep and lament, but the world will rejoice; you will be sorrowful, but your sorrow will be turned into joy. . . . In the world you have tribulation, but be of good cheer, I have overcome the world" (15:18; 16:20.33).

"I have overcome the world." I myself was victorious in the testing. Your testing will be a sharing in my testing, your victory a sharing in my victory. The tribulation and the sorrow of which Jesus is speaking is the great eschatological test which begins with our Lord's own testing in his Passion and Death. It is continued till the end of time in the Church, his members. In this trial of his people the new creation comes into being. When Jesus compares his disciples' sorrow and tribulation to the sufferings of a woman in labor, he is evoking a frequent theme of the Scriptures in which Jerusalem, the People of God, is personified as a woman in childbirth bringing forth the new creation (cf. Isa. 26:17; 66:7–14). Out of the tribulation comes forth the so-called "things to come," the eschatological or new era in contrast to the old order which is dominated by Satan.[1]

The eschatological tribulation, then, ("the present distress" (I Cor. 7:26), is the sufferings of the people of God in which their redemption is accomplished by the power of Christ's victory in his personal testing. In this distress through fidelity to Christ "a man is born" (Jn. 16:21) who is the new man, redeemed man, in contrast to fallen man. God's people become a rejoicing mother by the power of Christ's Resurrection. Christ has overcome the world and has cast out the prince of the world and his people must continue with him in his trials (Lk. 22:28) to share in his kingdom.

It is necessary, then, that his Apostles and his whole Church be put to the test of tribulation: "I do not pray that thou shouldst take them out of the world, but that thou shouldst keep them from the Evil One."

Wherever he preached, St. Paul taught the necessity of enduring trial: "They returned . . . reassuring the disciples and exhorting them to continue in the faith, and reminding them that through

1. See note on John 1:10, *Jerusalem Bible*.

many tribulations we must enter the kingdom of God!" (Acts 14:21).

In this whole context of the New Testament teaching on testing and tribulation we can express the meaning of the words, "lead us not into temptation," in this way: "We do not pray that there be no temptations in our lives, but that you will protect us in our trials so that we will not succumb to evil." Our assurance that our prayer is heard is Jesus who went through the test in its fullest bitterness and won the victory through his steadfast choice of the Father.

Who Are Victorious in the Test?

Who are delivered from the Evil One in the trial? The answer is found in a passage in the Apocalypse of St. John, which is like a homily on "the liturgy of the word" of the Last Supper:

Write to the angel of the Church in Philadelphia. . . . I know that though you are not very strong, you have kept my commandment and not disowned my Name. . . . You are the people I love. . . . Because you have kept my commandment to endure trials, I will keep you safe in the time of trial which is going to come for the whole world, to test the people of the world (Rev. 3:8–10,j).

Because they have been faithful in enduring lesser trials, they will be kept safe for Christ in the severe eschatological trial.

"You have not disowned my Name. . . . I will keep you safe in the time of trial." This corresponds to our Lord's petition at the Last Supper, "Holy Father, keep them in thy name which thou hast given me, that they may be one even as we are one" (Jn. 17:11). The Father has given his Name, that is, his divinity, to Jesus, and so they are one. Keep them in the power of my divinity which you have given to me; preserve them through their faith in my divinity.

In "the liturgy of the word" at the Last Supper, Jesus had called for a faith in himself which is on a par with our faith in God.

"Believe in God; believe also in me" (Jn. 14:1). This is because Jesus is on a par with God as Son of God sent for our salvation. With such faith we need not fear in our tribulations. We will be safe from evil: "Let not your hearts be troubled; believe in God; believe also in me." Anyone whom the Father wills to keep safe, he entrusts to Jesus. He gives him to Jesus through faith in him as Son of God: "They shall never perish, and no one shall snatch them out of my hand. My Father who has given them to me is greater than all, and no one is able to snatch them out of the Father's hand. I and the Father are one" (Jn. 10:28–30).

"Lead us not into temptation but deliver us from evil" is thus a participation in our Lord's prayer. It means "Keep them in thy name which thou hast given me"; keep them in my divinity; preserve them in their faith in me. For ultimately, the only evil is loss of faith, apostasy from Christ. The eschatological temptation is a temptation to reject Jesus. "By this you know the Spirit of God: every spirit which confesses that Jesus Christ has come in the flesh is of God, and every spirit which does not confess Jesus is not of God; this is the spirit of antichrist" (1 Jn. 4:2–3).

He who disowns the name of Christ has fallen into the hands of the Evil One. He who believes in Jesus till the end will be victorious in the eschatological test.

This faith in Jesus is possible only through the interior witness of the Holy Spirit. In "the liturgy of the word" at the Last Supper, the long passage in which Jesus foretells that all his followers will be put to the great test is included between two statements: "If the world hates you, know that it has hated me before you. . . . Take courage, I have overcome the world" (Jn. 15:18;16:33). Highlighted in the center of this literary "inclusion" is our Lord's promise of the Holy Spirit, the Advocate who will enable them to make the right choice in the eschatological test.

When the Apostles and Christians are cast out of the synagogues (16:2); when the religious leaders will condemn them as they had condemned Jesus before them, the great temptation will be to think that perhaps Jesus was wrong after all, and that the leaders who put him to death as a sinner were right. For these leaders have the whole force of their office behind them; "the scribes and Pharisees sit on Moses' seat" (Matt. 23:2).

But the Holy Spirit will convict the world of sin and will vindicate Jesus whom the world had convicted (16:8–11). He will show that the victory belongs to Christ, not to the world (16:11, 33). The disciples, through their faith in Jesus inspired by the witness of the Holy Spirit, will have the victory with him.

"Consecrate Them in the Truth"

In the eschatological test, we said, one is tempted to abandon the faith. This is a temptation to apostasy. Our Lord had to pray in a special way for his apostles because they in a special way are involved in the eschatological battle, and above all, Peter: "Simon, Simon, behold Satan demanded to have you, that he might sift you like wheat, but I have prayed for you that your faith may not fail; and when you have turned again, strengthen your brethren" (Lk. 22:31).

In John 17:15–17, the prayer for Peter is expanded to include all the apostles: "I do not pray that thou shouldst take them out of the world, but that thou shouldst keep them from the Evil One. . . . Consecrate them in the truth." Keep them so firm in the truth that their faith will not fail.

The prayer of the people of God, "lead us not into temptation but deliver us from evil," especially when it is said in the eucharistic liturgy, is a participation in our Lord's prayer for the faith of the Apostles and "also for those who believe in me through their word" (Jn. 17:20). Thus, in the Roman Canon, an expression of the Lord's Prayer, we pray for the pope, for our bishop and "for all who hold and teach the Catholic faith that comes to us from the apostles." In the original Latin of this Canon, it is more strikingly clear that this is a prayer not just for the pope and bishops, the present day apostles, but also for those who believe through their word: "All the authentic (Orthodox) and Catholic and apostolic

worshippers in the faith." Jesus wills to save his flock through his
shepherds, the bishops, united with "the sweet Christ on earth,"[1]
the pope: *"Ecclesia . . . una cum famulo tuo Papa nostro"* (the
Church . . . one with your servant our pope).

1. The "sweet Christ on earth" is St. Catherine of Siena's description of
the pope; and the popes she knew personally were surely the frailest of
frail men.

29

Why Jesus Prayed Alone

An Angel Strengthening Him

In his temptation in the Garden of Olives did Jesus pray for personal strengthening? There is no doubt of the reality of his fear, his anxiety, his experience of human helplessness. His very acceptance of the cup of suffering, "Nevertheless, not my will, but thine, be done" (Lk. 22:42), was an implicit prayer for strength: "And there appeared to him an angel from heaven strengthening him" (22:43). This answer from heaven brought true encouragement for his suffering human spirit, and was a sign to us of the kind of strength and relief that all of us can find in prayer.

Some readers of the Gospels have suggested a resemblance between the prayer of Jesus in his agony and Elijah's prayer to be relieved of his difficult mission through death: "He asked that he might die, saying, 'It is enough; now O Lord, take away my life'" (1 Kgs. 19:4). Jesus, too, would have found welcome relief in death: "My soul is very sorrowful, even to death" (Mk. 14:34). Was Jesus tempted to abandon his mission? His prayer expresses only the desire to be excused from it: "He fell on the ground and prayed that, if it were possible, the hour might pass from him" (Mk. 14:35).

Just as an angel gave Elijah the food and drink which enabled him to walk forty days and forty nights to the mountain of God, so an angel appears to Jesus to strengthen him for his journey to the mountain of the cross. The angel and the bread and drink of Elijah suggest the eucharistic nourishment by which all of us are strengthened in our trials by the journey of Jesus, by the power of his sacrifice, by his steadfast love of the Father which kept him courageous in his trial. That is why before Holy Communion, the food for our journey, we pray, "Lead us not into temptation," the temptation to abandon Christ and our mission when our difficulties are great.

Jesus Prayed Alone

"Now it happened that as Jesus was praying alone, the disciples were with him" (Lk. 9:18). Why did Jesus pray alone, if his disciples were there with him?

Jesus seemed to prefer to pray alone. Luke says that when the people began to crowd about Jesus to hear the word and to be cured of their ills, "he withdrew to the wilderness and prayed" (5:16). The pressing needs of his apostolate did not excuse him from the necessity of seeking solitude and prayer. To go apart to pray was not to abandon the poor and the hungry. It was to come to their aid. Every single benefit which Jesus bestowed upon his fellowmen he received from the Father in prayer. Feeling the weight of mankind's miseries upon his heart, he felt compelled to go to the Father in prayer to obtain relief for all his suffering brothers.

After laboring all day for his fellowmen and bearing all their infirmities in his compassionate heart, he would spend the night in prayer: "He went up the mountain by himself to pray," says St. Matthew. "And when it was late, he was there alone" (Matt. 14:23).

But even when he took his disciples with him, he prayed alone. On the night of his agony when he came to Gethsemane, he said to his disciples, "Sit here, while I go yonder and pray" (Matt. 26:36). Even though he took Peter and James and John deeper into the Garden with him, "he withdrew from them about a stone's throw, and kneeling down, he began to pray" (Lk. 22:40).

Why did Jesus pray alone? Both St. Augustine and St. Ambrose give answers to this question, each bringing out a different facet of the divine mystery involved.

Jesus prays alone because he is our Priest, our Mediator, who alone has access to the Father. We can go to the Father only in him. "No one comes to the Father but by me" (Jn. 14:6), he says at the Last Supper. He had expressed the same idea on an earlier occasion in his discourse with Nicodemus: "No one has ascended into heaven but him who has descended from heaven, the Son of Man who is in heaven" (Jn. 3:13).

We see, then, why Jesus goes to the mountain alone to pray. The mountain symbolizes heaven; "but no one ascends to heaven except him who has descended from heaven, the Son of Man." That is St. Augustine's explanation of this mystery. Augustine adds: "Even though he must come at the end and gather all together as his own members to raise us to heaven, even then he ascends alone because the Head with his body forms only one Christ." We ascend only in Jesus. We are taken by him to the Father.

St. Augustine finds in these words an allusion to the reality of the Mystical Body of Jesus. If we would have access to heaven, that is, to the Father, we must go to him in the Son, who came from the Father to take us to the Father. Truly, there is only one Son, only one heir of God. We are sons in the Son; we are heirs in the heir. We go to the Father only in him. Our prayers find acceptance only in him.

The aloneness of Jesus in his prayer for us is especially poignant in the Garden of Gethsemane. Though Jesus is the Son of God who has descended from heaven, he is nonetheless true man, like us in all things except sin. In the Garden he is alone and lonely, and this very loneliness reveals to us why Jesus has to go it alone in working our salvation. In his true human need as one of us, in his need for human comfort and human help in his suffering, he comes to his disciples for a bit of encouragement, but he finds them asleep. He is alone. The disciples cannot help him. They cannot understand what is going on.

In seeing Jesus seeking this support from his disciples we see how truly human he is, even though he is Son of God. But the very inability of the disciples to understand what was going on, and, therefore, their inability to enter into his saving work, accentuates the fact that Jesus really did have to do it alone. Only he could understand the salvific plan of the Father. Only he could understand why there must be a suffering Messiah. Once before, Peter had showed his inability to understand the ways of God when he took Jesus aside and chided him for speaking of sufferings.

It is along these lines that St. Ambrose approaches the question of why Jesus prayed alone. "He prayed alone," writes Ambrose. "Nowhere, if I am not mistaken, does one find that he prayed with the Apostles; everywhere he prays alone. It is because the design of God cannot be grasped by human desires, and no one can have part in the intimate thought of Christ."

"For my thoughts are not your thoughts, neither are your ways my ways, says the Lord. For as the heavens are higher than the earth, so are my ways higher than your ways, and my thoughts than your thoughts" (Isa. 55:8–9). Man is so earthbound by nature and by sin that he cannot rise to God unless Jesus sends the Holy Spirit from above. "Unless one is born anew—of water and the Spirit—he cannot see the kingdom of God" (Jn. 3:3,5).

The very fact that Jesus said, "You will be scattered, every man to his home, *and will leave me alone*" (Jn. 16:32), indicates that he felt deeply the loneliness of his abandonment by his friends. Yet he knew also how to fill his loneliness by turning to his Father in prayer. "Yet I am not alone, for the Father is with me." In the loneliness of the Garden, isolated by the incomprehension of his disciples, he prayed the more. And he who found no comfort from men is comforted by an angel of his Father.

Though Jesus prayed alone, he did not pray only for himself. In his prayers were contained those of all mankind. This truth is revealed to us in that cry of Jesus on the Cross: "My God, my

God, why have you forsaken me?" In this cry Jesus was really praying the twenty-first psalm. The psalm had been the cry of a suffering man of the Old Testament, a man seemingly abandoned by God, and it had become the prayer of the suffering people of Israel. All during his life on earth, Jesus had been praying the psalms of his people with these people when he took part in the synagogue worship. He had made their prayers his own because he had made their needs his own. He had become like them in all things except sin.

So much was he one with them that he made his own their very need for redemption. St. Augustine notices that the second line (in his Latin version) of the psalm, "My God, my God, why have you forsaken me?" is the cry of a sinner—"the voice of my sins keeps salvation far from me!" And momentarily he hesitates to believe that Jesus on the cross prayed that line, too. Because we have heard it said of Jesus, "In the beginning was the Word, and the Word was in God's presence, and the Word was God," we find it hard to grasp the full reality of his humanity. We hear it said of him, says Augustine, "the Word was God." "When in another passage of Scripture we hear him groan, pray, confess his humanity before God, acknowledge himself a sinner," says Augustine, "we hesitate to attribute these words to him . . .".

But we must not hesitate. "When a word, especially a prophetic word, which expresses a humiliation unworthy of God, is spoken of the Lord Jesus Christ, let us not hesitate to attribute it to him, who has not at all hesitated to become one with us. . . .

"As our priest he prays for us; as our head he prays in us; as our God he is prayed to by us. Let us, therefore, recognize our voice in him; let us recognize his voice in us. . . .

"Let no one, therefore, in hearing these words say, 'It is not Christ who speaks.' Neither let him say, 'It is not I who speak.' Whoever recognizes that he is a member of the body of Christ will say both: 'It is Christ who speaks' and 'It is I who speak.'

"Say nothing without him; he says nothing without you."[1]

1. On Psalm 85.

All the cries of Jesus—though he prayed alone—were our cries. Our cries find no admission to the Father in heaven except in the cries of anguish of Jesus himself. Though he was the Word of God who had descended from heaven, let us not forget for an instant the full reality of his human suffering. Each time we hear a cry of anguish in the liturgy, each time we hear someone cry out for help in the words of the psalms, let us hear the voice of Jesus. Let us try to realize the full reality of his sufferings in his Passion.

At the same time, let us recognize our own cry in his. Let us recognize the cries of all his suffering members, all the members of mankind who are suffering in the world this day. "In the days of his flesh," says Hebrews, "Jesus offered up prayers and supplications, with loud cries and tears, to him who was able to save him from death, and he was heard for his reverent submission" (Heb. 5:7). Into the reality of his own sufferings and tears, Jesus gathered the needs and anguish and prayers of all mankind, and within his own tears and petitions he presented them to the Father, and gained a hearing for all.

Prayer, says St. John Damascene, is "the interpreter of desire." And desire, of course, springs from need. Jesus gathered into his own prayer the prayers and desires and needs of all mankind— and not only our explicit prayers and desires, but even our unknown needs which have not yet given rise to desire and prayer. In a sense, need is already an implicit prayer, even before we become conscious of that need and ask God to fulfill it. There are countless members of our race who are not yet aware of their greatest of all needs, i.e., their need for God, their need to see him face to face and to embrace him in love. They do not know what they need, but Jesus knew. And he asked the Father to give them what they need.

In a sense, our whole being is a prayer, a hunger for God. "For you have made us for yourself, O God, and our hearts are restless, till they rest in you." For many years before he wrote these immortal words Augustine had hungered for God without knowing what he was hungering for. He tried to satisfy his hungry soul in every imaginable earthly love, but he found his needs unsatisfied.

Because Jesus on Calvary knew what Augustine needed, and offered this need to the Father, Augustine at last discovered and obtained what he was hungering for.

This is what St. Ambrose meant in saying that Jesus had to pray alone: "It is because the design of God cannot be grasped by human desires, and no one can have part in the intimate thought of Christ."

It was not only men like Augustine before his conversion who did not grasp the design of God. Men like St. Paul even after *his* conversion still found the ways of God beyond their comprehension. For, writes Paul to the Romans, "We do not know what we should pray for as we ought, but the Spirit himself pleads for us with unutterable groanings. And he who searches the hearts knows what the Spirit desires, that he pleads for the saints according to the will of God" (Rom. 8:26–27).

We see then why *we* cannot pray alone. We do not know what to desire and ask for. We must pray, therefore, in Jesus by the inspiration of his Holy Spirit.

"Let us, therefore, recognize our voice in him; let us recognize his voice in us." As a member of the body of Jesus, say, "It is Christ who speaks, and it is I who speak."

30

To a Loveless World

Pray Not To Be Put to the Test

St. Luke's way of telling about the prayer of Jesus in the Garden
of Olives differs from that of the other Evangelists. Luke puts the
emphasis on our joining Jesus in his prayer. He frames the whole
story between the exhortation of Jesus, "Pray not to be put to the
test" (Lk. 22:40,j) and its repetition: "Get up and pray not to be
put to the test" (22:46). The other Evangelists record the exhortation to pray only after their account of the prayer of Jesus.

As always, Luke is teaching us how to pray by showing us
Jesus at prayer. This time he is insisting that we must pray our
Lord's prayer with him. By placing the prayer of Jesus between
the two appeals of Jesus to his disciples to pray, Luke is telling us
to enclose our prayer within the prayer of Jesus. Our victory in
temptation is the fruit of his victory in his temptation. Our Lord's
prayer for himself in his agony was implicitly a prayer for us, since
his whole passion and death was a sacrifice, a prayer for our victory. All that he endured was for our sake. His prayer in the
Garden for his own strengthening was for our strengthening. "Because he himself has suffered and been tempted, he is able to help
those who are tempted. He had to be made like his brethren in
every respect, so that he might become a merciful and faithful

high priest in the service of God, to make expiation for the sins of the people" (Heb. 2:18,17).

Luke puts a strange statement on the lips of Jesus in his Last Supper account: "You are they who *have continued* with me in my trials" (Lk. 22:28). Jesus knew very well that his disciples would *not* continue with him in his way of the cross and crucifixion: "You will be scattered, every man to his home, and will leave me alone" (Jn. 16:32). So the words, "You *have* continued with me in my trials," seem meaningless.

They are not meaningless; they are timeless. Jesus suffered his passion alone as the sole propitiation for the sins of the world, but *later on,* after his Resurrection, his disciples and Christians in all centuries persevered with him in his trial in the sense that through their faith in him and by the power of his sacrifice they united their own sufferings with his and were victorious in their testing.

The double appeal of Jesus, "Pray not to be put to the test," is an appeal to all of us to pray with him and to prayerfully unite our trials with his. The very effort of our faith to be faithful, the very faith by which we continue with him in our trials is a prayer within his prayer. "This is the victory that overcomes the world, our faith. Who is it that overcomes the world, but he who believes that Jesus is the Son of God" (1 Jn. 5:4–5).

For the only real evil, we said, is apostasy from faith in Jesus, failing in the eschatological test. "Pray not to be put to the test." Perseverance in prayer will be a steady strengthening and purifying of your faith so that you will not be able to fall away.

The words of Jesus, "You are they who have continued with me in my trials," are placed in the midst of the Last Supper at which the Eucharist was instituted as if to suggest that those who participate in the eucharistic banquet and those who watch and pray will remain faithful to Jesus in all their trials. For after giving the disciples his body to eat and his blood to drink, he takes them out to pray with him.

"Pray Continually and Never Lose Heart!"

Persistence in prayer is our Lord's most insistent lesson about prayer. He tells many parables to this point. For instance, just after the eschatological discourse in St. Luke's Gospel (17:20–37), a parable is framed between these two statements: "Pray continually and never lose heart. . . . When the Son of Man comes, will he find any faith on earth?" (18:1,8).

The widow in this parable is not only suffering injustice from an adversary, but her tribulation is compounded by a judge "who neither feared God nor regarded man" and was unjust through his failure to vindicate her. Not for love of justice, but because of her persistence, he says at last, "I will vindicate her, or she will wear me out by her continual coming."

Finishing the parable, Jesus says, "Hear what the unrighteous judge says. And will not God vindicate his elect who cry to him day and night?" The very word "elect" is an eschatological term.

God is not an unrighteous, negligent judge who needs to be spurred to action by our persistence in praying to him. It is for our own benefit that we must cry to him day and night. It is our *perseverance in faith* which is at stake. "When the Son of Man comes, will he find faith on earth?" Will the suffering of repeated tribulations tempt us to abandon the faith? Pray continually and never lose heart in the midst of your hardships. Persistent prayer will keep your faith strong.

This is brought out still more powerfully in St. Matthew's eschatological discourse. The multiplication of wickedness will tempt man to abandon faith and love:

Then they will deliver you up to tribulation, and put you to death; and you will be hated by all nations for my name's sake. And then many will fall away, and betray one another, and hate one another. And many false prophets will arise and lead many astray. And because wickedness is multiplied, most men's love will grow cold. But he who endures to the end will be saved (Matt. 24:9–13).

Except for the first sentence, this passage refers chiefly to dissensions within the Church: the giving of scandal, mutual distrust, betrayal and hatred, deception by false prophets within the fold, rampant wickedness causing the love of the majority to grow cold, Christianity falling apart because charity is extinguished.

The widespread wickedness will tempt men to abandon faith in God's love. All evidence of divine love will seem to disappear. *Is* there a God of Love? "My adversaries taunt me while they say to me continually, 'Where is your God?'" (Ps. 42:10). Oppression and injustice are themselves a voice crying, "There is no God!" (Ps. 42:10). God has no love and concern for you: "Yahweh sees nothing." They say, "The God of Jacob takes no notice!" (Ps. 94:7).

Where there is no love, one is indeed tempted to give up loving. But this would be to deny the God of love. It would be to deny his fatherhood and to be disloyal to his people: "If I had said, 'I will speak thus,' I would have been untrue to the generation of thy children" (Ps. 73:15).

"Temptations to sin are sure to come, but woe to him by whom they come. . . . If your brother sins, rebuke him, and if he repents, forgive him; and if he sins against you seven times in a day, and turns to you seven times, and says, 'I repent,' you must forgive him" (Lk. 17:1,3–4). Failure to forgive is to multiply sin, and the multiplication of sin is the extinguishing of love. "Forgive us our trespasses, as we forgive those who trespass against us!"

When men in their wickedness give no evidence of God's love, when they are hateful and unforgiving, his love will be experienced only in persevering prayer. One can continue to love in the midst of wickedness only if he prays persistently, "Our Father!"

The eschatological temptation, then, is to abandon God and to abandon love because wickedness abounds (Matt. 24:12). The word used by Matthew for "wickedness" is really "iniquity," the eschatological sin, the rejection of Christ and the falling under the domination of Satan.[1] Iniquity is the sin of anti-Christ, the "man of iniquity" (1 Thess. 2:3).

1. Cf., *The Jerome Biblical Commentary* on 1 John 3:4.

It is from this sin that Jesus would like to save us when he insists that we persevere in prayer: "Pray not to be put to the test" (Lk. 22:40). God's elect are they who persevere till the end no matter what evils they may have to suffer. Like the persistent widow crying for vindication, they are persistent in prayer and therefore persevere in faith and love, loving even their enemies, proving themselves children of the Father in heaven (Matt. 5:44–45).

The parable of the persistent widow, then, corresponds to the petition, "Lead us not into temptation, but deliver us from evil," while the two parables in Luke eleven teaching perseverance in prayer correspond to the petition, "Give us this day our daily bread." In the first of these two, the man knocks persistently on his neighbor's door till the neighbor rises from bed and gives him the three loaves he asks. In the second, we are told that no man gives his son a stone when he asks for bread. "How much more will the heavenly Father give the Holy Spirit to those who ask him!" (Lk. 11:13).

"Pray continually and never lose heart!" Persistence in praying for our daily bread will serve to strengthen our faith and hope so that we will not fail in the severe testing when it comes our way. Asking the little daily needs of our Father in heaven bears witness to our hope in him and deepens our faith in his love. But the ultimate perfection of the cry, "Our Father," will be our hope in him in the moment of utter hopelessness, the time of severe trial, above all, the moment of death: "Father, into thy hands I commit my spirit" (Lk. 23:46). Jesus did not fail in the eschatological test. This loving surrender into the hands of his Father proves it. In spite of all his distress in the face of sufferings and death, he did not lose heart; for he prayed to the Father!

Death will be an eschatological test for all of us. When he comes to take us, will the Son of Man find faith in our heart? Pray always and do not lose heart!

We are put to the eschatological test any time in life when we are faced with a decision for or against Christ. For the choice of the *eschaton,* "the last things," is a choice of the kingdom present and working among us in the person of Jesus Christ.

"The beginning of the birthpangs" (Matt. 24:8) in which "the new man," redeemed mankind, is born, was the agony of Jesus. Not only at the end of the world will abounding iniquity tempt men to lose heart and abandon faith, unless *now* we are at the end of the world! Failure in the eschatological test seems to be rather common these days. Frequently, of late, we hear people saying that there is no God of love. If there were, he would not permit the terrible evils of the wars of this century. We hear even religious say that they have given up prayer. The lack of love among fellow religious, they claim, proves that prayer is of no avail! Because evil has abounded, they have failed in faith![1]

To be scandalized by wickedness, real or imagined, is to be scandalized in the Suffering Messiah. To refuse to suffer injustice for him is like denying that he suffered unjustly. "If the world hates you, know that it has hated me before it hated you. A servant is not greater than his master. If they persecuted me, they will persecute you" (Jn. 14:18,20).

This is the reason for our Lord's insistence in the Garden of Olives that we watch and pray with him and that we enclose our prayer within his lest we fall away from the faith when iniquity abounds among us. We must keep before our eyes the humility of the Son of God. "Let us run with perseverance the race that is set before us, looking to Jesus the pioneer and perfecter of our faith, who for the joy that was set before him endured the cross, despising the shame, and is seated at the right hand of the throne of God" (Heb. 12:1–2).

To a loveless world we must bring love. We must bear witness to the God of love so that our fellowmen may have a restored faith in God who *is* love.

1. In our previous book, *Prayer: The Search for Authenticity* (Sheed and Ward, 1969), we wrote a chapter, "The Compatibility of Authentic Prayer and Human Sinfulness," after hearing different religious speak in this way. The attitude is not uncommon.

Love on a Vietnam Battlefield

On September 8, 1967, four Americans in the Vietnam War were pinned down in a shell crater by enemy fire: the company commander, his radioman, a medic, and a chaplain, Father Vincent Capodanno. The wounded beyond the crater's rim could be heard screaming and dying. The medic and the chaplain jumped out of the crater and ran forward on their spiritual and corporal works of mercy, their missions of redemption. They went among the wounded and dying, the medic working to save lives, the chaplain soothing, praying, administering the sacrament of divine forgiveness and the anointing which gives the courage and vigor of divine love.

In a burst of machine-gunfire, the two men of divine mercy themselves were killed. Certainly, they must have been received immediately into the kingdom of God: "Happy the merciful: they shall have mercy shown them. . . . Insofar as you did this to one of the least of these brothers of mine, you did it to me. . . . Come, you whom my Father has blessed, take for your heritage the kingdom prepared for you since the foundation of the world" (Matt. 5:7; 25:40,34).

After reading this story in the New Orleans *Times-Picayune* on the morning of September 9, 1967, I took up my breviary to pray the Divine Office. Psalm ninety-four came alive for me, and brought me onto the Vietnam battlefield. The horror of the war and the greed and selfishness of men which spawn wars seemed to be crying out in the words of the psalm: God does not care! God does not love! "Yahweh, they crush your people, they oppress your hereditary people, murdering and massacring widows, orphans and guests. 'Yahweh sees nothing,' they say, 'the God of Jacob takes no notice.' . . . Are these evil men to remain unsilenced, boasting and asserting themselves?" (Ps. 94:5-7,4,j). The war was crying out, "God does not care. There is no God of love!" Was the cry to remain unsilenced?

The medic and the chaplain by their action of love silenced the lie, crying more eloquently: "God himself has taught us by his

Holy Spirit to love one another!" (1 Thess. 4:9). "Greater love has no man than this, that a man lay down his life for his friends" (Jn. 15:13). Such love is Christ's own love in a man's heart. "This is my commandment, that you love one another as I have loved you" (15:12).

The two men were redeemers, "redeeming the time, for the days are evil" (Eph. 5:16,Douay). The murderous, merciless war was the fruit of sin. It stemmed from the unthinking blind greed which has no eyes to see the misery of the poor, from the machinations of established business to safeguard their sources of wealth, though it means the increasing poverty of the underprivileged. It originated from the ambition of those who exploit the misery of the poor and who stir up hatred and strife to win power and influence. Where iniquity abounds, love grows cold unless there are redeemers.

The medic and the chaplain had won the victory which overcomes the world of sin and hatred—their faith in God's love (1 Jn. 5:4). Each man was a message of divine love counteracting the hopelessness and despair engendered by the sinful destruction and death all about. Each was a word from God making it possible for the dying soldiers to respond in love and hope, "Father, into your hands I commit my spirit!" Each was a redemptive sacrifice accepted by the Father in the sacrifice of Jesus.

My prayer that morning sprang fom the newspaper as much as from the Psalms, the inspired word of Scriptures. The situation in which one finds himself must enter the very texture of his contemplation. Prayer springs from life, from a consciousness of the solidarity of suffering mankind with the suffering Christ. Jesus made the sufferings of all sufferers his own: whatever injury you have done to the least of these my brothers you have done to me! He prayed the psalms of his people as he hung on the cross: "My God, my God, why have you forsaken me" (Psalm 22); "Into your hands I commit my spirit" (Psalm 31). He prayed them not only because he had learned them as a child while praying with his people in the synagogue, but because he had become like his people in all things except sin. He could suffer as they suffered, and he could truthfully express in their very own words his pain and torture endured for them.

He could offer to the Father in his cries on the cross the cries of mankind in every time and place. The words of the Psalms are perennially true. They are true whether they are on the lips of the men who composed them centuries before the time of Jesus, on the lips of Jesus himself, or on our lips as we cry out in union with Jesus and in communion with the victims of the wars in Biafra or Vietnam. The words express our communion with anyone else who is suffering, whether from his own sins, from the social injustice which breeds wars, or from any other cause. The eschatological battle, as fought by the medics and chaplains and dying soldiers on the firing line, or by anyone who labors by word or deed for justice and love, is helped by those who fight the battle behind the lines by their prayers for them in union with Christ in his battle on the cross.

And, of course, prayer for our suffering fellowmen is answered best when, to the extent of our possibilities and in keeping with our proper vocation, we become personally involved in the work of Christ, building a new world in justice and in love.

Such are the fruits of Christian contemplation of the Lamb of God. Prayer and contemplation is a fullness of baptismal participation in Christ's own light and love. They involve us dynamically in his paschal mystery, make us redeemers with the Redeemer and continue his mission to bring all mankind into communion with his Father.